STATISTICAL METHODS IN GEOGRAPHICAL STUDIES

DEDICATED
TO
THE MEMORY OF MY PARENTS
LATE SAYED BASHIR AHMAD
AND
LATE ZAKIA BEGUM

STATISTICAL METHODS IN GEOGRAPHICAL STUDIES

ASLAM MAHMOOD
Jawaharlal Nehru University, New Delhi

Introduction by

PROF. MOONIS RAZA
Former Vice - Chancellor
Delhi University, Delhi

RAJESH PUBLICATIONS
NEW DELHI - 110002

Statistical Methods in Geographical Studies

Published by :
Sanjay Gupta
RAJESH PUBLICATIONS
1, Ansari Road, Darya Ganj, New Delhi - 110002
Email : rajeshpublications@gmail.com, rajeshpubdelhi@gmail.com
Website : www.rajeshpublications.com

First Published in India	:	1977
Second Edition	:	1986
Third Edition	:	1993
Fourth Revised Edition	:	1998
Reprint	:	2002
Reprint	:	2008
Reprint	:	2012
Reprint	:	2013
Reprint	:	2016
Reprint	:	2017
Reprint	:	2019
Reprint	:	2021
Reprint	:	2023
Reprint	:	2025

ISBN 10 : 81-85891-17-6
ISBN 13 : 978-81-85891-17-0

Printed in India at :
R.K. Offset Process, Delhi

PREFACE

The book is an attempt towards presenting a lucid account of some of the quantitative methods commonly used in spatial analysis. Most of these methods may be found in several text books on basic statistics, multivariate statistical analysis and matrix algebra, while some of the more sophisticated methods, however appear only in various journals. The purpose of this book is, therefore, to collect and provide all these scattered methods and techniques in a fairly self-contained book, making them easily accessible to interested users.

While preparing this book I have tried to be careful enough in using minimum mathematical expressions and terminology and easily comprehenadable language. To make the book more practical and usable generally the final forms of the formulae used in different methods have been presented and the dredgery of their derivation has been avoided. The relevant references, however, have been given for the advantage of those readers who attempt an in-depth study. Major emphasis, here has been laid on their assumptions, computations and interpretations. The application of these methods in the real situation has been demonstrated by taking real examples of problems relevant to Indian situation. Taking the census map of 1971 as base many of the results have been mapped also to provide visual grasp of the space.

The book is primarily intended to be used as a reference work for geographical research, but I hope that other social scientists would also find it equally useful and interesting. First nine chapters of the book may be used for a post graduate level course on quantitative methods in Geography, chapters X to XII include some complex methods requiring elaborate and tedious calculations but can be used successfully, provided that, the facility of a personal computer (PC) is available.

I am highly indebted to Professor Moonis Raza for writing the introduction of this book. It would have not been possible for me to prepare this book without his encouragement and valuable guidance. I express my sincere gratitude to him. I also take this oppurtunity to express my thanks to Prof. G.S. Bhalla, Dr. M.K. Premi and Dr. A. Ahmad for their encouragement and help rendered at various stages. Thanks are also due to Dr. M.H. Qureshi for his valuable comments on the draft. I also wish to thank messers A. Malik and Z. Anwar, Miss C.K. Chauhan and Mrs. Kiran Banga also for their help, and to all other students who provided me the intermediate results of their various projects referred to in the book.

Lastly, I am thankful to my wife Rana Shahin also for her unbounded help. I am, however, alone responsible for any mistake.

New Delhi
February, 1977

ASLAM MAHMOOD

PREFACE TO THE REVISED EDITION

Continuous demand for the book for more than two decades, in spite of some problems in its distribution, has been highly encouraging. The book was written at a time when 'Personal Computers' were not in existence and most of the Computer work for the book was carried on the mainframe computers using punch cards. Revolutions in the field of data processing have made the book more relevant and useful with the help of a 'PC' and a good statistical package persons living in any part of the country can use these techniques equally well.

There were some printing errors brought to our notice in the original edition, which have been removed in the present revised edition. Few paragraphs have been added or rewritten in some of the Chapters to highlight their context in the changing situations. One full Chapter has been added on network analysis.

The examples, however using 1961 or 1971 data have not been changed or updated simply due to the fact that their emphasis is on techniques and method which have not change.

I am extremely thankful to all my colleagues and students who contributed in the improvement of this book through their suggestion.

New Delhi
15th August, 1998

ASLAM MAHMOOD

CONTENTS

INTRODUCTION

1.0 Aslam Mahmood's Statistical Methods in Geographical Studies is a most welcome addition to the hitherto to slender collection of Indian text-books on problems of methods and techniques in geography and is a pioneering work—the first of its kind—to present statistical methods in the context of Indian experiences in geographical studies.

1.1 The teaching of methods and techniques in geography curricula of Indian colleges and universities ha been, unfortunately since its very emergence on the academic scene, "imprisoned" within the four walls of what had come to be designated as "practical geography"—a projection of the British academic tradition which continues to persist within the spongy organism of Indian geography, decades after the British themselves have given it up. What in other scientific disciplines was lab and field work with a view to underline, exemplify and validate theory was transformed, within the imitative ethos of geographical academia, into an autonomous sub-discipline. It is not difficult to imagine that the patently naive suggestion to introduce a course in practical physics or practical economics would be met by a spontaneous sneering response. Not that physics, for example, does not have a strong lab based "practical" component. But at the undergraduate level, it is *Physics* Practical not *Practical Physics*. In fact, at every stage, the share of physics practical in the total curricular load is twice as much as that of its counterpart in geography. What, however, makes it meaningful and relevant for the learning experience is its intrinsic link with the theoretical components of the curriculum. It is not looked upon as an autonomous realm of pedagogy but as flowing out of and subservient to theory. It is, unfortunately, the non-adherence to this basic principle of the unity of theory and practice which has reduced "practical geography" into a mechanical aggregate of disparate elements—ranging from triangulation to rock identification, from barometric readings to astronomical calculations, from choropleth mapping to the use of chain and tape, from pie-diagrams to land use surveys. It is not being suggested that any of the above is infructuous, redudant or useless. On the contrary, each one of them has some role play in the training of a geographer. It is, however, open to question whether, within the time constraint of a curricular programme, *all* of this has to be necessarily taught to *every* student. Their utility having been conceded, it must be clearly and explicity stated that teaching all of these as a part of an ombnibus course called "Practical Geography" becomes entirely irrational and disfunctional—irrational because disparate elements get clubbed together in an amorphous aggregate without a logical system to articulate it, and disfunctional because the intrinsic links of each of these elements with that which provides meaning and purpose to it have been cut. It is heartening to note that geography departments in many Indian universities are increasingly realizing the inadequacy (and, perhaps, also the absurdity !) of organising their curriculum round this queer academic species—"Practical Geography" and are, alternatively, experimenting with developing lab and field based components for each course. It is in this direction that the solution of one of the major problems of geographical pedogagy lies. More strength to those who dare to innovate and experiment in an essentially conservative ethos and strike against vested interests in the established curriculum "thc textbook lobby"!

2.1 The essential tools of analysis and synthesis in geography—as in all scientific disciplines—is logic. Logic may be either qualitative or quantitative/symbolic. The use of the latter on a significant scale is late arrival on the academic landscape of geography. It is a most welcome phenomenon. But its emergence should not be mistaken for the institutionalisation of a new sub-discipline, sometimes mistakenly designated as Quantitative Geography—with a capital Q and a capital G. This caution is necessary for one comes across—not quite often though—academic snobs with turned up noses calling themselves "quantitative geographer," looking down from the rarifield atmosphere of the elysian heights of their social irrelevance upon ordinary mortals, smelting of the earth. There is not and cannot be a quantitative geography; for this would lead to the acceptance of a taxonomy wherein the categories of the first order would be quantitative geography and qualitative geography. Who in his right senses would accept the position that there is a geography, which has no use for quantification ; or a geography, which shuns all quantitative assessments.

2.2 Both quality and quantity are aspects of objective reality. Quality refers to that which makes a particular object what is; it reflects its identity. It cannot, therefore, be broken up into homogeneous parts, the moment that is done the identity is lost. Consequently, in itself it cannot be measured. Since quantity, however, is capable of being increased or reduced without changing its character, one has to select *quantitative indicators of quality*, in order to make qualitative assessments. Let us take the example of health, which is an integrated quality, cannot be broken up into homogeneous parts, and therefore, cannot be measured directly. What does the physician do to get over this difficulty ? He selects quantitative indicators of health which can be measured - for example, for a tubercular patient : body temperature, blood pressure, body weight, ESR, RBC, WBC. The values and magnitude of these quantitative indicators help him to diagnose, i.e. to make an analogous situation from the field of geography of regional development. To start with, the geographer has to diagnose - to identify the nature of the health of region, which is quality and cannot be measured directly. Depending on his analytical system, he may select the following quantitative indicators that can be measured : for example, *(i) land capability index, (ii) aridity index, (iii) per capita income, (iv) percentage share of the secondary sector in the working force, (v) index of urbanization, (vi) literacy rate, (vii) index of income inequality, (viii) share of the deprived communities in the total population and (ix) share of working women in the total female population.* The values of these indicators either singly or after composition help him to arrive at a qualitative assessment about the "health" of the region. Having completed the diagnostic part of his work, he takes up the next task - that of prescription. Once again, he goes to the quantitative indicators within the framework of his theory of development and picks out the crucial constraints - environmental, technological and institutional. Having done this, he works out the elements of the proposed operational strategy to remove the constraints and generate the desired rates of growth. It is clear from the above, that the geographer moves back and forth from qualitative assessments to quantitative measurements. They are both necessary components of research strategy. Qualitative evaluation provide purpose and direction to quantification and gets back from it accuracy, precision and depth.

2.3 Geography has been and continues to be a unified field of study which has been using, from the times of Herodotus, quantitative judgements. The "quantitative revolution" in modern geography has now made it possible to measure phenomena with greater precision and/or accuracy; to develop explanatory mechanism of greater sophistication so as to make qualitative judgements of a higher order and to uncover or unfold deeper layers of meaning in objective phenomenon, which less sophisticated tools were unable to reach; and to facilitate the process of abstraction from emphirical facts so as to generate concepts and theories.

2.4 Geographers have been using quantitative methods for identification, explanation and decision - making. Their endeavors in this direction generally take the following forms :

(i) to tabulate data methodically and systematically;

(ii) to extract sample from a large and unmanageable universe in such a manner that the analysis with the sample become valid for the universe;

(iii) to identify, classify and extract the inherent characteristics of phenomena;

(iv) to study distributions : frequency, variance and measures of inequality inherent therein — growth and development along the temporal scale; variation, concentration, clustering and dispersion along the spatial scale;

(v) to analyze the matrix of flows across space and the characteristics of networks;

(vi) to identify association and correlation between and combination of phenomena across space and/or through time;

(vii) to composite and synthesis relevant variables in hierarchical regional systems;

(viii) to explain : to relate causes with their effects and/or effects with their causes in a system of uni-directional, bi-directional or multi-directional relationships;

(ix) to project processes in time and to predict;

(x) to simulate and build spatial models;

(xi) to optimize in the light of given constraints;

3.0 The more geography moves from the descriptive to the analytical, from the ideographic to the nomothethic, the more would be the need for the use of quantitative tools. However, recent experience has shown that there are some serious dangers inherent in their use against which a clear warning needs to be given.

3.1 First, there is an increasing tendency to hide the paucity of thought by weaving a cobweb of mathematical signs and formulae. Not long ago, a doctoral thesis proved, on the basis of a computer intensive exercise that urban centres in India and the US have a common feature — their population are larger than those of their rural counterparts. If such a statement were to have been made without the use of terms and phrases like "matrix of correlation" or "orthogonalisation of a whole set of variables into mutually independent components," even the kid of Anderson's tale would have cried out in embrassment : "But, Mummy, the emperor hasn't got anything on !" Spate, in his unimitatable style, has quoted a "most sublime" example from our sister discipline - Sociology:

> ".......such epoch-making generalization (and this is not a parody !) as that 'perhaps people have more frequent cordial and intimate contacts with their personal friends than with those who are not their personal friends; or that while one usually marries some one of one's own creed and class, quite often he or she is of somewhat opposite temperament. Although this last conclusion on mate—selection was arrived at by impeccably quantitative methods-with 15 variables (variably dichotomized and double dichotomize) into 44 sub-variables, the complete inter-spousal correlation elements.....' - it is perhaps not fair to quote it against respectable quantifiers, since

the generalization is based on 25 university couples, a restricted sample not likely to be of practical use of colleagues with adolescent daughters."

3.2 Secondly, statistical relationships are, not rarely, confused with causal relationships. From the given data, wherein every time X undertakes a railway journey the train is late, one cannot conclude that the travel of X is the cause of the train being late or the lateness of the train is the cause of the journey of X-whatever be the value of the coefficient at whatever level of significance. Causal relationships should be rooted in logic, in the conceptual frame of the scholar which is evolved through the rigours of intellection and not through statistical exercises. Quantitative methods validate theory; they do not generate or replace it.

3.3 Thirdly, it is something inadequately realized that while statistical methods are positivistic and value neutral, the premises underlying them are not. Let us take the example of the valuable monograph of the 1961 census entitled *Levels of Regional Deveopment in India,* wherein the indicators of distributive trade, manufacturing and infra-structure — which constitute Block V in the study — are assumed to move together in the same direction. How do we interprete this result? It is well known that the Colin Clark hypothesis of the share of the tertiary sector as an indicator of economic development is just not tenable in most of the developing economics, wherein it is an indicator of disguised unemployment rather than of economic development. The preponderence of tertiary activities in the Indian urbanization process is more an indicator of the dysfunctional character or urbanization, as the growth of centres of consumption rather than production. It is clear that an essentially erroneous assumption cannot be validated by being stamped under the seal of Kendell's Method of Ranking Co-efficients.

3.4 Fourthy, there is a serious danger of falling a prey to what C. Wright Mills calls the "perversity of abstracted empiricism," *i.e.* to minimize the *initiating role* of a hypothesis and an analytical frame in the strategy of research and ultimately to end up by denying their role altogether. To begin with, the cart is put before the horse and then the horse is dispensed with altogether with the fond (but naive) hope that the cart would ultimately "generate" its own horse! Experience has, time and again, demonstrated the sterlity of such an approach, and has shown that, in the field of social science research, tools and methods are subervient to and flow from the analytical frame and cannot be developed autonomously, of and for themselves. The indicators chosen and the sophisticated multivariate techniques used by Soja, for example, to analyse economic development in Kenya are rooted in his theory which states that imperialism has been the major instrument of modernization in that country. If one is able to show that Soja's basic theoretical assumption itself is erroneous, the entire house of (computer !) cards collapses ! Theory is of the essence, "Abstracted empiricism" is based on the rejection of this essential element; and leads to the blind alley wherein the task of the researcher is reduced to the punching of cards, or getting them punched @ I paisa a card; and lo and behold ! the computer provides the answer. The dangers inherent in such an "impirical" approach are more so in a discipline-like geography where the tradition of theory building is already quite weak. The overwhelming concern with the specific minutae has inhibited the development of concepts in general — the discipline tending to acquire the dimensions and the characteristics of a dinosaur, a huge body, a long tail and a tiny little head. Geographical science, having failed like *Hanumana* to identify *Sanjivani*, carries the whole mountain of infinitesimal facts on its hefty shoulders. In such a state of theoretical anamia of the discipline, quantitative methods and computer-based tools provide an easy escape from the rigours of intellection into the world of figures and mechanical calculations. Let us take the example of a fairly sophisticated exercise based on the data provided by the census monograph cited above but using the computer — intensive principal component analysis instead of the comparatively simpler method of Kendell's ranking coefficient. To start with the twenty four variables, used in the earlier study, were reduced to fifteen more efficient ones on the basis of a study of the correlation martix. It would be reasonable to accept that in measuring the levels of the development, the choice of indicators or thier abridgment would have been given far greater attention since it constitutes the crux of the methodology; it is through this that the pertinent questions that need to be asked of the data are indentified. The data base in itself is inert and passive; it only responts to active questioning. In this case, the questions were not formulated through an understanding of the social situation — at least, there is no indication that they were. The indicators selected for an earlier study were accepted lock, stock and barrell and the inefficient ones were discarded on the basis of their external properties, without a critical examination of their relevance to the analytical frame; in fact, the whole exercise has proceeded without any analytical frame without any initial hypothesis. The results obtained through the "intellection" of the computer, suffer from two basic lacunae:

(i) the components are not "identifiable" — in the sense that no economic interpretation (which preforce the scholar and not the computer has to do !) in terms of real variables is possible: and

(ii) there is an underlying assumption that it is sufficient for a subset of variables simply to move together to be represented by a component. It is, for instance, stated therein:

"It is clear that the following variables - income, literacy, minorities (*sic*), immigration, retail, manufacturing and registered factory workers, number of establishments run on electricity, roads per mile, irrigated area, tenancy and the rate of increase in population are positively associated with development; on the other hand, scheduled castes and tribes, hired workers, agricultural labourers, proportion of labourers and cultivators and rural population are negatively associated with development."

We have a parodoxical situation on hand:

(i) the incidence of tenancy, moves in the *same* direction as the general index of economic development.

(ii) indices of development of capitalism in agriculture — such as incidence of hired workers, agricultural labourers move in a direction *opposite* to the level of economic development. The method obviously assumes that there is nothing fundamentally counter — development about the dynamics indicated by the above; and that the logic of the developmental process obtaining in any given situation is, in some way, optimal also. It amounts to assuming that the logic of the under — development process is, in some way, also rational and legitimate. And, that is swallowing — hook, line and sinker — the neo-imperialist bait of "modernization" ideology.

4.0 The dangers inherent in the use of quantitative tools of analysis— some of which have been discussed above—do not indicate that they should be left like hot potatoes or touched, if at all, by a long pair of tongs. Such a conservative attitude would seriously restrict the development of geography and inhibit its interactions with other disciplines. It should, however, be clearly realized that quantification is not a convenient substitute for thinking; and that the more sophisticated the statistical tool, the more sophisticated analytical frame it requires. It is only through the interwined process of the development of theory and sophistication of analytical tools that the dicipline is destined to develop.

5.0 It is in this background that the present volume acquires both its relevance and its significance.

Its chief merit lies in the fact that it is both a textbook and a work book, and can, therefore, be directly used for organising work in the class; that its exercises are based on Indian data and therefore are linked with the live experience of the learner; and that most of its exercises have a strong geographical bias, dealing with the kind of problems that geography students are required to handle as a part of their training. Its strength lies in the fact that it embodies the five years experience of teaching statistical methods to geography students at the M.A. and M.Phil, levels in the Centre for the Study of Regional Development of the Jawaharlal Nehru University. The curriculum and the instructional techniques in this important area of our academic work have been evolved through prolonged discussion among the faculty and regular feed back from students. Gone are the days, fortunately, when 714 and 920 (the numbers identifying compulsory coursed on quantiative methods) were dreaded words for geography students. Much of the credit for this rightly goes to Amitabh Kundu and to Aslam Mahmood, the author of the present volume. It is hoped that students in other universities would make use of this instructional material and they, as well as our colleagues, would point out to us its shortcomings and inadequacies so that they may be removed in the next edition.

ITHACA
February 8, 1977 **MOONIS RAZA**

1
DESCRIPTIVE STATISTICS

The preliminary analysis of a research problem starts with identifying the salient features of a given phenomenon and comparing and contrasting them in different situations. Several statistical methods can be used for this purpose, provided that, the related charecteristics of the phenomenon under consideration can be transformed into quantitative variables, like density of population, percentage of urban population to total population, consumption of fertilizers per acre of sown area, etc. The data related to these variables may be obtained either from primary sources (field surveys) or from secondary sources (official reports such as census, National Sample Surveys, statistical abstracts and other important reports etc.)

Such data collected in the raw form is a set of numbers not arranged in any systematic form, so it is not of much help. Firstly, it is not easily manageable and secondly, as such it does not tell us its underlying pecularities. In order to get more meaningful information from the raw data the steps in which a quantitative analysis proceeds are as follows:

(*a*) Tabulation of data
(*b*) Graphical Representation
(*c*) Comparison of Distribution

(*a*) THE TABULATION OF DATA

The Data in which the underground raw data is arranged in a systematic form is known as Frequency Distribution table. In any grouped frequency distribution table we divide the whole range of the values of the variable into some smaller groups, known as classes and note the number of observations falling in each class. These numbers are called as the frequencies of the particular classes.

As an example, consider the daily rainfall record (in mm.) of a rain gauge station for 90 days as

50	60	55	58	59	61	63	54	52	59
48	51	59	58	60	63	62	58	55	63
52	54	55	51	54	55	60	62	61	64
49	50	56	52	55	54	51	63	31	41
42	44	68	70	30	43	42	39	43	41
74	31	51	52	51	48	47	45	38	45
37	38	49	54	38	40	43	42	48	50
32	33	51	50	57	58	48	45	47	39
47	49	55	42	47	48	42	45	49	50

Here the lowest value is 30 mm. and the highest is 74 mm., so the range is 74–30=44. If we take 5 mm. as the class interval, the nine classes which we will get are given with frequencies in Table 1.1.

Table 1.1

Rainfall in mm.	*No. of days*	*Cumulative Frequencies*
30-35	5	5
35-40	6	11
40-45	11	22
45-50	18	40
50-55	19	59
55-60	15	74
60-65	13	87
65-70	1	88
70-75	2	90
	Total 90	

Here class *a-b* is defined as *a* and above but less than *b*. Each class has two values known as upper and lower class limits, for example 35 and 40 are the lower and upper limits of the second class. The difference between upper and lower class limits is known as class interval which may or may not be equal for all the classes. In the present example there is an equal class interval of 5 mm. in all the classes.

An ungrouped frequency distribution is that in which, instead of classes, the fixed values of the variable are given. An ungrouped frequency distribution may look like a distribution as given below in Table 1.2.

Table 1.2
Distribution of the size of 100 families of a locality

Size of family (x)	Number of families (f)
1	4
2	12
3	26
4	20
5	17
6	15
7	6
	Total 100

Total number of observations whose values are less than the upper limit of a class is known as cumulative frequency (less than type) of that particular class. Similarly the total number of observations greater than the lower class limit of a class is also known as cumulative frequency (more than type) of that particular class.

The following points should be kept in mind while preparing a frequency distribution table.

(1) For the sake of convenience in computation and comparison the class intervals should be kept equal unless there is some specific reason against it.

(2) The number of classes should not ordinarily exceed 20 and should not, in general, be less than 10.

(3) The class limits as well as class interval should be a multiple of 5, as far as possible.

Important Notations:

Variables : The characteristics whose values vary from one observation to another observation are known as variables. For example, rainfall is a variable because it varies from one point to another point over space, as well as, over time. Other examples of the variables may be districtwise data on density of population, area sown, urban population, per acre consumption of fertilizers, percentage of irrigated area to total cropped area, number of towns, number of tube-wells, number of primary schools etc. etc.

In mathematics, for the sake of compactability, the different variables are represented by some symbols. Generally the symbols used to denote the variables are the alphabets U, V, X, Y and Z etc.

Subscript of the variables : After denoting the different variables by *x, y, z* etc. we may distinguish between two or more variables, but we can not differentiate between the different values of the same variable. This difficulty is easily removed by attaching a small number with a variable which correspond to the serial number of the value. For example if x denotes the per capita income of n districts x_1, x_2, x_3........... x_n will denote the per capita income of 1st, 2nd, 3rd and so on up to the nth district in the list. These small numbers are known as subscript of the variables. We may use double subscripts also as:

$$\begin{matrix} x_{11} & x_{12} & x_{13} \\ x_{21} & x_{22} & x_{23} \\ x_{31} & x_{32} & x_{33} \\ \cdots & \cdots & \cdots \\ \cdots & \cdots & \cdots \\ x_{n1} & x_{n2} & x_{n3} \end{matrix}$$

They show the n values of three variables. Here the first subscript shows the number of observations (or rows) and the second subscript shows the number of variables (or columns). Thus x_{32} means 3rd value of the second variable and in general term x_{ij} means value of the jth column or ith value of ijth variable.

Summation Sign :

Suppose we want to represent the sum of the annual income of 100 persons which is denoted by x, we would have to write all the x_s right from x_1, to x_{100} and put a plus sign in between each of them. Such lengthy expressions can be conviently written with the help of the summation sign sigma (Σ).

Using the Sigma sign it can be written as

$$\sum_{i=1}^{100} xi$$

which means all the values from x_1 to x_{100} have been added. Thus :

$$\sum_{i=1}^{100} xi = x1 + x2 + x3 \ldots\ldots\ldots\ldots + x100$$

The summation sign can operate over algebric expressions also. For example :

(1) $\sum_{i=1}^{3}(xi + yi) = (x1 + y1) + (x2 + y2) = (x3 + y3)$

(2) $\sum_{i=1}^{50} yixi = y1x1 + y2x2 + y3x3 + \ldots\ldots\ldots\ldots + y50x50$

(3) $\sum_{i=1}^{4} Cxi = Cx1 + Cx2 + Cx3 + Cx4 = C(x1 + x2 + x3 + x4)$

$$= C\sum_{i=1}^{4} xi$$

(4) $\sum_{i=1}^{n} C = C + C + C + \ldots\ldots\ldots C(n\ times) = nC$

(5) $\sum_{i=1}^{n} x_{ij} = x_{1j} + x_{2i} + \ldots\ldots\ldots\ldots + x_{ni}$ = Sum of Jth column n

(6) $\sum_{j=1}^{3} x_{ij} = xi1 + ix2 + xi3$ = Sum of the ith row

(7) $\sum_{j=i}^{3} \sum_{i=1}^{n} x_{ij} = \sum_{i=1}^{n} x_{i1} \sum_{i=1}^{n} x_{12} + \sum_{i=1}^{n} x_{13}$

= Sum of 1st column + Sum of 2nd column + Sum of 3rd column

= Sum of all the values given in three columns

(b) **Graphical Representation**

Once the raw data are converted into a frequency distribution, it can be represented on a graph also for a quick visual assessment and comparison. The common graphs are generally of the following types :

1. Histogram
2. Frequency Polygon
3. Frequency curve
4. Cumulative Frequency curve or ogive

Histogram : A histogram is obtained by first making off, along the *x*-axis, all the class intervals on a suitable scale. With the class interval as bases, we draw rectangles with heights proportional to all the frequencies of the classes which have equal intervals. For the classes of unequal

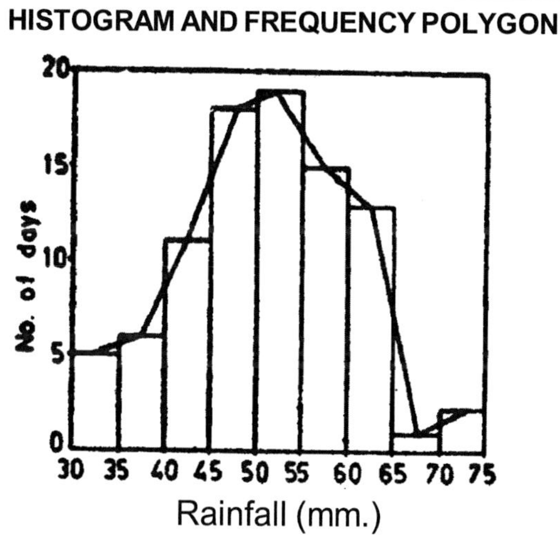

Fig. 1.1

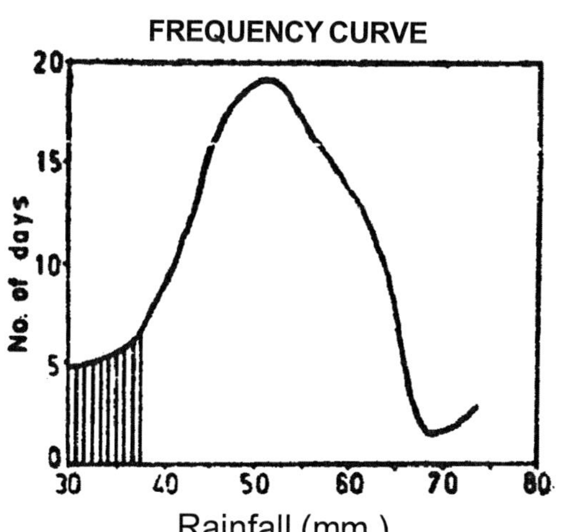

Fig. 1.2

intervals, the heights will be proportional to the ratios of the frequencies to the class intervals. Thus area under each such rectangles will be proportional to the frequencies of the corresponding classes. Figure 1.1 is the histogram prepared from the data given in Table 1.1.

Frequency Polygon and Frequency Curve

The frequency polygon can be obtained by joining the middle points of the upper sides of the adjacent rectangles of a histogram with straight lines. For ungrouped frequency distribution, the frequency polygon is obtained by plotting the points with abscissa (values on x-axis) as the value of the variable and the ordinate (values on y-axis) as the corresponding frequencies and joining them by means of a straight line. In Fig. 1.1 the frequency polygon of the frequency distribution as given in Table 1.1 is also plotted by thick lines.

If the class intervals are small, the frequency curve can be obtained by drawing a smooth free hand curve through the vertices of the frequency polygon. A frequency curve of data in table 1.1 is also given in Fig. 1.2. On the basis of their shapes the frequency curves are broadly divided into five different forms as given in Fig. 1.2 (a) and (b). These forms are : (1) Symmetrical (2) Positively skewed (3) Negatively skewed (4) Extremely asymmetrical and (5) *U*-Shaped.

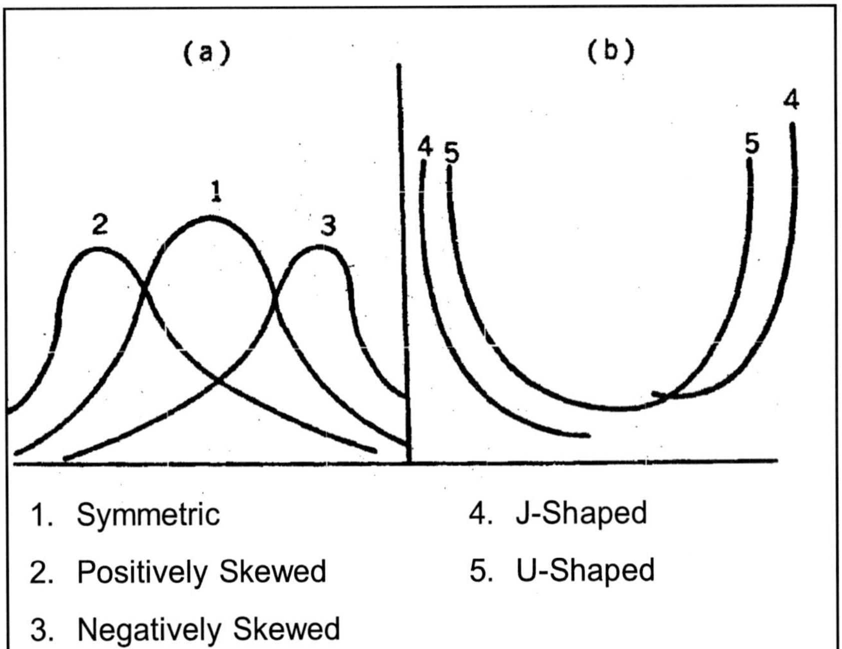

Fig. 1.2

Cumulative Frequency Curve : Cumulative frequencies are the numbers of observations whose values are less than (greater than) the upper limits (lower limits) of each class. The less than type or more than type cumulative frequencies of any class are obtained by adding the frequencies of all the preceding or following classes respectively up to the frequencies of the particular class. Points are then plotted with the upper limits of the classes as abscissa and cumulative frequencies of less than

CUMULATIVE FREQUENCY CURVE

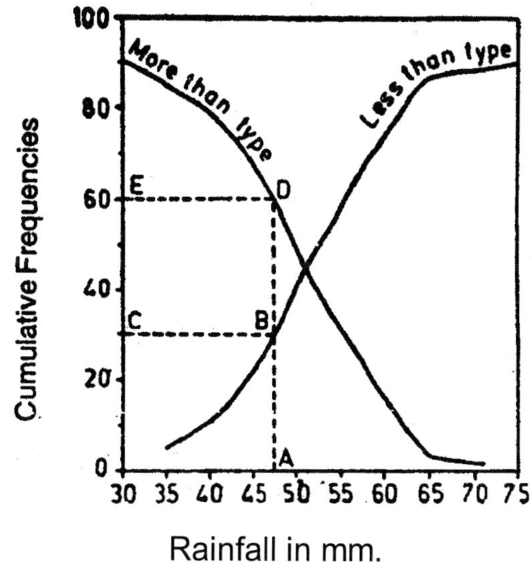

Fig. 1.3

type as ordinate. When these points are joined by a smooth free hand curve, we get a cumulative frequency curve of less than type. For a more than type cumulative frequency curve lower class limits are plotted with the cumulative frequencies of more than type. The cumulative frequency curves of both the types have been prepared for the data given in table 1.1 and are shown in Figure 1.3. Table 1.3 contains the cumulative frequencies of both the types for each class.

Table 1.3
Cumulative Frequencies

Rainfall (in mm)	*Frequencies (no. of days)*	*Less than type*	*More then type*
30-35	5	5	90
35-40	6	11	85
40-45	11	22	79
45-50	18	40	68
50-55	19	59	50
55-60	15	74	31
60-65	13	87	16
65-70	1	88	3
70-75	2	90	2

The following points should be noted when a graphical representation of data is attempted :

(1) The area of the constituent rectangles of a histogram is proportional to the number of observations falling in the corresponding classes.

(2) From any Point on a frequency curve if a perpendicular is drawn on the x-axis, the area between the x-axis and the frequency curve on the left hand side and right hand side of this perpendicular is proportional to the number of observations whose values are less than, or equal to or greater than the value at which the perpendicular cuts the x-axis.

In figure 1.2 from a point on the frequency curve a perpendicular has been drawn on x-axis which cuts it at a point whose value is 37.5 according to the given scale. Thus the shaded area is proportional to the days in which rainfall was less than 37.5 mm. and the unshaded area is proportional to the days in which rainfall was 37.5 mm. or above.

(3) In a cumulative frequency curve from any point (A) on x-axis erect a perpendicular which will cut the cumulative frequency curve at a point B. From B draw a perpendicular on y-axis which will cut it at some point C. The value of C would be the number of observations whose value is less than or greater than A, depending on whether a less than type curve or a more than type curve has been used. In figure 2, A has been taken as 47.5 and the corresponding C values from less than type curve is 30 and from more than type curve it is 60. Thus there are 30 days in which the rainfall is less than 47.5 mm and 60 days in which it is more than or equal to 47.5 mm.

Comparison of different distributions by graphs has a limited scope as it cannot be further analysed mathematically. More accurate statistical comparisons, which can be used in further quantitative analysis also, are discussed below :

(C) COMPARISON OF FREQUENCY DISTRIBUTIONS

In order to make further quantitative comparisons of frequency distributions, a distribution is initially characterised statistically by certain parameters. These Parameters are such that their differences bear a meaningful interpretation. Such important parameters of any distribution, which are used at later stages for further analysis also, are :

I Measures of Central Tendency
II Measures of Dispersion
III Measures of skewness.

Measures of Central Tendency

The frequency distribution of the raw represents the variations of a variable. The differences between these distributions may be highlighted in terms of their various characteristics. One of these characteristics is the value around which each distribution tends to have the maximum concentration of observations. This value is the best representative of the whole distribution and the different ways through which it is measured are known as the measures of central tendency or the measures of location.

Three such measures of central tendency are discussed below with a brief summary.

Mean

Mean or arithmetic mean is the simple average of the different values of a variable. In case of ungrouped data, mean is the sum of all the observations divided by the number of observations. Thus if a variable has *n* different values, the mean $\bar{x}$ is given by

$$\bar{x} = \frac{\Sigma x}{n} \qquad ...(1.1)$$

In case the data are in the grouped form of distribution as given in Table 1.2, the mean is given by :

$$\bar{x} = \frac{\Sigma fx}{f} = \frac{\Sigma fx}{n} (\text{where } \Sigma f = n) \qquad ...(1.2)$$

A short cut of this method is

$$\bar{x} = A + \frac{\Sigma fu}{n} h \qquad ...(1.3)$$

Where
A is any arbitary value in the middle range and

$$ui = \frac{xi - A}{h}$$

h is the class interval of the distribution (which should be equal for this formula)

or $$\bar{x} = A + \frac{\Sigma fu}{n} \qquad ...(1.4)$$

when the class intervals are not equal. Here

$u_i = (x_i - A)$ only

In case of grouped data with classes the middle values of each class are considered as *x* and the rest of the method remains the same.

Example 1.1 The record of rainfall in a month at 10 stations of a district is given below. Compute the average rainfall of the month in the district.

Station	*A*	*B*	*C*	*D*	*E*	*F*	*G*	*H*	*I*	*J*
Rainfall (in m.m.)	10.2	15.3	18.9	9.9	12.5	11.5	10.5	10.4	10.5	10.7

Solution : A.M. $= \frac{10.2+15.3+18.9+9.9+12.5+11.5+10.5+10.4+10.5+10.7}{10}$

$= \frac{120.0}{1010} = 12.00 \text{ mm}$

Example 1.2. The following table gives the distribution of salaries of 132 workers in a factory. Calculate the average salary of the workers in the factory.

Salary (in Rs.)	50-60	60-70	70-80	80-100	100-120	120-150	150-200	Total
No. of workers	8	12	15	20	22	25	30	132

Solution

Classes (Salary in Rs.)	No. of Workers (f)	Midvalue of classes (x)	$u = x$-90	fu	fx
50-60	8	55	-35	-280	440
60-70	12	65	-25	-300	780
70-80	15	75	-15	-225	1125
80-100	20	90	0	0	1800
100-120	22	110	+20	440	2420
120-150	25	135	+45	1125	3375
150-200	30	175	+85	2550	5250
	n = Σf = 132			+3310	15190

As the class interval in this exercise is not the same for all the classes, the A.M. of the above example may be computed either by using the formula (1.2) or (1.4) as below (both methods will give similar results)

$$\text{(1)}\quad \text{A.M.} = \frac{\Sigma fx}{n} = \frac{15190}{132} = \text{Rs. } 115.07$$

$$\text{(2)}\quad \text{A.M.} = A + \frac{\Sigma fu}{n} \quad \text{where } A = 90 \quad u = x - 90$$

$$= 90 + \frac{3310}{132} = 90 + 25.07 = \text{Rs. } 115.07$$

Example 1.3. Compute the Arithmatic mean from the rainfall data given in Table 1.1.

Solution

Classes (Rainfall in mm.	No. of days (f)	Mid. value of the classes (x)	$u=\frac{x-52.5}{5}$	fu
30-35	5	32.5	–4	–20
35-40	6	37.5	–3	–18
40-45	11	42.5	–2	–22
45-50	18	47.5	–1	–18
50-55	19	52.5	0	0
55-60	15	57.5	+1	+15
60-65	13	62.5	+2	+26
65-70	1	67.5	+3	+3
70-75	2	72.5	+4	+8
	$N=\Sigma f=90$			$\Sigma fu=-26$

Using formula (1.3), since the class interval of 5 is common in all the classes :

$$\bar{x} = A+\frac{\Sigma fu}{n}h = 52.5+\left(\frac{-26\times 5}{90}\right) = 52.5-\frac{130}{90}$$

$=52.5–1.44=51.06$ mm

Median : The arithmetic mean of a distribution, in which there are some extremely high or low values, will either over estimate or under estimate the average position and Hence is not a best representative value. The measure of central tendancy suitable in such situations is Median, which is defined as the middle most value of the observations after arranging them in an ascending or descending order.

Formula

(1) *For ungrouped data* : If n values of a variable are arranged in ascending or descending order, median is the $\frac{n+1}{2}$th, value provided that, n is an odd number. It is taken to be the arithmetic mean of the two middle values if n is an even number.

(2) *For grouped data* : It involves cumulative frequencies also alongwith the class frequencies and is denoted by

$$\text{Median} = 1+\frac{\frac{n}{2}-c}{f}\times h \qquad ...(1.5)$$

where
n is the total number of frequencies, l is the lower class limit in which the median lies.

c is the cumulative frequency, of the class preceding the median cass (the class in which the median lies)

f is the class frequency of the median class

h is the class interval of the median class

Example 1.4
The monthly income of 20 families in a small locality is given below. What is their most representative family income?

(Income in Rs.)
200, 150, 300, 1,280, 253, 260, 233, 301, 315, 285, 276, 304, 308, 380, 319, 307, 4,989, 100, 305, 403

Solution
Since there are some extremely high values, the arithmetic mean will give a misleading impression of a high level of family income. The median income therefore would be the better representative value. To compute the median, first we arrange the values in ascending order as below ;

100, 150, 200, 233, 253, 260, 276, 285, 300, 301, 304, 305, 307, 308, 315, 319, 380, 403, 1,280, 4,984

The number of observation n in this case is even, so there are two middle values in the series which have been underlined. The median would be the mean of these two middle values :

$$\text{Median} = \frac{301+304}{2} = \text{Rs. } 302.5$$

Thus the most representative family income of the locality is Rs. 302.5.

Example 1.5
The distribution of 2462 Indian towns in 1961 according to their size of population is given below, what is the most representative size of the towns in India?

Population	Below 5000	5000-10,000	10,000-20,000	20,000-50,000	50,000-1,00,000	More than 1,00,000
No. of towns	218	761	748	484	138	113

Solution
In this example A.M. will not serve the purpose because of the two reasons : (*a*) the distribution involves extreme values at both ends (*b*) the middle value of the last class cannot be determined. Thus median is a better measure here and is computed as below :

Population	*Frequencies (no. of towns)*	*Cumulative Frequencies*
Below 5,000	218	518
5000-10,000	761	979
10,000-20,000	748	1,727
20,000-50,000	484	2,211
50,000-1,00,000	138	2,349
1,00,000 and above	113	2,462

$$\frac{n}{2} = \frac{2462}{2} = 1231$$

The median class in which the cumulative frequency $\frac{n}{2} = 1{,}231$ falls is 10,000–20,000.

Thus using the formula (1.5)

$$\text{Median} = l + \frac{\frac{n}{2} - c}{f} \times h$$

where $l = 10{,}000$ $c = 976$ $mf = 748$ and $h = 20{,}000 - 10{,}000 = 10{,}000$

$$= 10{,}000 = \frac{1{,}231 - 979}{748} \times 10{,}000$$

$$= 10{,}000 = \frac{252}{748} \times 10{,}000$$

$$= 10{,}000 + 33{,}68.98$$

$$= 13{,}368.98 \text{ persons}$$

Partitioned Values

Median divides the number of observations such that half the values will be less than median and half will be more than median. Similar interpolation method can also be used for dividing the range of the vlaues of the observations into four parts, ten parts and 100 parts, such that 1/4th, 1/10th and 1/100th of the observations fall within each division respectively. These values are known as quartiles, deciles and percentiles. The formula of computing them are slightly different and are given below.

Quartiles : The values which divide the number of observations into four equal parts are known as quartiles. There are only 3 quartiles Q_1, Q_2 and Q_3 given by :

Ist Quartile, $$Q_1 = l + \frac{\frac{n}{4} - c}{f} \times h \qquad ...(1.6)$$

2nd Quartile, $$Q_2 = \text{Median} \qquad ...(1.7)$$

3rd Quartile, $$Q_2 = l + \frac{\frac{3n}{4} - c}{f} \times h \qquad ...(1.8)$$

Deciles : There are nine deciles which divide the observations into ten equal parts, the *j*th decile is given by :

$$Dj = l + \frac{\frac{jxn}{10} - c}{f} \times h \qquad j = 1, 2 \quad ...9 \qquad ...(1.9)$$

The 5th decile is median.

Percentiles : There are 99 percentiles which divide the observations into hundred equal parts. The *r*th percentile is given by :

$$Pr = l + \frac{\frac{rxn}{10} - c}{f} \times h \qquad r = 1, 2 \quad ...99 \qquad ...(1.10)$$

The 50th percentile is the median.

Note that the values of *l*,*c*, *f*, and *h* will be determined according to the class in which the particular value lies.

Example 1.6

Find out the Ist and 3rd quartiles, 4th and 9th deciles and 3rd and 80th percentiles of the data given in the previous example.

Solution

$$Q1 = l + \frac{\frac{n}{4} - c}{f} - h$$

$$= 5,000 + \frac{615.5 - 218}{761}(5,000)$$

= 7,611.695 or
7,612 person

As

$$\frac{n}{4} = \frac{2462}{4} 615.5$$

which lies in 5,000-10,000

so $l = 5,000, f = 761$
$c = 218, h = 5,000$

$$Q3 = l + \frac{\frac{3n}{4} - c}{f} h$$

As

$$\frac{3n}{4} = \frac{3 \times 2,472}{4} = 18,465$$

which lies in the class

$$= 20,000 + \frac{18,46.5 - 1727}{484}(30,000)$$

$= 37,40.02$ or 37,407 person

20,00,00–50,000

so $l = 20,000$, $c = 1,727$

$f = 484$ and $h = 30,000$

4th Decile,

$$D4 = l + \frac{\frac{4n}{10} - c}{f} h$$

As

$$\frac{4n}{10} = \frac{4 \times 2.462}{10} = 984.5$$

which lies in the class 10,000–20,000 and so

$l = 10,000$, $c = 979$, $f = 748$

$h = 10,000$

$$= 10,000 + \frac{984.8 - 979}{748}(10,000)$$

$= 10,077.54$ or 10,078 persons

9th Decile

$$D9 = l + \frac{\frac{9n}{10} - c}{f} .h$$

As

$$\frac{9n}{10} = \frac{9 \times 2.462}{10} = 2,215.8$$

which lies in the class 2,000–50,000 and so

$l = 20,000$, c–1,727, $f = 484$

$h = 30,000$

$$= 20,000 + \frac{2,215.8 - 1,727}{484}(30,000)$$

$= 50,297.52$ or 50,298 persons

3rd percentile

$$P3 = l + \frac{\frac{3n}{100} - c}{f} .h$$

As

$$\frac{3n}{100} = \frac{3 \times 2,492}{100} = 73.86$$

which lies in the class

so $l = 0$, $c = 0$, $f = 218$

and $h = 5,000$

$$= 0 + \frac{73.86 - 0}{218}(5,000)$$

$= 1,694.04$ or 1,694 persons

and 80th percentile

$$P80 = 1 + \frac{\frac{80n}{100} - c}{f} h$$

As

$$\frac{80n}{100} = \frac{80 \times 2,462}{100} = 1,969.6$$

which lies in the class 20,000-5,000, so $l = 20,000$, $c = 1,727$, $f = 484$ an $h = 30,000$

$$P80 = 20,000 + \frac{1,969.6 - 1,727}{484}(30,000)$$

$= 35,037.19$ or 35,037 persons

Mode : The mode or modal value of the distribution is that value which has the maximum frequency. In case a frequency distribution the mode is computed by the following formula :

$$\text{Mode} = 1 + \frac{fm - f1}{2fm - f1 - f_2} h \qquad ...(1.11)$$

where l is the lower limit of the modal class (i.e. Class having maximum frequency), fm is the maximum frequency, f_1 and f_2 are frequencies of the classes preceding and following the modal class and h is its class interval.

Example 1.7 The following table gives the size of land holding of 357 families in a village. Find out the modal holding size.

Area of Land (in acres)	5-10	10-15	15-20	20-25	25-30	30-35
No. of families	20	35	150	70	44	38

Solution

$$\text{Mode} = 1 + \frac{fm - f1}{2fm - f1 - f_2} h$$

Here $fm = 150$

$$= 15 + \frac{150 - 35}{2 \times 150 - 35 - 70}(5)$$

$t = 15, f_i = 35$

$= f_2 = 70$ and $h = 20–15 = 5$

$$= 15 + \frac{115}{195} \times 5$$

$= 17.94$

Measures of Dispersion : Any measure of central tendency alone is not capable of specifying the distribution sufficiently, because it does not take into consideration the internal variations in the data. For example, if the rainfall of 4 months in two districts *A* and *B* is as given below, we see that the mean monthly rainfall of this season in both the districts is equal.

Month	*1st*	*2nd*	*3rd*	*4th*	*Mean*
Rainfall (mm) District A	50	40	15	15	30
Rainfall (mm) District B	31	29	28	32	30

It is obvious from the above data that although the two districts have equal mean monthly rainfall, they differ in terms of the variability of rainfall in the given season. Thus, in order to further specify a distribution, the values of the central tendency should be supplemented by some measure of dispersion also.

The measures of dispersion, measure the internal variability of the values of the variables. There are generally four knids of measures of dispersion, *viz.*,

(1) Range

(2) Quartile Deviation

(3) Mean Deviation

(4) Standard Deviation

(5) Relative Dispersion

Formula (using the notation used in measures of central tendency)

1. Range=highest value-lowest value

2. Quartile Deviation $= \dfrac{Q_3 - Q_1}{2}$

3. Mean Deviation $= \dfrac{\Sigma|x-a|}{n}$ (for ungrouped data) ...(1.12)

(About any value a)

$= \dfrac{\Sigma|\text{f}x-a|}{n}$ (for grouped data) ...(1.13)

sign | | stands for the absolute value.

Example 1.8

The rainfall in a district for 4 months is given as 50, 40, 15 and 15 mm. Find out the mean deviation of rainfall about mean for the given four months.

Solution

The mean of rainfall (x) in the four months is

$$\bar{x} = \frac{50+40+15}{4} = \frac{120}{4} = 30 \text{ mm.}$$

Because it is an ungrouped data, using formula (1.12)

$$\text{M.D.} = \frac{|50-30| + |40-30| + |15-30| + |15-30|}{4}$$

$$= \frac{20+10+15+15}{4} = \frac{60}{4} = 15 \text{ mm.}$$

Example 1.9

The following table shows the size of coalmines in a coalfield. Compute the mean deviation about mean to show the extent of variations in the size of units.

No. of persons employed	0-100	100-200	200-300	300-400	400-500	500-600	600-700
No. of units	30	45	50	120	100	112	80

Solution

As the data is in a grouped form, we have to use formula (1.13)

Classes (No. of persons employed	No. of Units (f)	Mid value of classes (x)	$u = \frac{x-350}{10}$	fu	$\lvert x-412.2\rvert$		$f\lvert x-412.2\rvert$
0—100	30	50	–3	–90	| –362.2 |	=362.2	10866.2
100—200	45	150	–2	–90	| –262.2 |	=262.2	11799.0
200—300	50	250	–1	–50	| 162.2 |	=162.2	8110.0
300—400	120	350	0	0	| 62.2 |	=62.2	7464.0
400—500	100	450	+1	100	| +37.8 |	=37.8	3780.0
500—600	112	550	+2	224	| +137.8 |	=137.8	15433.6
600—700	80	650	+3	240	| +237.8 |	=237.8	19024.0
Total	537		$\Sigma fu = 334$		$\Sigma f\lvert x-\bar{x}\rvert$		=76476.6

$$\bar{x} = 350 + \frac{334}{537} \times 100$$

$$= 350 + 62.20 \text{ approx.}$$

$$= 412.2$$

$$\text{M.D. about Mean} = \frac{\Sigma f\left|x-\bar{x}\right|}{n} = \frac{76476.6}{537} = 142.414$$

4. Standard Deviation :

Mean deviation gives equal importance to all the deviations about mean or about any other point (median or any other number). Standard deviation is another measure of dispersion in which greater weightage is given to higher deviations about mean.

Standard Deviation is the positive square root of the average of squares of deviations about mean and is given by

$$\text{S.D.} = \frac{\sqrt{\Sigma\left(x-\bar{x}\right)^2}}{n} \text{ (for ungrouped data)} \qquad ...(1.14)$$

or

$$= \sqrt{\frac{\Sigma x^2}{n}-\left(\frac{\Sigma x}{n}\right)^2} \qquad ...(1.15)$$

and

$$\text{S.D.} = \frac{\sqrt{\Sigma f\left(x-\bar{x}\right)^2}}{n} \text{ (for grouped data)} \qquad ...(1.16)$$

or

$$= \sqrt{\frac{\Sigma fx^2}{n}-\left(\frac{\Sigma fx}{x}\right)^2} \qquad ...(1.17)$$

Formula (1.14) and (1.15) will give equal results for ungrouped data and (1.16) and (1.17) will also give equal results for grouped data. Formula (1.15) and (1.17) are shorter in computation than (1.4) and (1.6).

Example 1.20

Find out the S.D. of data in example 1.8.

Solution

$$\frac{\Sigma\left(x-\bar{x}\right)^2}{n} = \frac{\left(50-30\right)^2+\left(40-30\right)^2+\left(15-30\right)^2+\left(15-30\right)^2}{4}$$

$$= \frac{20^2+10^2+15^2+15^2}{4} = \frac{400+100+225+225}{4}$$

$$= \frac{950}{4} = 237.5$$

$$\text{S.D.} = \frac{\sqrt{\Sigma f\left(x-\bar{x}\right)^2}}{n} = \sqrt{237.5} = 15.41 \text{ mm.}$$

Second method : Using formula 1.15

$\Sigma x^2 = 50^2+40^2+15^2+15^2 = 2500+1600+225+225 = 4550$

$\Sigma x = 50+40+15+15 = 120$

$$\text{S.D.} = \sqrt{\frac{\Sigma x^2}{n} - \left(\frac{\Sigma x^2}{n}\right)} = \sqrt{\frac{4550}{4} - \left(\frac{120}{4}\right)^2} = \sqrt{1137.5 - 30^2} = 15.41 \text{ mm.}$$

It should be noted that both the methods yield the same result.
We also observe that the standard deviation is higher than mean deviations.

Example 1.2
Find out the standard deviation of data in Example 1.9.

Classes	No. of Units (f)	Middle Values (x)	fx	fx^2
0—100	30	50	1,500	75,000
100—200	45	150	6,750	1,012,500
200—300	50	250	12,500	3,125,000
300—400	120	350	42,000	14,700,000
400—500	100	450	45,000	20,250,000
500—600	112	550	61,600	33,880,000
600—700	80	650	52,000	33,800,000
	537		221,350	106,842,500

Using (1.17)

$$\text{S.D.} = \sqrt{\frac{\Sigma fx^2x^2}{n} - \left(\frac{\Sigma fx}{n}\right)^2} = \sqrt{\frac{106842500}{537} - \left(\frac{221350}{537}\right)^2}$$

$$\sqrt{198961.824 - (412.197)^2} = \sqrt{198961.824 - 169906.367}$$

$$\sqrt{29055.457} = 170.46 \text{ persons}$$

A short cut method of computing standard deviation is often used, as it saves considerable time. The method is given below :

$$\text{Standard Deviation} = h\sqrt{\frac{\Sigma fu^2}{n} - \left(\frac{\Sigma fu}{n}\right)^2} \quad \text{...(1.18)}$$

where $u = \frac{X - A}{h}$, A is any value of X in the middle and h is the common class interval.

The above example can be solved more easily using the short cut method, as below.

Short cut method :

Classes	(f)	(x)	$u = \frac{x-350}{100}$	fu	fu^2
0—100	30	50	–3	–90	270
100—200	45	150	–2	–90	180
200—300	50	250	–1	–50	50
300—400	120	350	0	0	0
400—500	100	450	+1	+100	100
500—600	112	550	+2	+224	448
600—700	80	650	+3	+240	720
	537			+334	=1768

$$\text{S.D.} = h\sqrt{\frac{fu^2}{n} - \left(\frac{fu}{n}\right)^2} = 100\sqrt{\frac{1.768}{537} - \left(\frac{334}{537}\right)^2} = 100\sqrt{3.2929 - (.6230)^2}$$

$$= 100\sqrt{3.2924 - .3869} = 100\sqrt{2.9055} = 100 \times 1.704,527$$

$$= 170.5 \text{ persons}$$

Note that this method takes considerably less time than the previous method but gives the same result. A difference of 0.01 units in the two methods is just because of the rounding error.

5. Measures of Relative Dispersion

The units of measurement of variability are the same as the units of measurements of the original data. Thus the variability of the two variables measured in different units cannot be compared. Secondly, variability becomes more meaningful if given in relation to the mean of the variable. For example, the variability of Rs. 150 in the income distribution of a community whose average family income is Rs. 1000 is not as undesirable as in a community whose average family income is only Rs. 200.

Thus there is a need to measure the dispersion in a distribution in relation to its central value for expression the consistency in the data. The most commonly used measure of such relative variability is the coefficient of variation, defined as $\frac{\text{S.D.}}{\text{Mean}} \times 100$. As the S.D. and mean have the same dimension, C.V. is a dimension less quantity and so the different values of C.V. are comparable. A higher value of C.V. shows higher inconsistency in the data, whereas a lower value of C.V. shows higher consistency in the data.

Example 1.18

The average annual rainfall (in inches) for Bikaner and Jodhpur is given below for 10 years. In which district is it more consistent?

Bikaner : 6.4, 27.4, 8.1, 16.1, 19.0, 7.2, 10.0, 4.7, 12.4 and 18.9
Jodhpur : 8.7, 14.6, 25.1, 30.6, 22.7, 9.4, 15.0, 15.3, 9.0 and 11.3

Solution
Computing the mean and standard deviation in usual manner, we get

	Bikaner	Jodhpur
Mean	13.92 inches	16.17 inches
S.D.	6.83 inches	7.16 inches
C.V.	$\frac{6.83}{13.92}\times 100 = 53.00$	$\frac{7.16}{16.17}\times 100 = 44.00$

As the C.V. is smaller for Jodhpur we can say that the rainfall is more consistent in Jodhpur than in Bikaner (it is interesting to note that the absolute variability as reflected in S.D. is smaller in Bikaner).

Measures of Skewness

A concentration of relatively larger number of observations on higher (or lower) side causes inequality in any distribution. This inequality is reflected in the shape of its frequency curve. A positively skewed curve shows the concentration of observations at lower end, whereas a negatively skewed curve shows the concentration at higher end. A symmetric curve on the other hand, shows the concentration at the middle.

In order to measure the nature and extent of skewness, the coefficient of skewness (SK) as suggested by Karl Pearson is given as :

$$SK = \frac{\text{Mean–Mode}}{\text{Standard Deviation}}$$

There is no limit to this measure in theory. But generally its value lies in between +1 to –1. When the distribution is symmetrical, the values of mean, median and mode coincide and therefore, the coefficient of skewness will be positive and when it is negatively skewed coefficient of skewness will be negative. The degree of skewness is proportional to the value of the coefficient of skewness. A higher value of it means a higher skewness and a lower value of it means a low skewness.

In case the standard deviation and mean of any distribution cannot be worked out, as is the case in open end distributions, the coefficient of skewness, as suggested by Bowley, can be used. His coefficient of skewness is given as :

$$\text{Bowley's SK} = \frac{Q_3 + Q_1 - 2\ \text{Median}}{Q_3 - Q_1}$$

This measure is called as Quartile Measure of skewness, and it varies exactly from +1 to –1.

Apart from the above two measures of skewness and variability, few more methods have been discussed separately in Chapter VIII.

EXERCISES

1. The daily minimum temperature record of a weather reporting station is given below for 80 days in °F. Construct a frequency distribution table using a class interval of 5°F. Show the distribution by a Histogram and cumulative frequency curve and from that find in how many days the minimum temperature was

   1. 75°F or higher
   2. Below 80°F
   3. 65°F and above but less than 85°F

Temperature in °F									
68	84	75	82	68	90	62	88	76	93
73	79	88	73	60	95	71	59	85	75
61	65	75	87	74	62	95	78	63	72
66	78	82	75	94	77	69	74	68	60
66	78	89	61	75	95	60	79	83	71
96	62	67	97	78	65	76	65	71	76
79	80	73	57	88	78	62	76	53	74
65	67	73	81	72	63	76	75	85	77

2. The production of rice per acre in 130 districts of a region is given below. Construct a Histogram and cumulative frequency curve.

Production in Kgs.	Less than 100	Less than 200	Less than 300	Less than 400	Less than 500	Less than 600
No. of Districts	8	18	34	54	84	130

3. Write each of the following expressions in full

   (a) $\sum_{i=1}^{5} X_1$ (b) $\sum_{i=1}^{6} X_1^2$ (c) $\sum_{i=1}^{4} (X_1 + Y_1)$

   (d) $\sum_{i=1}^{6} (X_1 + a)$ (e) $\sum_{i=1}^{3} X_1 Y_1$ (f) $\sum_{i=1}^{8} X_1 Y_1$

4. Write each of the following expressions in summation signs

   (a) $X_1 + X_2 + X_3 + \ldots\ldots\ldots\ldots + X_{15}$

   (b) $(X_1 - Y_1) + (X_2 - Y_2) + \ldots\ldots\ldots + (X_n - Y_n)$

   (c) $X_2 + X_3 + X_4 + \ldots\ldots\ldots\ldots + X_{10}$

   (d) $X_3^2 Y_3 + X_4^2 Y_4 + \ldots\ldots\ldots\ldots + X_{11}^2 Y_{11}$

5. Given $X_1 = 3,\ X_2 = 2,\ X_3 = 1,\ X_4 = 0,\ X_5 = 2$

   $F_1 = 2,\ F_2 = 8\ ,\ F_3 = 20,\ F_4 = 12,\ F_5 = 3$

   $Y_1 = 7,\ Y_2 = 4,\ Y_3 = 8,\ Y_4 = 5,\ Y_5 = -3$

   Evaluate

   (a) $\sum_{i=1}^{5} X_1 F_1$ (b) $\sum_{i=2}^{4} X_1 F_1$ (c) $\sum_{i=1}^{4} (Y_1 - X_1)_1$

   (d) $\sum_{i=2}^{4} (X_1 Y_1)_1$ (e) $\sum_{i=2}^{4} X^2{}_1 Y_1$

6. The Production of wheat in 10 plots of equal size is given below. Find the average production of wheat per plot.

Plot	1	2	3	4	5	6	7	8	9	10
Production (in MT)	50	35	65	67	73	81	95	32	87	57

7. The following table gives distribution of salaries of workers in a factory. Work out the most representative salary of worker in the factory, also prepare a frequency curve of the salaries of workers and comment on it.

Salary in Rs.	50-60	60-70	70-80	80-90	90-100	100-110	110-120	120-130	130-140
No. of workers	8	12	55	65	73	72	81	62	46

8. The average yield of barley (in maunds) per acre and the area (in acres) under barley in 4 districts is given below. Compute the combined average yield of barley for 4 districts.

Districts	A	B	C	D
Mean yield of barley	20.0	23.0	26.0	27.0
Area	200	205	85	119

9. Daily rainfall record of a district for 40 days is given below. Compute the median and the mean rainfall and compare them.

Rainfall in inches	11.8-12.6	12.7-13.5	13.6-14.4	14.5-15.3	15.4-16.2	16.3-17.1
No. of days	3	5	9	12	5	6

10. The classification of 1085 families according to their monthly income is given below. Compute, the median family income, the 2nd and the 3rd quartile, the 8th decile and the 30th percentile.

Among mean, median and mode, which is the best representative of the family income and why ?

Income in Rs.	150-160	160-170	170-180	180-190	190-200	200-210	210-220	220-230	230-240	240-250	Total
No. of families	62	65	71	83	90	95	110	180	168	161	1085

11. The frequency distribution table of agricultural holdings in a village is given below. Compute the model agricultural holding of the village.

Area of land (in acres)	5-10	10-15	15-20	20-25	25-30	30-35
No. of families	20	35	50	55	40	38

12. Calculate the model wage for the following distribution of daily wages of workers in a certain factory.

Daily Wages (in Rs.)	No. of Employees	Daily Wages (in Rs.)	No. of Employees
60-80	22	140-160	85
80-100	45	160-180	190
100-120	67	180-200	64
120-140	73	200-220	55

13. The average annual rainfall of 66 districts is given below. Compute 1st and 3rd Quartile and the median, then work out the semi-inter quartile range.

Rainfall (in inches)	0-10	10-20	20-30	30-40	40-50	50-60
No. of Districts	22	10	8	15	5	6

14. The monthly salary of 20 workers in a factory is given below. Compute the mean deviation about mean and median.

Monthly Salary (in Rs.)

84	95	96	93	87	79	73
69	68	67	78	82	83	89
95	103	108	117	130	97	

15. The following table gives the distribution of 40 farms by size. Compute the standard deviation and the skewness of the size of the farms :

Farms acreage to nearest acre	1—10	11—50	51—100	101—200	201—300	301—400	401—500
No. of farms	13	9	10	7	4	5	2

16. The following table gives the distribution of land in two tehsils. In which tehsil the land is more unequally distributed ?

Size of Holdings in acres	No. of Households Tehsil I	Tehsil II
1	2	3
3—6	42	28
6—9	78	292
9—12	35	389
12—15	49	212
15—18	200	59
18—21	150	18
21—24	140	2

17. The following table shows the districtwise density of population (per sq. mile) of two states of India, *i.e.*, J & K and Kerala in 1961. In which state the variations in districtwise density of population are more ?

S. No.	J. & K. State	Density (persons per sq. mile in 00)	Kerala State	Density (persons per sq. mile in 00)
1.	Anantnag	3	Cannanore	8
2.	Srinagar	5	Kozhikode	10
3.	Baramula	5	Palghat	9
4.	Ladakh	1	Trichur	14
5.	Doda	1	Ernakulam	14
6.	Udhampur	1	Kottayam	7
7.	Jammu	1	Alleppey	25
8.	Kathua	1	Quilon	11
9.	Poonch	2	Trivandrum	21

(Density is given in round figures)

2
THEORY OF PROBABILITY

It is said that "Statistics is The mathematical study of probability." It is, therefore, not possible to proceed into analytical aspects of statistics without introducing the basic concepts of probability.

The need of the theory of probability arises when we deal with a phenomenon whose future behaviour cannot be predicted precisely *i.e.* the random phenomenon. For example, we do not know the amount of rainfall Delhi is going to receive next year. We also do not know that if a coin is tossed whether we will get head or tail or if a district is randomly chosen what will be the proportion of its urban population to the total population etc. In all such problems we cannot predict the exact position.

Before any such phenomenon occurs, it may be considered to occur in many different ways. Delhi, for example, in the next year may receive rainfall equal to 25 cms., 100 cms., more than 100 cms., or any value in between. A person who is well aware of the climatological conditions in India, however, would say that it is extremely unlikely that the rainfall in the next year would be 25 cms. or 100 cms. The rainfall below 20 cms. and above 100 cms. in a year may also be considered very unlikely for Delhi. The chances are more, in fact, that the rainfall would be around 40 to 60 cms.

We make several such conclusions in our daily life. In this case, we measure the possibilities of the different outcomes of an event (rainfall) on the basis of our past experience.

The theory of probability provides us a mathematical basis of measuring the chances of the occurrence of the random events.

The Empirical Defination of Probability

If an event is repeated a great number of times under the same conditions then the ration of the number of times that a particular from of the event occurs to total number of trials is known as the probability of that event. Suppose, the average annual rainfall in a region for 200 year is as given below in Table 2.1. The probabilities of the different intervals of rainfall can be computed simply by taking the ratios of the frequencies in each class to the total 200 frequencies. These probabilities are also given in the last column of Table 2.1.

Table 2.1

Rain fall (in cms.)	No. of Year	Probability		
0—10	1	1/200	=	.005
10—20	9	9/200	=	.045
20—30	16	16/200	=	.080
30—40	39	39/200	=	.195
40—50	70	70/200	=	.350
50—60	40	40/200	=	.20
60—70	15	15/200	=	.040
70—80	8	8/200	=	040
80+	2	2/200	=	.010
	Total 200	1.000		

Mathematically, if an event can occur in n total number of mutually exclusive and equally likely[1] cases and m of them are in favour of a particular event A (case), the probability of the event A is given by

$$P(A) = \frac{m}{n}$$

provided that n is sufficiently large.

Tossing of a coin, for example, can occur in two mutually exclusive and equally like cases of heads and tails. As there is only one case in favour of heads, the probability of heads $P(H)$ will be ½. Similarly the probability of getting 5 in a throw of a dice, $P(5)$ is

$$P(5) = \frac{1}{6} \qquad \text{(Here } n=6, m=1\text{)}$$

Axioms of Probability

On the basis of the above definition of the probability the following exioms are important to know.

(1) The value of any probability ranges from zero to unity. In extreme cases, when the occurrence of an event is impossible, its probability is zero and when the event is sure to occur, its probability is unity. In all other cases it varies in between zero and unity.

(2) If $A_1, A_2 \ldots\ldots\ldots A_n$ are the total number of cases in which an event can occur, the sum of their probabilities is unity, i.e.

$$P(A_1) + (PA_2) + \ldots\ldots\ldots + P(A_n) = 1$$

1. The events which cannot occur simultaneously are known as mutually exclusive events and are said to be equally likely if the probability of their occurrence is equal.

To illustrate it, consider a dice on which number 1, 2, 3, 4, 5 or 6 can occur with a probability $\frac{1}{6}$

$$P(1)+P(2)+P(3)+P(4)+P(5)+P(6)$$

$$=\frac{1}{6}+\frac{1}{6}+\frac{1}{6}+\frac{1}{6}+\frac{1}{6}+\frac{1}{6}=1$$

3. The Probability of not occurrence of an event A is

$$P(A^{6})=1-P(A)$$

Thus the probability of not getting number 5 in a throw of dice

$$=1-\frac{1}{6}=\frac{5}{6}$$

Probabilities of Compound Events

(1) If $P(A_1), P(A_2)$.............$P(A_n)$ are the probabilities of n independent events, the probability of the simultaneous occurrence of A_1 and A_2 is $P(A_1)\text{x}P(A_2)$ and is denoted by $P(A_1{\times}A_2)$. Similarly $P(A_1\text{x}A_3)=P(A_1)\text{x}\,P(A_2)\text{x}P(A_2)$ and will mean the probability of the simultaneous occurrence of A_1, A_2 and A_3. Thus, if two coins are tossed the probability of getting heads on both the coins is

$$P(H\,x\,H)=P(H)\,x\,P(h)=\frac{1}{2}\times\frac{1}{2}=\frac{1}{4}=0.25$$

Where it is given that $P(H)=\frac{1}{2}$

(2) If there are two events A_1 and A_2 the probability that any one of them (or both) would occur is denoted by $P(A_1{+}A_2)$

$P(A_1{+}A_2)=P(A_1)+P(A_2)$ when
A_1 and A_2 are mutually exclusive, and
$P(A_1{+}A_2)+P(A_1)+P(A_2)-P(A_1{+}A_2)$
when A_1 and A_2 are not mutually exclusive.

'According to this the probability of getting either 3 or 6 in the throw of a dice is

$$\text{P}(3{+}6)=\text{P}(3){+}\text{P}(6)=\frac{1}{6}+\frac{1}{6}=\frac{2}{6}=\frac{1}{3}$$ (since on only one dice 3 and 6 are mutually exclusive)

Probability Distribution

It has been shown earlier that the probabilities in any distribution are the relative frequencies. These proportions (realtive frequencies) reflect the probability with which any observation may fall in any one of the given classes. In Table 2.1 for example, when the 200 frequencies distributed in different classes are converted into proportions, they give the probabilites with which different values of rainfall may occur-the probability for example, that the average annual rainfall in year would be between 10 to 20 cms. is .045. What follows from this argument is that if the frequencies of different values of the observations are expressed as the ratios to the total number of observations, the frequency distributions may be considered as probability distributions also. The shape of the frequency curve, however, remains unchanged if the frequencies are conversted into probabilities.

The Nature of the distribution of any variable depends on the particular process which generates it. For example, the process of urbanization has generated the distribution of percentage of urban population to total population in the districts of India which is skewed to the right. The climatological process on the other hand is such that the distribution of the average annual rainfall of an area over large number of years will be almost symmetric. In other words, we can say that the probabilities of the different values of a variable depend on the underlying process.

The functional form a relationship between the values of a variable and their probabilities is known as probability distribution function. There are several forms of these probability distribution functions, depending on certain underlying assumptions through which a particular process is characterized. Making a hypothesis about any process and using its underlying assumptions, we can choose a probability distribution function for given phenomenon. The probabilities or proportional frequencies are then estimated according to the chosen probability distribution function. These estimated frequencies are then compared with the actual values. If the difference between the actual and estimated values is found to be large, the process and its underlying assumptions are supposed to be incorrect, otherwise it may be taken to be true. Probability distributions have an important role to play in the whole theory of statistical inference. The important probability distributions are given below with their underlying assumptions.

1. Binomial Distribution

Consider a hypotherical process of tossing n coins, as a result of which we can get either no head, 1 head, 2 heads....or n heads. Each of the above n outcomes have some probability.

Here the number of heads may be considered as the variable x which can assume different integer values between zero and n, and hence, the process of tossing the coin may be defined by the following assumptions :

1. The different values of the variable x are discontinuous.
2. Probability of head is, say, p, and so probability of tail q is 1-p (i.e. $q = 1—p$).
3. The result of a coin does not affect the results of the other coins (*i.e.*) events are independent)
4. The number of coins (n) is not very large.
5. Neither p nor q is very small.

A normal process of tossing the coins will follow the above assumptions, in the light of which the probabilities with which the variable x will occur with different values $P(x)$ can be determined theoretically as given below.

$$P_{(x)} = {}^nC_x P^x q^{n-x} \qquad x=0, 1, 2....n$$

Where $nC_x = \dfrac{n!}{x!(n-x)!}$ and $n! = n(n\text{-}1)(n\text{-}2)....1$

Properties of the Binomal Distribution

1. It is symmetrical when $p = q$ and when $p \neq q$ it is skewed.
2. Its mean = np and standard deviation = $\sqrt{npq}$

2. Poisson Distribution

The binomial distribution assumes a convenient form in the limiting case when :

1. Either p or q is very small.
2. n is large.
3. np *i.e.* the average, is finite.

The probability distribution function $P(X)$ is given by

$$P(x) = \frac{e^{-m} m^x}{x!} x = x = 0, 1, 2............,$$

Where m is the mean of the variable X and e = 2.718.

It is must be noted that the condition that either p or q is very small makes it suitable only for rare events *i.e.* for those events whose occurrence is more frequent in smaller number and their occurrence in larger number is limited to only few observations.

Properties of Poisson Distribution

1. Mode of the Poisson variate is the integral value in between m and m-1.
2. Mean an variance of a Poisson variate are same and are equal to m.
3. It is not symmetric.

3. Normal Distribution

The above two distributions are discontinuous distributions. The normal distribution to which a large number of distributions approximate is a continuous distribution and may be considered as another limiting form of the bonomial distribution when :

1. Neither p nor q is very small
2. n is very largre.

The normal probability distribution function $P(x)$ is given by :

$$P(x) = \frac{1}{\sigma\sqrt{2\pi}} e^{-\frac{1}{2}\left(\frac{x-m}{\sigma}\right)^2}$$

X varies from minus infinity to plus infinity.

Where e = 2.718

n = 3.1416

σ = S.D. of the variable x and m is its mean

The normal probability curve is a bell-shaped symmetric curve (Fig. 2.1) about the ordinate at $X=m$. The medium of the distribution coincides with mean and mode. The value of $P(x)$ decreases rapidly as X deviates from the mean. The curve extends to infinity on either sides of the mean. In terms of real situation it has been said that if there appear to be two groups of factors affecting a variable such that one group acting consistently and another acting randomly, there are a priori grounds for expecting that the variable in the long run will follow the normal distribution.[1]

Normal distribution is the most important distribution in statistics, because it has an important bearing on the whole theory of parametric statistical analysis. Most of the statistical analyses are valid only if the data is normally distributed. It has its importance in the theory of sampling also, where it has been found that the distributions of a sample mean, standard deviation and other sample characteristics are normal even if the distribution of the original data deviates from normal it. Thus the properties of normal distribution are also used in drawing inferences from samples.

NORMAL CURVE

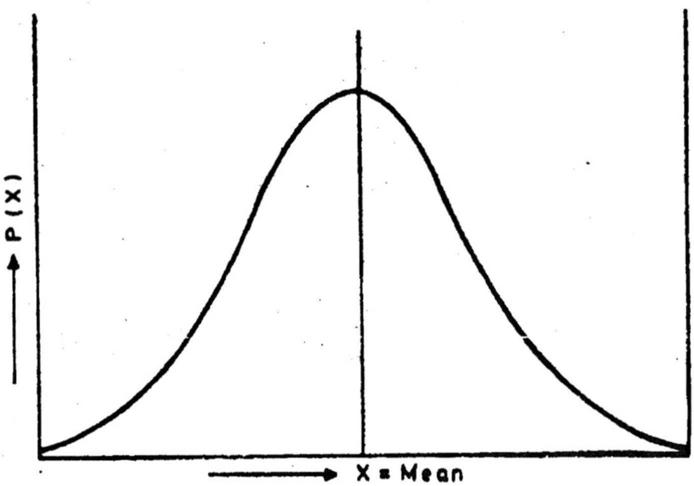

Fig. 2.1

1. R. Hammond and P.S. Macullagh. *Quarantitative Methods in Geography*. Clarendon Press Oxford, 1974. p. 98.

Important Properties of Normal Distribution

Apart from the properties given above the following properties are important to know because of their application in making statistical inferences.

The different values of a normal variable with mean and S.D.=will be distributed as below.

1. Half of the values will be less than the mean and half will be greater than the mean.
2. The 68.26 per cent values will be greater than or equal to *m*-3 and less than m+σ
3. The 95.46 per cent values will be greater than or equal to *m*-2 and less than m+σ
4. The 99.73 per cent values will be greater than or equal to *m*-3 and less than m+σ.

Thus, if a variable is normally distributed with mean 50 and S.D.=8, there will be 68.26 per cent values in between 42 and 58,95.45 (or 95 in round figures) per cent values in between 34 and 66 and 99.73 (or 99 in round figures) per cent values will be in between 26 and 34.

3
THEORY OF SAMPLING

In many studies, which consist of a large number of observations, often it is not possible to collect the information for each and every unit because of the lack of resources, time and trained peronnnel, etc. Such cases can be tackled by observing a manageably smaller portion of it, instead of the whole. While using a smaller portion of the total observations the researcher, however, has to be assured that is the best representative of all the observations included in his study. Another important aspect of any such exercise is that the researcher has to make a compromise between manual labour saved and the amount of information lost in using this sample short cut. The above concepts in terms of sampling theory may be explained as below.

The larger group of observation required for a study is known as the universe or the population of the study. For example, in study of the rural settlement pattern in a region all the villages (which may be several thousands in number) in the region will form the universe or population of the study. Similarly, a large set of households, industrial units, agricultural farms and steel plants, etc. may form the universe or population of different studies (note the population here has nothing to do with the people). The summary measures of the population like mean, median and standard deviation etc. are known as the parameters of the population. A part of the population selected as its representative is called the sample and the process of such selection is known as sampling. The summary measures of sample are known as statistic (s).

Types of Sampling

Maximum representation of the population by a sample may be achieved by the method of drawing the sample. The different methods of sampling which ensure better representation of the population under different situations are given as below :

Simple Random Sampling. It is a method of drawing the sample in which every member of the population has equal chance of being selected in the sample. This method is useful only when the members of the population are fairly homogeneous. The procedure of simple random sampling is just like drawing a number in a lottery.

The random sampling is very much facilitiated by the use of random numbers table prepared by Tippet, Kandall, Smith, Fisher and Yeats or by Rand Corporation. A page of one of them is given in appendix-I as an example. A random numbers table is such arrangement of numbers in which randomness has been ensured by some method. Any number on any page is either taken from any row, column or from any diagonal to constitute the random sample of numbers. In a practical exercise of sampling, first the members of the population are assigned a serial number and then the set of chosen random numbers is considered as the serial numbers of the members in the population to be selected in the sample. If the total number observation are between 10 to 99 two adjoining columns (or rows) of the random numbers have to be taken. In case it is more than 99 but less than 1000 three adjoining columns have to be taken, and so on. For example, suppose the population observations are 88, we will take two columns. Thus if we take the 7th and the 8th columns of the random number given in appendix-I, the first numbers of the two columns are 2 and 8 which makes 28, similarly the other numbers are 49, 31, 15, 18, 97, 49... we can choose as many numbers as we want to include in the sample. The observations corresponding to the serial numbers 28, 49, 31, 15, 18, 49... will constitute the random sample of the given population. Note that the random numbers more than 88 have to be rejected.

Areal Random Sampling : Geographers often consider location as an essential part of the variability of individual observations, and it is therefore, important that samples are representatives of the full range of locational variability.

The procedure of areal random sampling is slightly different from the ordinary random sampling. By using a grid overlay on a map a population of coordinate points can be generated. By using a random numbers table a set of points may be selected as random sample of all the points. The areas around the sample points may be considered as sample areas. The procedure for this would be to chose any four columns of a random number table (if the grids numbers are between 1 and 99). From these four random numbers sample points can be chosen by assigning two consecutive

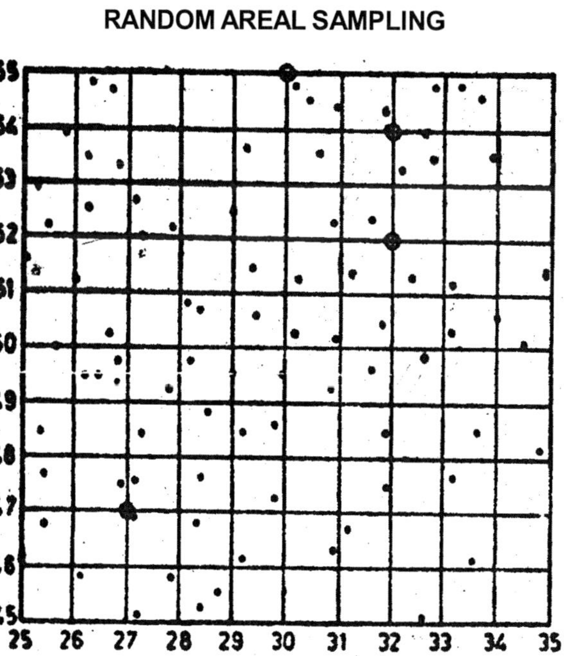

Fig. 3.1

columns to the x-coordinate and next two columns to the y-coordinate. For example, for a hypothetical map of settlements in Fig. 3.1, there are 11 rows and 11 columns and their serial numbers (given arbitrarily) range from 45 to 55 and from 25 to 35 repectively. From four randomly chosen columns of a random number table, we have to fix two digits for x-coordinate and two for y-coordinate. Suppose we randomly choose columns 13th to 16th, read them down, then the next four columns down to up and so on till we get the desired number of points. The points so obtained are 32, 52, 30, 55, 54, 27, 47... Thus the intersection of 32nd row and 52nd column will be the first sample observation. Intersection of 30th row and 55th column will be the next sample observation and so on. Four such points selected are shown on the map given in Fig. 3.1 (other numbers fall outside the range).

Whenever the units of observation are points, it is not necessary that the observational points will coincide with the chosen grid points. In such cases we can always frame some rule for getting them and follow it consistently. For example, we may decide that from the sample point the nearest observational point in the south-east direction will be chosen as member of the sample. When a patch of land is the unit of observation, we may also choose the whole grid on the south-east or south-west etc. of the sample point.

Systematic Sampling : Many times a random sample does not have the good coverage of the area of study. A systematic sampling selects the population at regular intervals. Each tenth name on an electoral list, every 5th household, every alternate grid intersection etc., will yield the systematic

SYSTEMATIC AREAL SAMPLING

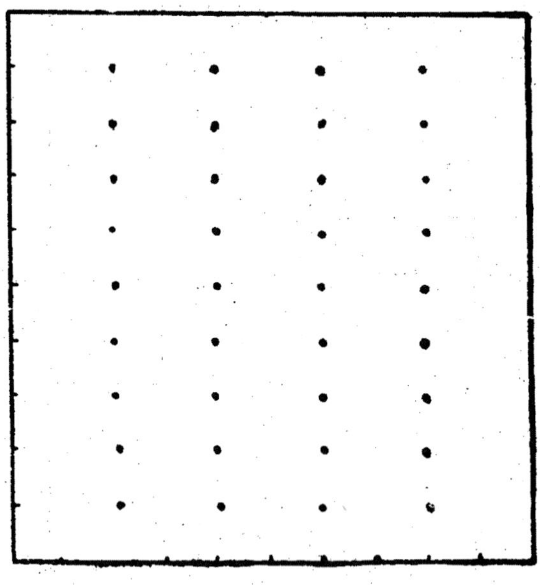

Fig. 3.2

sample. It also gives a more uniform coverage of the population. A systematic sample is generally used when the background population is itself randomly distributed. On the other hand if there are regularities in the population distribution, a systematic sample may be biased.[1] A systematic sample of points on the previous map is shown in Fig. 3.2.

Stratified Sampling : A random sample is good only when there are not marked differences in the population. Problem arises when the population is composed of highly varied observations. Suppose for a family planning survey in a district a sample of 1000 households has to be selected from the total 25000 households living in both rural and urban areas. In a random sample there is no surety that both urban and rural part will have proper representation. Random selection of the sample households may give us either more or less urban representation than its proportion in the total population. A balanced representation may be ensured by dividing the population into two sets of urban and rural households and then drawing a random sample of appropriate size from each set. Whenever a population is first divided into some sub-populations (strata) to ensure the representation of each sub group and then from each sub-group a sample is drawn in any suitable way, it is known as stratified sampling.

Apart from the three important sampling procedures frequently used in geographical studies, the other sampling methods like Hierarchical Sampling, Cluster Sampling and Quota Sampling, etc. may also be used. A further discussion on these sampling methods may be found in many good book on sampling.[1]

Sampling Distributions

Let $x_1\ x_2\ x_3$............ be the sample means of large number of random samples of equal size, each drawn from the same population after replacing the previous sample observations into population. The distribution of these hypothetical sample means is known as standard error of sample means. Similary we can have sampling distribution of median, standard deviation or any other statistics also. The standard deviation of the sampling distribution of any statistics is known as the standard error of that statistics.

Sampling distributions have an important bearing on the of theory sampling in establishing a relationship between population measures (parameters) and sample measures (statistics).

IMPORTANT SAMPLING DISTRIBUTIONS

Sampling Distribution of Means : If a random sample of size n>30 is drawn from a population with mean μ and finite standard devisation σ the sampling distribution of mean would be a normal distribution with mean μ and standard devation σ_n. Here there is no assumption about the distribution of population except that it should have a finite standard deviation which is not very unlikely.

The degree of approximation of a sampling distribution of mean to the normal distribution depends on (*a*) the degree of departure of the parent population from the size of a sample is less than 30, the sampling distributions will rather approximate to students' *t*' distribution than to normal,

---

1. R. Hammond and P. Macullagh, "Quantitative Techniques in Geography : An Introduction" Clarendon Press 1947, p. 115.

2. Reader, may refer to : Tarayamane, *Elementary Sampling Theory*, Prentice Hall, Englewood cliffs, N.J. 1967 or W.G. Cochram, *Sampling Techniques*, Asia Publishing House, New Delhi, 1953.

even if the population is normal. Because of this reason, in case of the sampling distributions of mean, a sample of size 30 an more is supposed to be a large sample.

Sampling Distribution of the Difference of Two Sample Means : If two large samples to size n_1 and n_2 are drawn from the poulations with mean μ_1 and μ_2 and standard deviations σ_1 and σ_2, the sample distribution of the difference of these sample means x_1 and x_2 will be normally distributed with

mean = $\mu_1 - \mu_2$ and standard deviation $\sqrt{\frac{\sigma_1^2}{n_1}+\frac{\sigma_2^2}{n_2}}$ (also known as the standard error of the differences

of two sample means). If the sample is more than 100, σ^2_1 and σ^2_2 may be replaced by their sample variances.

Sampling Distribution of Proportions. The sampling distribution of the proportions p of an attribute will also be normal with mean equal to the proportion of the attribute in the population and

standard deviation $=\sqrt{\frac{pq}{n}}$ where $q = 1\text{-}p$ and $n>30$ is the size of the sample. Similarly the sampling

distributions of the difference of two sample proportions q_1 and p_2 will be normal with mean equal to

the difference of those proportions in the population and standard deviation = $\sqrt{\frac{p_1q_1}{n_1}+\frac{p_2q_2}{n_2}}$ where

n_1 and n_2 are the sizes of the large samples.

The main objective of any sampling exercise is to get as much information as possible about the population from which it has been drawn. The sampling theory identifies important relationships between the population parameters and sample statistics. These relationships help us in making conclusions about the parameters with the help of statistics only. The logic of the theory of sampling is the logic of induction, the is, we pass from particular to general and hence all results will have to be expressed in terms of probability.

These concepts of probable results of any sampling exercise are explained as below :

Suppose we have to test whether a sample is drawn from a population or not. We start with a null hypothesis,[1] that the sample has been drawn from a given population, whereas in reality it may or may not be true. We can make the decision of accepting or rejecting the hypothesis using some tests. If in reality the hypothesis is true (i.e. sample has been drawn from the population) and our test rejects it (i.e. on the basis of the test we conclude that sample might not have been drawn from the given population, we commit an error. The chances of such error to be reduced in any sampling problem. A technical term "level of significance" is being used in place of the probability of this error. The chances of such error to be reduced in any sampling problem. A technical term "level of significance : is being used in place of the probability of this error. Thus the level of significance can be defined as probability of rejecting a correct hypothesis.

1. A null hypothesis is defined as the hypothesis with probable rejection.

TEST OF SIGNIFICANCE BASED ON LARGE SAMPLES

On the basis of the properties of the sampling distributions of means and proportions as given above the following useful tests have been designed for large samples.

1. *Test of Significance between the mean of large sample and population mean* : Given a sample of size n drawn from a population with standard deviation σ we can test the null hypothesis that the mean of the population is μ. The procedure of this test is to compare the absolute difference between the sample mean $\bar{x}$ and the population mean μ with the standard error of mean $\sigma/\sqrt{n}$. If the difference $|\bar{x}-\mu|$ is less than $3\sigma/\sqrt{n}$ it is said to be insignificant at 1% level of signicicane[1] and population mean may be considered equal to μ (*i.e.* the null hypothesis may be accepted). The population mean are just attributed to the chance or random factors. On the other hand, if $|\bar{x}-\mu|$ is greater than or equal to $3\sigma/\sqrt{n}$ the null hypothesis is rejected and the population mean cannot be considered equal to. Note that if Population S.D. σ is not given the sample S.D., is generally taken as an estimated value for σ when the size of sample is fairly large $n \geq 100$). For small samples the estimate of σ is

$$S\sqrt{\frac{n}{n-1}}$$

Example 3.1

A random sample of 100 farms from a region gives the average farm size of 50 acres with a standard deviation (s) of 26 acres. Can the average farm size in the region be taken as 60 acres?

Solution

Given $\bar{x} = 50$, $\mu = 60$, $n = 100$, we do not know the value of the population standard deviation. Since the size of the sample is large, the samples standard deviation (s) may be taken as good estimate of σ

Thus,

$$= |50\text{-}60| = 10 \text{ acres}$$

$$3.\text{S.E.} \quad = \frac{3\times 26}{\sqrt{100}} = \frac{3\times 26}{10} = 7.8$$

As the difference of sample mean and the given population mean (10 acres) is more than 3 times of the S.E. of mean (7.8 acres), the difference is significant at 1% level of significance. Hence, we cannot take the average farm size in the region as 60 acres.

2. *Testing the Significance of the Difference between the Means of Two Large Samples* : Suppose we are interested in knowing whether the two population have the same mean or not. We draw two random samples one from each population. Let the results be as below :

1. 3 S.E. is being used because of the property of normal distribution that one per cent observations of a distribution will fall out side the limit-3 standard deviation. We can use 2 S.E. limit for 5 per cent of level of significance.

	First Sample	*Second Sample*
Size	n_1	n_2
Mean	$\bar{x}_1$	$\bar{x}_2$
S.D.	s_1	s_2

Under the hypothesis that the means of two populations from which the two samples have been drawn are equal, the absolute difference of sample means $|\bar{x}_1 - \bar{x}_2|$ should not exceed 3 times the S.E.

of $|\bar{x}_1 - \bar{x}_2|$ which is $\sqrt{\frac{\sigma_1{}^2}{n_1} + \frac{\sigma_2{}^2}{n_2}}$. If the values of the S.D. of the two populations σ_1 and σ_2 are not known, the two sample S.D. s_1 and s_2 may replace them.

Example 3.2

A random sample of 100 rural settlements from region A gives the mean size of the settlements equal to 600 persons with a S.D. of 85 persons. Another random sample of 150 settlements from region *B* gives the mean size as 630 persons with a S.D. of 100 persons.

Test whether the two regions have equal mean size of the settlements?

Solution

	Region A	*Region B*
Sample Size	100	150
Mean	600 persons	630 persons
S.D.	85 persons	95 persons

The absolute difference between the sample means is | 600—630 | = 30 persons

The S.E. of this difference $|x_1 - x_2| = \sqrt{\frac{85^2}{100} + \frac{95^2}{150}} = \sqrt{\frac{7225}{100} + \frac{9025}{150}}$

$$= \sqrt{72.25 + 60.17} = \sqrt{132.42} = 11.51 \text{ persons}$$

3 times of this S.E. = $3 \times 11.51 = 34.53$

Since the difference of means is less than its 3 S.E., the differnce is insignificant 1% level of confidence. Thus we can conclude that the two regions *A* and *B* may equal mean Size of the rural Settlements. However, whatever difference in the sample mean size is observed may be attributed to the random factors.

3. Test of significance between sample proportion and population proportion of an attribute :

If the members of any population either posses an attribute or not, the number of observations possessing the attribute divided by the total number of observation is denoted as *p*, the proportion of that attribute.

As we know that the sample proportion p will have a S.E. $\sqrt{\frac{pq}{n}}$ as defined ear-sample proportion p may have a population proportion P only when the difference between the two is insignificant i.e. $|P-p| < 3\sqrt{\frac{pq}{n}}$. Otherwise the population proportion cannot be considered as equal to P.

Example 3.2

A random sample of 100 villages from a region gives 45 villages of population 1500 and above. Can we conclude that half of the villages in the whole region may be of population 1500 and above?

Solution :

Given $n = 100, p. = \frac{45}{100} = .45,\quad q = .55$

The proportion in population P ½ = .5

$$|P-p| \quad = |.5-.45| \quad = .05$$

$$3\text{ S.E.} \quad = 3\sqrt{\frac{pq}{n}} \quad = 3\sqrt{\frac{.45\times.55}{100}} = 3\sqrt{.002475} = 3\times.049$$

$$= 0.147$$

Since the difference is much less than the 3 S.E. so it is insignificant and we can say that half of villages in the region may be of population 1500 and above.

Confidence Limits

While estimating the mean by a random sample, we do not get the exact value for the population mean. However, a random sample gives us a close interval within which the population value of the mean falls with some probability. These limits are known as confidence limits and are given below.

$$\bar{x} - \frac{3\sigma}{\sqrt{n}} \text{ to } \bar{x} + \frac{3\sigma}{\sqrt{n}} \text{ for 99\% confidence limit} \qquad (3.1)$$

$$\bar{x} - \frac{2\sigma}{\sqrt{n}} \text{ to } \bar{x} + \frac{2\sigma}{\sqrt{n}} \text{ for 95\% confidence limit} \qquad (3.2)$$

where n and $\bar{x}$ are the size and the mean of the random sample respectively, and σ is the S.D. of the population. In case of fairly large samples the S.D. of the population may be taken as equal to the S.D. of the sample.

Example 3.4

A random sample of 100 boring points has been selected from an area and the depth of water below the suface is recorded. The mean and the S.D. of this depth are 950 cm. and 460 cm. respectively. Find out the 99% and 95% confidence limits for the mean depth of water in the whole area.

Solution

Here $\bar{x} = 950, \quad n = 100$

$\sigma = 460$ (Sample S.D. = Population S.D. for large samples).

So 99% confidence limits are

$$950 - \frac{3 \times 460}{\sqrt{100}} \text{ to } 950 + \frac{3 \times 460}{\sqrt{100}} = 912 \text{ cms. to } 1088 \text{ cms.}$$

and 95% confidence limits are

$$950 - \frac{2 \times 460}{\sqrt{100}} \text{ to } 950 + \frac{3 \times 460}{\sqrt{100}} = 858 \text{ cm. to } 1042 \text{ cm.}$$

Determination of size of Sample : As we have seen in the above example the range of estimate of 99% and 95% confidence limits are $\frac{6\sigma}{\sqrt{n}}$ and $\frac{4\sigma}{\sqrt{n}}$ respectively. These ranges are inversely proportional to n, the size of the sample.

Thus fixing a desired range of limits one can work out the appropriate size of the sample (ignoring other considerations like cost, time, etc.) Note that if σ is not known an estimate of it from a small sample may be used.

Example 3.5

An interval of the mean depth of underground water has to be estimated from a random sample of some boring points. What should be the size of sample such that the upper and lower values of 99% confidence estimates do not differ by more than 50 cms. The estimate of the S.D. of the depth of water is given to be 100 cm.

Solution :

We know that for 99% confidence interval

$$\frac{6\sigma}{\sqrt{n}} = \text{Range}$$

Given maximum Range = 50, $\sigma = 100$

$$\frac{6 \times 100}{\sqrt{n}} = 50$$

$$\frac{6 \times 100}{50} = \sqrt{n}$$

$$\sqrt{n} = 12$$
$$n = 144$$

Thus the appropriate size of the sample is 144 boring points.

Test of significance based on small samples :

Whenever the size of sample is less than 30, the sampling distributions of mean will not be normal and hence the tests of significance given above cannot be used. The shape of the sampling distribution of these means will not be symmetric but flatter than the normal curve. As the size of sample increases it gradually converges into a normal curve. Thus the value of confidence limits varies as n, the size of the sample varies till $n \geq 30$.

W.S. Gosset,[1] whose pen name was Student, studied the ratio 't' as given below :

$$t = \frac{\bar{x} - \mu}{\sigma\sqrt{n}} \qquad ...(3.3)$$

Where n and $\bar{x}$ are the size and mean of a random sample drawn from a normal population with mean = μ and S.D. = σ

Under the assumption that μ is the population mean, he gave the probability distribution of 't' mainly as function of n. Fisher and Yeates have tabulated the values of 't' for various degrees of freedom at different levels of significance. These values are given in appendix II. In the persent single sample problem degrees of freedom is number of observations minus one, (n-1).

This t distribution of small samples is being used in the following ways.

1. *Testing the significance of the mean of a random sample drawn from a normal population.* Consider a random sample of size n and mean $\bar{x}$, being drawn from a normal population of S.D. σ To test the hypothesis that the population mean may be considered as μ, we use the following statistics.

$$t = \frac{\bar{x} - \mu}{\sigma / \sqrt{n}} \quad \text{When S.D. of population is known} \qquad ...(3.4)$$

or

$$t = \frac{\bar{x} - \mu}{S / \sqrt{n-1}} \quad \text{When S.D. of population is not known but}$$

S, the S.D. of the sample is known ...(3.5)

Under the null hypothesis that the population mean is μ the calculated absolute value of it should not exceed the t value given in appendix 11, for (n-1) *d.f.* at an appropriate level of significance. If the calculated value exceeds the tabulated value, the null hypothesis is rejected and population mean cannot be taken as.

1. Student, "Probable Error of the Mean," Biometrika, 6, 1908, p.1.

Example 3.6

The size of households in a locality is normally distributed. A sample of 10 households is drawn randomly and the number of persons in each household is found to be 14, 9, 8, 4, 14, 5, 11, 10, 12 and 3. In the light of these data can we consider the mean size of households in the locality as 12 person ?

Solution

Household	Size (X)	$(X\text{-}x)$	$(X\text{-}\mu x)^2$
1	14	+5	25
2	9	0	0
3	8	-1	1
4	4	-5	25
5	14	+5	25
6	5	-4	16
7	11	+2	4
8	10	+1	1
9	12	+3	9
10	3	-6	36
			142

$X = 90,\ \Sigma(X - \bar{x})^2 = 142$

$$\bar{x} = \frac{90}{10} = 9$$

$$s = \sqrt{\frac{\Sigma(X-\bar{x})^2}{n}} = \sqrt{\frac{14.2}{10}} = \sqrt{142} = 3.768$$

Using the second expression for t (since only sample S.D. is known)

$$t = \frac{9-12}{3.768/\sqrt{10-1}} = \frac{-3}{3.768/\sqrt{9}} = \frac{-3}{3.768/3} = \frac{-3\times 3}{3.768} = \frac{-9}{3.9}$$

$= -2.3085$ taking absolute value $t = 2.3085$

The value of t for 9 d.f. at 1% level of significance is 3.25 and 5% level of significance it is 2.26.

Thus the null hypothesis that the mean size of the locality is 12 persons cannot be rejected at 1% level of significance however it is rejected only at 5% level of significance. In other words we may conclude that the mean size of households in the locality cannot be 12 persons only if we agree to sacrifice some accuracy (i.e. hypothesis is rejected at 5% level of significance), but more accurate conclusion would be that it might be equal to 12 persons.

2. *Test of equality of two population means from samples* : Consider the two random samples of size n_1 and n_2 drawn from two normal populations *having equal S.D.* but unknown means. Let $\bar{x}_1$ and $\bar{x}_2$ be the means and *S*1 and *S*2 the S.D. of first and second samples respectively. The following ratio '*t*' will be distributed as students *t* distribution with (n_1+n_2-2) d.f.

$$t = \frac{\bar{x}_1 - \bar{x}_2}{\sqrt{S^2\left(\frac{1}{n_1}+\frac{1}{n_2}\right)}} \qquad ...(3.6)$$

provided that,. the null hypothesis that the two population have equal mean is true.

where $$S^2 = \frac{\Sigma(X_1-\bar{x}_1)^2+\Sigma(X_2-\bar{x}_2)}{n_1+n_2-2} \text{ or } \frac{n_1S_1{}^2+n_2S_2{}^2}{n_1+n_2-2}$$

Example 3.7

The per acre yield of wheat is given to be normally distributed in both the regions R_1 and R_2 with equal variance. The yield of wheat per acre of a random sample of 8 plots of equal size from region R_1 and 10 plots of the same size from region R_2 is given below. In the light of these data can we conclude that the two regions have equal mean of yield of wheat per acre.

Yield of Wheat per acre in Metirc Tons in

Plot	Region R_1 (X_1)	Plot	Region R_2 (X_2)
A	1.9	M	1.3
B	1.8	N	1.2
C	1.8	O	1.4
D	1.9	P	1.5
E	2.4	Q	1.2
F	2.1	R	1.3
G	1.9	S	1.6
H	2.2	T	1.4
		U	1.5
		V	1.6

Solution

$$\bar{x}_1 = \frac{\Sigma X_1}{n_1} = \frac{16}{8} = 2.0\,\bar{x}_2 = \frac{x^2}{n^2} = \frac{14}{10} = 1.4$$

$$\Sigma(X_1-\bar{x}_1)^2 = (1.9-2)^2+(1.8-2)^2+(1.8-2)^2+(1.9-2)^2+(2.4-2)^2+ (2.1-2)^2+(1.9-2)^2+(2.2-2)^2=0.32$$

$$\Sigma(X_2-\bar{x}_2)^2 = (1.3-1.4)^2+(1.2-1.4)^2+(1.4-1.4)^2+(1.5-1.4)^2+$$

$(1.2-1.4)^2+(1.3-1.14)^2+(1.6-1.4)^2+(1.4-1.4)^2+$

$(1.5-1.4)^2+(1.6-1.4)^2=0.20$

$$S=\sqrt{\frac{\Sigma(X_1-\bar{x}_1)^2+\Sigma(x_2-x_2)^2}{n_1+n_2-2}}=\sqrt{\frac{0.32+0.20}{8+10.2}}$$

$$=\sqrt{0.325}=0.1802$$

$$t=\frac{\bar{x}_1-\bar{x}_2}{s\sqrt{\frac{1}{n_1}+\frac{1}{n_2}}}=\frac{2.0-1.4}{0.1802\sqrt{\frac{1}{8}+\frac{1}{10}}}$$

$$=\frac{0.6}{.1802\sqrt{.125+.1}}=\frac{.6}{.1802\sqrt{.225}}$$

$$=\frac{.6}{.1802\times.4743}=\frac{.6}{.0854}=7.0257$$

tabulated value of t for 16 degrees of freedom at 1% level of significance = 2.92

Since the calculated t (7.025) is greater than tabulated value (2.92) the difference of sample means is significant. Hence the hypothesis that the two resions have equal mean of yield per acre of wheat is rejected at 1% level of significance.

Note that before applying that 't' test the researcher should first ascertain the essential condition of normality of the populations. The equality of variances of the two populations, can be tested by using their sample estimates and applying F-ratio test as discussed in the following section.

3. *F. Distribution* : Let the two samples of size n_1 and n_2 are drawn from a normal population and their sample variances be s_1^2 and s_2^2. The F-ratio is defined as :

$$F=\frac{S_1^2}{S_2^2}=\frac{\frac{n_1}{n_1-1}s_1^2}{\frac{n_2}{n_2-1}s_2^2}$$

Where S_1^2 and S_2^2 are the independent estimates of population variance such that :

$$S_1^2=\frac{\Sigma(x_1-\bar{x}_1)^2}{n_1-1}=\frac{n_1S^2{}_1}{n_1-1}$$

$$S_2^2=\frac{\Sigma(x_2-x_2)^2}{n_2-1}=\frac{n_2}{n_2-1}S^2{}_2$$

Under the hypothesis that the two samples have same population variance, the F-ratio will form a particular distribution which is a funcion of degrees of freedom (n_1-1) and (n_2-1) and is known as Snedecors's F distribution. Tables have been prepared which give the values of f ratio for different combinations of (n_1-1) and (n_2-1) for various levels of significance. These tables are given in Appendix-III.

Testing whether the two samples have equal population variance :

If S_1^2 and S_2^2 are the two independent sample estimates of the variance of two normal populations such that $S_1^2>S_2^2$ then under the null hypothesis that their population variances are same, the statistic F as defined above will follow F-distribution with n_1-1 and n_2-1 degrees of freedom. Thus if the computed value of F is less than the tabulated value, F-ratio is insignificant and the two populations may have equal variances. In case the computed value is greater than the tabulated value the null hypothesis that the two populations have same variance is rejected.

Example 3.8

In the previous example, it has been assumed that in the two regions the yield of wheat per acre has equal variance. using the F ratio test the validity of this assumption.

Solution

$$S_1^2 = \frac{\Sigma(X_1-\bar{x}_1)^2}{n_1-1} = \frac{0.32}{8-1} = .0457$$

$$S_2^2 = \frac{\Sigma(X_2-x_2)^2}{n_2^2-1} = \frac{0.20}{10-1} = 0.0222$$

$$F = \frac{S_1^2}{S_2^2} = \frac{0.457}{0.0222} = 2.0586$$

The value of F for (7, 8) d. f. at 1% level of significance is 5.62. Since our computed value is less than the tabulated value of F ratio is insignificant and hence the hypothesis that the two sample come from the population having same variance is accepted i.e. the variance of yield of wheat per acre in region R_1 and R_2 are equal.

EXERCISES

1. The rough estimated value of the S.D. of the size of rural settlements in a district is given as 50 persons. In order to find out the estimates of the mean population of the rural settlements in the district with 95% level of confidence and (b) with 99% level of confidence, what should be the size of the sample. It is also given that the range of the estimates should not be more than 25 persons.

2. The mean production of wheat per acre is 2000 lbs for the entire region A. A random sample of 100 farms in region B gives the mean per acre production of wheat equal to 2100 lbs with a S.D.=224 lbs. Test whether the two regions have the same mean per acre production of wheat.

3. A random sample of 1000 labourers from region R_1 gives their mean daily wage as Rs. 3.50 with S.D.=Rs. 1.50. Another random sample of 1500 labourers from region R_2 gives the same as Rs. 3.00 with S.D.=Rs. 2.00. Use statistical reasoning to test the null hypothesis that the mean daily wages in both the regions R_1 and R_2 are same.

4. A sample of 6 households from a tribe from a region *A* and 10 households of the same tribe from the region *B* is selected at random. The agricultural land holdings of those two samples are given below in acres
   Region A : 6.3, 6.5, 6.8, 6.9, 7.1 and 7.2
   Region B : 6.1, 6.2, 6.5, 6.5, 6.9, 7.0, 7.1, 7.2 & 7.3
   Assuming the distribution of holdings in both the regions as normal, test whether the land holding pattern of the tribe differs regionally.

5. Out of a large universe of labourers a random sample of 10 labourers gives the mean monthly wage Rs. 56.80 with S.D.=Rs. 18.00 can the mean of all the labourer be considered as Rs. 50.00 (a) when the standard deviation of the universe is given to be Rs. 20/- (b) when the S.D. of universe is not given.

6. The mean size of the rural settlements in region *A* is 650 persons. *A* random sample of 200 settlements from another region *B* gives the mean size as 500 persons with a S.D. of 150 persons.

   Test whether the two regions may have equal mean size of the settlements ?

4
CORRELATION

Identification of the causal relationships among the different characteristics of any study is an essential concern of a scientific investigation. A causal relationship between the two characteristics exists only when one of them may logically be considered as the cause of the other.

The factor which is supposed to be the cause is known as the *independent variable* and the one which is supposed to be the effect is known as the *dependent variable*. Thus the variations in dependent variable may be explained in terms of the variations in the independent variables. In case there exists a causal relationship, both the values of independent and dependent variables will vary together. This property of co-variation is also termed as correlation.

In a bivariate case, if an increase in the independent variable also tends to cause an increase in the dependent variable, the correlation is said to be positive, For example, in a semi-arid area, a higher amount of rainfall may tend to cause a higher amount of crop production also, or better facilities of irrigation may lead to higher consumption of fertilizers. On the other hand if an increase in the independent variable tends to cause a decrease in the values of the dependent variable, the correlation is said to be negative. For example, the greater the distance between and two places, the smaller would be the number of persons moving between them. Another example of negative correlation could be between medical facilities and infant mortality. In case the variations of a variable are independent of the variations of the other variable, they are said to be uncorrelated. An example of this kind may be the *literacy* and *rainfall*, *death rates* and the *prices of coal* etc.

In case, there is no logical basis for a correlation between variables, it should not be taken as a casual relationship. Any such relationship is spurious and should not be attempted. This correlation is found only because of the influence of a third unknown variable on both the variables.

Measurement of the degree and direction of correlation helps particularly the geographers is explaining the variations in various spatial phenomena.

To represent the correlation between two variables visually, we consider the values of the independent and the dependent variables as X and Y coordinates of a two dimensional space. Each pair of observations can then be plotted on the graph paper, according to its X and Y coordinates. The graph so obtained is called as scatter diagram. Such a diagram is useful in giving us an intuitive idea of the relationships between independent variable X and the dependent variable Y as given in figure 4.1.

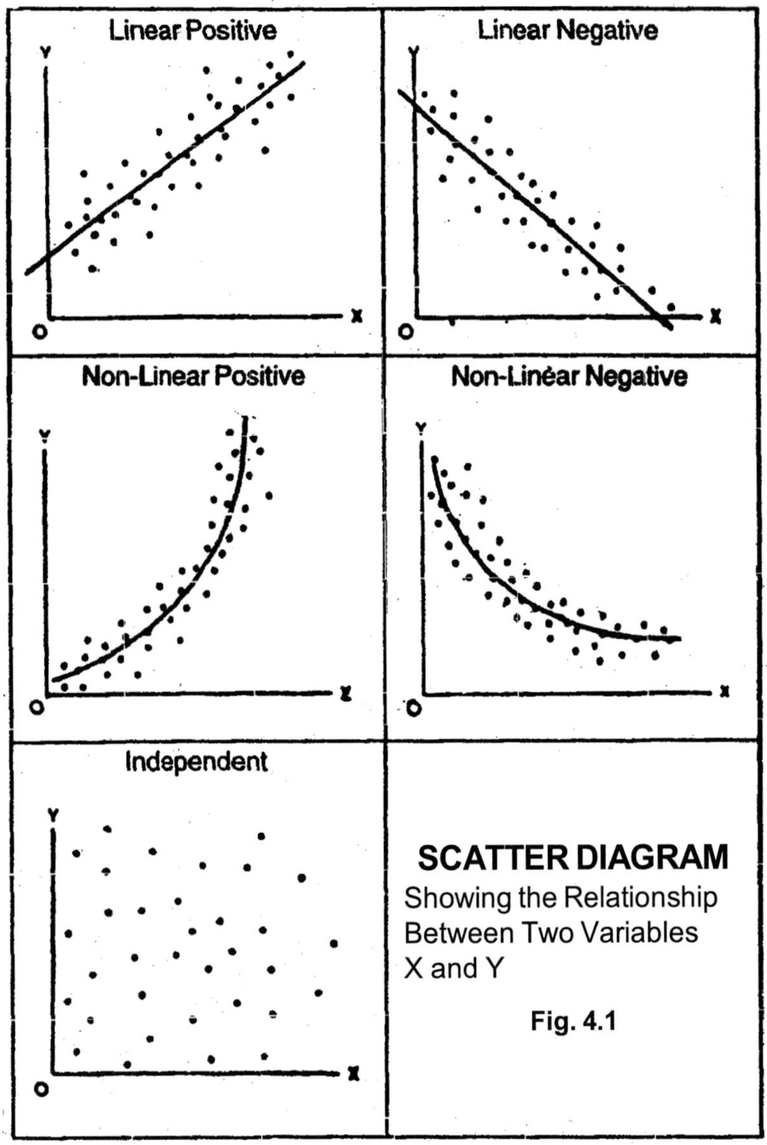

SCATTER DIAGRAM
Showing the Relationship Between Two Variables X and Y

Fig. 4.1

From Fig. 4.1 it is clear that some clusters of points move around a line and some move around a curve. There are several forms of the curves around which different clusters can move, but only one of them is depicted in Fig. 4.1.

On the basis of the curve around which the values of a bivariate data move, the correlations are classified into two broad categories, namely *linear correlation* and *non-linear correlation.* If the values of a bivariate data are moving around a line, the correlation between them is said to be linear. On the other hand if the values move around any curve the correlation is said to be non-linear or curvilinear.

The degree of relationship (linear or cuvilinear) between any two varibles on the closeness of the cluster of points to the straight line or to any curve. If the values of X and Y vary such that each point falls exactly on a straight line, (or curve) the relationship is said to be perfectly linear (or curvilinear). The higher the deviation of these points from the straight line, (or curve) the weaker will be the correlation between X and Y variables.

Methods of studying only the linear correlations are discussed below because of two reasons : (a) a majority of variables are generally correlated in linear fashion (b) many of the non-linear correlations become linear after the two variables are properly transformed.

Measurement of linear Correlation. As pointed out earlier a scatter diagram gives us an intuitive idea about the relationship between the two variables X and Y.

A more precise quantitative measurement of the degree and direction of a linear correlation was suggested by Karl Pearson, defined by :

$$r = \frac{\Sigma XY - \frac{\Sigma X \Sigma Y}{N}}{\sqrt{\Sigma X^2 - \frac{(\Sigma X)^2}{N}}\sqrt{\Sigma Y^2 - \frac{(\Sigma Y)^2}{N}}} \qquad ...(4.1)$$

This measure is known as product moment correlation coefficient or simply correlation coefficient. By symmetry it is clear that $rxy = ryx = r$.

Properites of Coorelation Coefficients (r)

1. If the sign of r is positive the variable X and Y are positively related and if the sign is negative, they are negatively correlated.

2. The value of r varies between -1 and $+1$. The value $+1$ or -1 indicates a perfect positive or negative correlation. As the extent of correlation decreases the value of r approaches zero.

Significance test of Correlation Coefficient

A coefficient of correlation based on a smaller number of observations is generally considered as a sample correlation. Using the test of significance of r it is possible to infer whether the correlation coeffcient of the bivariate normal population (the correlation between the same variables but bassed on a fairly large number of observations) will be zero or not. Under the null hypothesis, that the population correlation is zero, the expression as given below will follow 'the students 't' distribution with (n–2) degrees of freedom.

$$t = r\sqrt{\frac{n-2}{1-r^2}} \qquad ...(4.2)$$

where n is the number of observations used and r is the coefficient of correlation.

Thus if any computed value of 't' is less than the corresponding tabulated value the correlation coefficient is said to be insignificant, meaning thereby that over a larger number of similar observations the two variables will be independent, as the hypothesis that the population correlation coefficient is zero is accepted. Whatever sample correlation in this case we get may be attributed to the chance factors, only. On the other hand if the computed value of '*t*' is greater than the tabulated '*t*' the correlation coefficient is said to be significant, and the population correlation coefficient between the two variables in this case is not considered to be zero.

It is evident from this test that the significance of the correlation coefficient is directly proportional to not only *r*, but also to (*n*-2). In some cases, because of a larger value of '*n*' a smaller correlation coefficient may become significant, whereas in some other cases, a larger correlation coefficient may become insignificant because of the smaller value of '*n*'.

Example 4.1

The percentage of scheduled caste population to total population and the percentage of landless agricultural labourers to total agricultural workers are given below for 12 randomly selected villages of a district. Does there exist a linear correlation between them in the whole districts.

Village Code	(01)	(02)	(03)	(04)	(05)	(06)	(07)	(08)	(09)	(10)	(11)	(12)
%of S.C. to Total Population (X)	2.8	8.6	1.8	4.8	4.8	2.0	6.7	2.2	5.7	7.3	6.3	2.6
% of L,L. Labourers to total agr. workers (y)	38.9	33.7	40.6	22.0	29.5	4.9	37.6	2.6	28.2	33.2	65.8	3.7

Solution

The following tables gives all the intermediate results used in formula (14.1)

Village	X	Y	X^2	Y^2	YX
01	2.8	38.9	7.84	1513.21	108.92
02	8.6	3.37	73.96	1135.69	289.82
03	1.8	40.6	3.24	1648.36	73.08
04	4.8	22.0	23.04	484.00	105.60
05	4.8	29.5	23.04	970.25	141.60
06	2.0	4.9	4.00	24.01	9.80
07	6.7	37.6	14.89	1413.76	251.92
08	2.2	2.6	4.84	6.76	5.72
09	5.7	28.2	32.49	795.24	160.74
10	7.3	33.2	53.29	1102.25	242.36
11	6.3	65.8	39.69	4329.64	414.54
12	2.6	37.9	6.76	1437.41	98.54
	55.60	374.9	317.08	14759.58	1902.64

$$\text{Using } r = \frac{\Sigma XY - \frac{\Sigma X \Sigma Y}{N}}{\sqrt{\sqrt{\Sigma X^2} - \frac{(\Sigma X)^2}{N}}\sqrt{\Sigma Y^2 - \frac{(\Sigma Y)^2}{N}}}$$

$$= \frac{1902.64 = \frac{55.6 \times 374.9}{12}}{\sqrt{317.09 - \frac{55.6 \times 55.6}{12}}\sqrt{14759.58 - \frac{374.9 \times 374.9}{12}}}$$

$$= \frac{165.6}{\sqrt{59.47}\sqrt{3047.8}} = \frac{165.6}{7.71 \times 55.20} = \frac{165.6}{425.59} = +0.389$$

The results show that there exists a positive relationship between the p.c. of scheduled caste to total population and p.c. of L.L. labourers to total agricultural labourers in the present sample of 12 villages. However, without applying the test of significance, we cannot generalize this positive relationship for all the villages in the district, as the number of observations in the present case is very small. The test is carried out in the following manner :

$$t = r\sqrt{\frac{n-2}{1-r^2}} = .389\sqrt{\frac{12-2}{1-(.389)^2}} = .389\sqrt{\frac{10}{.8487}}$$

$$= .389\sqrt{11.783} = .389 \times 3.4324 = 1.3353$$

The tabulated value of t for 10 (12–2) degrees of freedom is 3.17 at 1% 2.23 at 5% and 1.81 at 10% levels of significance respectively.[1] The computed value is not greater than even the 10% tabulated value of t hence, the correlation coefficient is quite insignificant, *i.e.* the population correlation coefficient may be considered as zero.

Here we may conclude that even there exists a positive correlation in the 12 sample villages, but it is small in relation to the size of the sample and so may be attributed to the chance or random factors. Thus on the basis of this correlation coefficient we cannot conclude that the data supports a causal relationship between the two variables in whole of the district.

Rank Correlation

Spearman rank correlation is another measure of the relationship between two variables using the ranked data. For a rank correction the data may be collected either in ranked from of actual quantitative values may be converted into the ranked form. The index of rank correlation rho (ρ) is given as below:

$$\text{rho}(\rho) = 1 - \frac{6\Sigma di^2}{n^3 - n} \qquad \text{...4.3}$$

1. Refer appendix II.

Where *n* is the total numer of observations, and di is the difference in the ranks of the two variables in the ith observation.

Example 4.2

In the exercise given above if variable *X* and *Y* are converted into their ranks R*x* and R*y* respectively as given below, the coefficient of rank correlation may be computed in the following manner :

Village Code	Rx	Ry	di-Rx-Ry	di^2
01	8	3	5	25
02	1	6	–5	25
03	12	2	10	100
04	6.5	10	–3.5	12.25
05	6.5	8	–1.5	2.25
06	11	0	0	0
07	3	5	–2	4
08	10	12	–2	4
09	5	9	–4	16
10	2	7	–5	25
11	4	1	3	9
12	9	4	5	25
				247.50

$$e = 1 - \frac{6 \times 247.5}{12^3 - 12}$$

$$= 1 - \frac{1485}{1728 - 12}$$

$$= 1 - \frac{1485}{1716}$$

$$= 1 - .8653$$

$$= 0.1347$$

The same test of significance as mentioned before may also be applied here.

Point to note :

1. Whenever we say that a coefficient of correlation is significant, its level of significance shows the chances of its actually being not singnificant (i.e. the probability of error in the statement).

2. A coefficient of correlation, significant at a lower level of significance (say 1%) will of course, be significant at all the other higher levels of significance (*i.e.* 5% or 10% etc.) However, if

its is insignificant at a lower level of insignificance, it may or many not be insignificant at higher levels of significance.

3. The choice of the level of significance is the researcher's own choice, depending on the nature of the problem and the tolerable error.

4. If the universe is small it should be considered as a sample.

5. A significant correlation means that its population coefficient is not zero, an insignificant correlation, on the other hand, means that its population coefficient of correlation may be zero and hence whatever its sample value we are getting is just because of the chance factors or random error.

6. A correlation analysis starts with a theoretical formulation of different relationships and then coefficient of correlations are used only to see whether this formulation is supported by the data or not. <u>One should not start first with finding out a coefficient of correlation and then making a theory to fit into it.</u>

If a theoretically formulated relationship is not supported by the data (*i.e.* r is not found significant as it was expected), the following may be the reasons :

(1) Wrong formulation of relation

(2) Incorrect definition of variable

(3) Presence of non-linearity in data

A mistake in the theoretical formulation can be rectified by probing into the thoretical aspects in more detail. If one is sure about the theoretical formulation, specification of variables should be checked. For example, suppose we formulate a hypothesis that urbanziation and migrations are positively related. To test this hypothesis, we take the district-wise data for percentage of urban population to the total population, and for percentage of migrants to the total population, and compute the coefficient of correlation between them. Suppose, it is found to be insignificant everyone would agree that the formulation of relationship, by and large, is true, so we must get a good positive relation between urbanisation and migration. When we search for the mistake, it might strike us that we should have taken only urban migration and not the total migration. Thus, we would redefine our migration factor as percentage of urban migrants to total population or to total urban population. This altcration might improve the correlation coefficient. The third kind of mistake is possible when the two variables are correlated, as formulated theoretically, but in a linear fashion. In such cases, if we work out a coefficient of correlation (which measures only the degree and direction of linear correlation), we might get a very small insignificant value and that should not be taken to mean that the data do not support the hypothesis. Here we must say that do not support the hypothesis of a linear correlation only.

Association between Qualitative Variables : Computation of Pearson's coefficient of correlation requires the data in quantitative form for both the variables X and Y. Sometimes, however, either one or both the variables are in qualitative form. In such cases we are not in a position to work out coefficient of correlation and use chi-square instead of it.

Chi-square statistics is basically a method to test the correspondence between certain obseerved and estimated frequencies. In case of close correspondence between the two, the statistics chi-square (x^2) as given below will be statistically insignificant.

$$x^2 = \sum_{i=1}^{n}\left[\frac{(Oi - Ei)^2}{Ei}\right] \qquad ...(4.4)$$

where Oi and Ei are the observed and estimated frequencies respectively of the ith class.[1] The shape of the distribution will vary with $(n-1)$ which is known as its degress of freedom. For different values of degrees of freedom, the upper limits of the values of x^2 at different levels of significance are given in Appendix-IV.

Any value of x^2 based on the correctly estimated values will have to be less than the corresponding upper limit given in the table (*i.e.* it has to be insignificant). If any value of x^2 comes out to be greater than the value given in the table (i.e. it is significant), the assumptions under which the frequencies have been estimated may not be correct.

The following example will make this concept clearer. Suppose the map of an area is subdivided into five equal parts and the number of rural settlements (Oi) in each part is recorded as given in Table 4.2.

Table 4.2

Part	No. of Rural Settlement Qi	Expected No. of Settlement Ei	: O-E	$(O-E)^2$	$(O-E)^2/E$
I	20	50	–30	900	$\frac{900}{50} = 18.0$
II	20	50	–30	900	$\frac{900}{50} = 18.0$
III	50	50	0	0	0 0
IV	60	50	–10	100	$\frac{100}{50} = 2$
V	100	50	+50	2500	$\frac{2500}{50} = 50$
Total	250				$x^2 =$ 88.0

1. M.G. Kendall., *The Advanced Theory of Statistics,* Charles Griffin and Co., London

To study whether the distribution of settlements is even or not, we make a null hypothesis that the number of rural settlements in each part tends to be equally distributed. Under this assumption each part should have equal number of settlements (with a marginal deviation). Thus if the total number of settlements are 250 in five parts, each part should have 50 estimated settlements.

A close correspondence between the estimated and observed value will provide strength to the assumption under which the frequencies of each cell are estimated. In this case the calculated value of chi-square will be found to be statistically insignificant. A statistically significant value of chi-square will suggest complete divergence between estimated and observed values, challenging the assumption under which the values have been estimated.

In order to test the assumption made above we work out the value of chi-square as given in Table 2. The value comes out to be 88.0. The degrees of freedom (n-1) in this case are 5–1=4. For 5 d.f. tabulated value of chi-square at 1% level of significance is 13.28. Our computed value (88.0) is much more than the tabulated value and hence, it is statistically significant. Thus the hypothesis that the settlements are equally distributed in each part is rejected and we may conclude that the distribution of settlements is not even.

CHI SQUARE FROM A CONTINGENCY TABLE

If the two attributes are cross-classified into a contingency table, a value of chi-square can be computed under the assumption of the independence of the two attributes of rows and columns. If the row and column attributes are independent, the estimated frequency of the cell in the ith row and the jth column in a contigency table is equal to $\frac{Ri \times Cj}{N}$, where Ri and Cj are the totals of the row and jth column respectively and N is the total number of frequencies.[1] The degrees of freedom in case of a contingency table of r rows and c column is $(r–)$ $(c–1)$.

Example 4.3

The economic functions cross classified by the nature of distributions of 200 towns are given below. Test whether the two attributes are independent.

Economic Functions	Distribution: Random	Even	Cluster	Total
Industrial	20	25	27	72
Servicc	21	10	12	43
Diversified	25	30	30	85
Total	66	65	69	200

Solution

Under the null hypothesis that the economic functions and the nature of the distribution of towns are independent, the different cell, frequencies are estimated as below :

1. M.C. Kendall, op. cit., pp. 309.

$$E_{11} = \frac{72 \times 66}{200} = 23.8, \qquad E_{12} = \frac{72 \times 65}{200} = 23.4, \qquad E_{13} = \frac{72 \times 69}{200} = 24.8,$$

$$E_{21} = \frac{43 \times 66}{200} = 14.2, \qquad E_{22} = \frac{43 \times 65}{200} = 14.0, \qquad E_{23} = \frac{43 \times 69}{200} = 14.8,$$

$$E_{31} = \frac{85 \times 66}{200} = 28.0, \qquad E_{32} = \frac{85 \times 65}{200} = 27.6, \qquad E_{33} = \frac{85 \times 69}{200} = 29.3$$

The value of chi-square is :

$$X^2 = \frac{(20-23.8)^2}{23.8} + \frac{(25-23.4)^2}{23.4} + \frac{(27-24.8)^2}{24.8} + \frac{(21-14.2)^2}{14.2} + \frac{(10-14.0)^2}{14.0}$$

$$+ \frac{(12-14.8)^2}{14.8} + \frac{(25-28)^2}{28} + \frac{(30-27.6)^2}{27.6} + \frac{(30-29.3)^2}{29.3}$$

$$= 0.60 + 0.10 + 0.19 + 3.25 + 1.14 + 0.52 + 0.32 + 0.20 + 0.01$$

$$= 6.33$$

Degrees of freedom $= (r-1)(c-1) = (3-1)(3-1) = 4$

The value of x^2 for 4 d.f. at % level of significance in the table is 13.28. Since our computed value of x^2 is less than the tabulated value it is statistically insignificant. At 5% and 10% levels of significance the tabulated values are 7.78 and 9.49 respectively and our computed value is less than even these values, hence it is insignificant even at 10% level of significance. Because the computed value of chi-square is statistically insignificant, the initial hypothesis that the functions of towns and their nature of distribution are independent is accepted *i.e.* we may conclude that the economic funtions of these cities and the nature of their distribution are independent.

It is to be noted here that we prove the hypothesis of interdependence of two attributes by first framing a null hypothesis of independence (no interdependence) and then rejecting it and accepting the alternative hypothesis of dependence between the two attributes. We can not sart with a hypothesis of dependence and accepting it simply due to the fact that estimation of frequencies is possible under the assumption of independence (no interdependence) only.

Points to Note :

1. That chi-square test is not applicable if any of the cell frequencies the less than five and the total number of frequencies are less than 20. In case some of the cell frequencies are less than five, the two rows or the columns are pooled together such that after pooling, each of the cell frequency is more than 10.[1]

2. A quantitiative information can also be converted into qualitative statement like per acre consumption of fertilizer may be divided into two categories as less than 3 Kgs. or density

1. F.Kenney and E.S. Keeping, *Mathematical Statistics,* D. Van Nostrand East West Press, New Delhi, 1965, p. 118 and 230.

of population may be converted into 3 categories like, less than 300 persons, 300 to less than 500 persons and 500 persons and more.

3. It takes care of non-linearity also in the relationship.

EXERCISES

1. (a) Given

$\Sigma XY = 1399$, $\Sigma X = 2$, $\Sigma Y = 49$

$N = 11$ $\Sigma X^2 = 1414$, $\Sigma Y^2 = 1865$

Compute the coefficient of correlation.

(b) The number of vehicles per km. of road in a country and the maintenance cost (millions of pound) of roads are given below per 10 years. What is the degree and direction of linear relationship between vehicles/km. and the maintenance cost.

Vehicles/km.	20	22	24	25	26	28	30	34	36	39
Maintenance Cost	26	23	27	26	32	35	36	39	42	43

2. The following table gives the Index Number of industrial production and the number of registered unemployment in a region for 8 years. In what way the industrial production affects the unemployment?

Industrial Production (I.N.)	100	102	104	107	105	112	102	94
No. of Registered Unemployment	113	124	140	111	123	122	191	264

3. The following table shows the area sown more than once and the area irrigated more than once for 10 districts randomly selected from Western U.P. Is there any significant linear relationship between them? (Given that the bivariate population is normal)

S.No.	District	Area sown more than once (0000 acres)	Area irrigated more than once (000 acres)
1	Muzaffar Nagar	3	1
2	Meerut	16	4
3	Bulandshahar	14	7
4	Aligarh	23	11
5	Dehra Dun	19	5
6	Saharanpur	21	4
7	Mathura	10	2
8	Agra	9	1
9	Moradabad	14	2
10	Rampur	8	1
	Total	137	38

(Source : Indian Ag. Statistics 1967–68).

4. The following table gives the average rainfall and price of wheat in U.P. for different years. Find out the coefficient of rank correlation between them.

Prices of Wheat (Rs. 5 Kg)	3.5	2.6	1.6	1.6	2.6	1.5	1.2
Annual Rainfall (in inches)	27	27	26	39	32	35	40

5. The following table gives the percentage of urban population to the total population and percentage of literate to the total population of 10 randomly selected districts of Maharashtra. What is the direction and extent of relationship between education and urbanization ?

S.No.	District	% Urban Population	% of Literates
1.	Thana	68	40
2.	Nasik	71	36
3.	Dhulia	83	31
4.	Sangli	81	37
5.	Aurangabad	83	28
6.	Osmanabad	87	28
7.	Amravati	72	42
8.	Akola	76	40
9.	Chandrapur	89	27
10.	Nagpur	45	45

(Source : Census of India 1961)

5
SIMPLE LINEAR REGRESSION ANALYSIS

The study of a causal relationships between a dependent variable and one or more independent variables becomes more useful when the relationship is defined in terms of a mathematical form. These mathematical forms of the relationships are used in making predictions and also help us in assessing the relative influence of each of the independent variables on the dependent variable.

In this chapter we will be discussing first, how such a mathematical equation is worked out from a given set of bivariate data, and secondly, what statistical inferences can be derived from it. The bivariate case has been taken up here first only for the sake of simplicity. The methods which deal with the relationship of several independent variables with one dependent variable are discussed in Multiple Regression Analysis under the chapter on Multivariate Analysis.

As the relationships in social are not very exact, we have to tolerate a certain amount or error while approximating them into any exact form of relationships. The simplest form, in which the relationship between a dependent variable and an independent varibale can be approximated is that of a straight line. These linear forms of relationships are important because many non-linear forms of relationships also become linear after some kinds of transformation.[1] One such transformation, for example, has been used in rank-size rule given in chapter VI.

In case, there exists a relationships between a dependent variable Y and an independent variable X, the points of the scatter diagram will move around a curve which may be called the regression curve. In the particular case when the curve is a straight line it is said to be the regression line.

Through a scatter diagram one can draw a large number of straight lines. In these equations of straight lines, if we put different given values of X we get the corresponding estimated values for Y. These estimated values of Y would by different from the actual values of Y. Out of all these lines the line which gives the minimum sum of squares of differences between actual values of Y and their estimated values is supposed to be the most suitable line and is known as the line of regression of Y on X. The method by which we determine such equation is known as the least square method.

The form of any linear relationship between a dependent variable Y and an independent variable X is given as :

$$Y = \alpha + \beta X + U \qquad \text{....(5.1)}$$

Where the constants α and β are the intercept and slope of the straight line and u is the error term.

1. For further discussion on use of transformation please see Croxiton, F.E. Cowden, D.J. and Klein, S. *Applied General Statistics*, Prentice-Hall India, 1975, pp, 431-440.

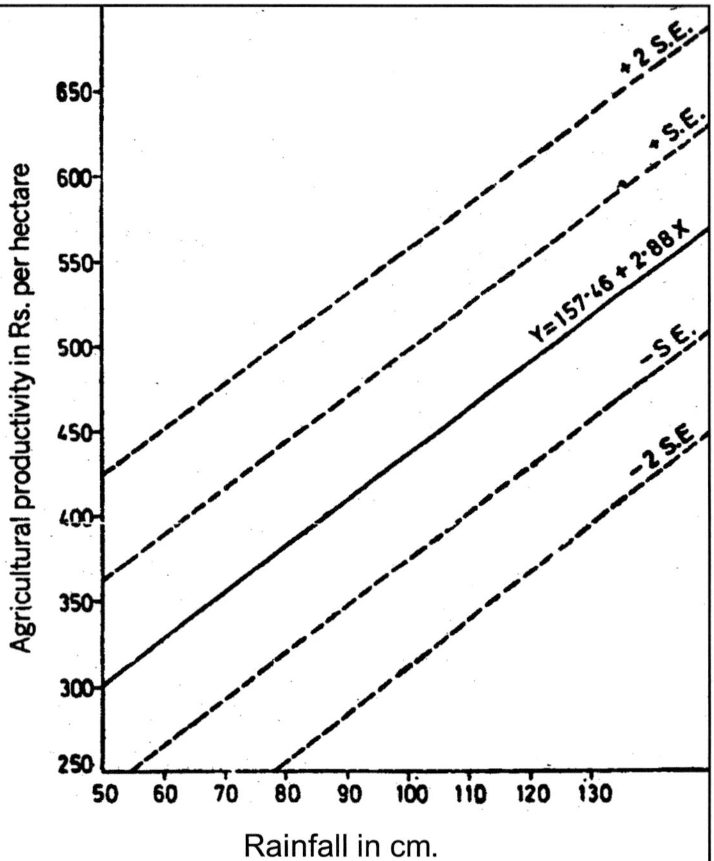

Fig. 5.1

The basic objective of a regression analysis is to estimate the values of α and β. The estimated least square form of the relationship is given by[1] :

$$Y = a + bx \qquad ...(5.2)$$

where $b = \dfrac{\Sigma xy - \dfrac{\Sigma X \Sigma Y}{n}}{\Sigma x^2 - \dfrac{(\Sigma X)^2}{n}}$ is an estimate of β ...(5.3)

and $a = \bar{y} - b\bar{x}$ is estimate of α

It has also been shown that if we make certain assumptions regarding the error term, the least square estimates become best linear and unbiased. These assumptions are given below :

1. For mathematical derivation readers may refer to J. Johnston, *Econometric Methods,* Mac-Graw-Hills, 1972, pp. 8-16.

(1) u is a random variable distributed normally

(2) $\bar{u} = 0$

(3) Variance of u is constant for all X and

(4) Each error term u, is independent of other random terms. It is also uncorrelated with the independent variable.

In many cases it is not difficult to meet these assumptions. When we deal with only one independent variable and leave out other variables, their intraction effect becomes unpredictable provided that they are large in number and uncorrelated with the independent variable already included. In such cases it will be close to the assumption that the left out part is a random variable. In the scatter diagram if the distance of the points from the regression line does not increase along the x axis, assumptions (3) and (4) can also be justified. If almost equal number of points fall above and below the line in a random fashion, assumption (2) may be justified.[1]

Thus the scatter diagram in relation to the regression line, helps, us in judging whether the assumptions are justified or not. Once it is established that the assumptions are not seriously violated one can use the line of regression for further analytical purposes.

The slope of the regression line β which is known as population regression coefficient also, shows an average change in Y for a unit change in X and the value of b is an estimate of it. If the dependent variable is indifferent to the given independent variable, it means that β=0. In such cases its estimated value b may be very close to zero. To worn against such cases the test of significance used is given as :

$$t = \frac{b-0}{S.E.(b)} \qquad ...(5.4)$$

with $(n-2)$ degrees of freedom

$$\text{where S.E. (b)} = \frac{\sigma_u}{\sqrt{\Sigma X^2 - \frac{(\Sigma X)^2}{n}}} \qquad ....(5.5)$$

$$\text{and } \sigma_u^2 = \frac{\Sigma Y^2 \frac{(\Sigma Y)^2}{n} - b\left\{\Sigma XY - \frac{\Sigma X^2 - Y}{n}\right\}}{n-2}$$

In the above analysis if the value of regression coefficient is found to be insignificant we conclude that the estimated value of the regression coefficient is so small that for all practical purposes it may be considered at zero and such a low relationship may be attributed only to the random or chance factors. In this case changes in the independent varibale may not cause any change in the

1. For further discussion on the test of these assumptions please refer to : A. Koutsoyinanis, *Theory of Econometric*, MacMillan 1973, pp. 173-193.

dependent variable (i.e. $\beta = 0$). On the other hand if it is found to be significant it may be attributed to the causal relationship between the dependent and independent variables.

Another important summary statistics in a regression analysis is the coefficient of determination R^2 which tells us the proportion of variations in Y as explained by X and is given by[1].

$$R^2 = \frac{\text{Explained S.S.}}{\text{Total S.S.}} \qquad \text{...(5.6)}$$

Where explained sum of squares $= b\left\{\Sigma XY - \frac{\Sigma X \Sigma Y}{n}\right\}$ and

Total sum of squares $= \Sigma Y^2 - \frac{(\Sigma Y)^2}{n}$

Example 5.1

In order to explain the agricultural productivity of the different districts of Tamilnadu by the rainfall in 1964-65 the varibales chosen are (1) Value of agricultural production in Rs. per hectare (y) and (2) annual average rainfall of the district in cms. (*x*) These data are given in Table 5.1 Find out the functional form of linear relationship between them. What is the average rate of change in agricultural productivity with respect to rainfall and how good is the relationship ?

Solution

The intermediate values used in (5.3) to (5.6) are given at the bottom of the Table 5.1.

Table 5.1

District	*Y*	*X*	*Y*	*X*	*XY*
1. Chingleput	364.6	101.3	132933.16	10261.69	36933.98
2. South Arcot	402.1	86.9	161684.41	7551.61	34942.49
3. North Arcot	416.1	99.7	173139.21	9940.09	41485.17
4. Salem	310.6	87.9	96472.36	7726.41	27301.74
5. Coimbatore	536.2	94.4	287510.44	8911.36	23630.25
6. Tiruchinapalli	367.5	64.3	135055.25	4134.49	23630.25
7. Thanjavur	448.7	85.3	201331.69	7276.09	38274.11
8. Madurai	420.5	89.2	176820.25	7596.64	37508.60
9. R.N. Puram	287.7	70.2	82771.29	4928.04	20196.54
10. Tirunelveli	366.1	52.1	134029.21	2714.41	19073.81
11. Kanyakumari	596.0	135.4	355216.00	1833.16	80698.40
	4516.1	966.7	1936964.27	89733.99	410662.37

N.B. Madras has been excluded because it is totally urban and Nilgiri has been excluded because of the tea plantations which give abnormally higher values of productivity.

1. Variation here means sum of squares of deviation from mean and is also known as sum of squares.

Using (5.3) and (5.4)

$$b = \frac{410662.37 - (4516.1 \times 966.7)/11}{89733.99 - (966.7)^2/11} = \frac{13779.29}{4778.64} = 2.88$$

$$a = \frac{4516.1}{11} - 2.88\left(\frac{966.7}{11}\right) = 410.55 - 253.09 = 157.46$$

Thus the regression equation of Y on X is $Y = 157.46 + 2.88X$

The slope of this regression line, b, which is also known as regression coefficient, shows the estimated average change in y with respect to unit change in X. Thus from the regression equation we can say that the relationship between agricultural productivity and rainfall is such that a centimeter change in rainfall by and large causes an increase of Rs. 2.88 in the agricultural productivity. The result indicates towards the fact that a great deal of agricultural productivity in the state depends on rainfall. This conclusion may further be ensured by testing the significance of b, as given in (5.5) and (5.6):

$$\text{Total } S.S. = \Sigma Y^2 - \frac{(\Sigma Y)^2}{n} = 193696427 - \frac{4516.1 \times 4516.1}{11} = 82858.89$$

$$\text{Explained S.S.} = b\left\{\Sigma XY - \frac{\Sigma X \Sigma Y}{\text{n}}\right\} = 2.88\{13779.29\} = 39684.33$$

$$\sigma^2_u = \frac{82858.89 - 39684.43}{11 - 2} = 4797.17 \text{ or } \sigma_u = \sqrt{4797.17} = 69.26$$

As defined by (5.5) and (5.6)

$$\text{S.E.(b)} = \frac{69.26}{\sqrt{89733.99 - \frac{966.7 \times 966.7}{11}}} = \frac{69.26}{69.12} = 1.002$$

$$t = \frac{2.88}{1.002} = 2.8742$$

The tabulated values of t at 1%, 2% and at 5% levels of significance for 9 degrees of freedom are 3.11, 2.72, and 2.20 respectively. It is obvious that our calculated value is significant only at 5% level of significance. Thus the existence of a causal relationship is supported by the data also.

To see how good is the assumption of linearity in the relationship we have to work out coefficient of determination R^2 given by (5.7) as below :

$$R^2 = \frac{\text{Explained S.S.}}{\text{Total S.S.}} \quad \frac{39684.33}{82858.89} = 0.479$$

The value of the coefficient of determination here shows that 47.9 per cent of the total variation in y is being explained by X. Although 47.9 per cent is not a bad explanation, a considerable percentage (52.1%) of variations in y are yet to be explained.

Note that in a bivariate case, R^2 is equal to the square of coefficient of correlation between the two variables. The coefficient of correlation, r, when worked out between y and x here is 0.692 and r^2=0.479 which is equal to the coefficient of determination. The coefficient of correlation in the present case is found to be significant at 5% level of significance.

Thus, the results show that although the independent variable X taken here is giving a good explaination of y, yet it is not the only determinant. An ideal situation in any such exercise would be to get cent per cent explanation, i.e. R^2=1.00 (all the points in the scatter diagram fall on a straight line not parallel to any of the axes). However, in social science where interaction among different variables are quite complex, a bivariate regression analysis is not expected to give us a very high value of R^2. This is because generally no social phenomenon is governed by only one variable. In spite of this fact, even if we try to explain it by only one variable, we shall be explaining it only partially and the value of R^2 is bound to be not very large. A better explantion of y has to be achieved through some more explanatory variables.

Residuals

When in a regression equation different values of x are substituted, we get the corresponding estimated values of Y. For example in our equation when X=101.3

$$\hat{Y}_1 = 157.46 + 2.88\ (101.3) = 449.2$$

and when $X = 86.9$

$$\hat{Y}_2 = 157.46 + 2.88\ (86.9) = 407.3$$

Similarly when all other values of X are substituted in the equation the corresponding estimated values of Y which we get are given in the 3rd column of Table 5.2 below.

These estimated values are the mean values of Y for the given value of X. As an example, suppose in few districts the rainfall (X) is equal, that does not mean that their productivity (Y) will also be equal. Each such district will have different values of Y. The mean of all these different values of Y would be equal to the estimated value $\hat{Y}$. Even if no two values of X are same Y maintains the average position.

Table 5.2
Residuals from regression of productivity on rainfall for Tamilnadu 1964-65

District	Y	$\hat{Y}$	$Y-\hat{Y}$	$\left(Y-\hat{Y}\right)^2$	$\frac{Y-\hat{Y}}{Y}\times 100$	Category
(1)	(2)	(3)	(4)	(5)	(6)	(7)
1. Chingleput	364.6	449.2	–84.6	7157.16	–23.2	High negative
2. South Arcot	402.1	407.3	–5.2	27.24	–1.3	Medium negative
3. North Arcot	416.1	444.6	–28.5	812.25	–6.8	Medium negative
4. Salem	310.6	410.6	–100.00	10000.00	–3.22	High negative
5. Coimbatore	536.2	429.3	+106.90	11427.61	+19.9	High positive
6. Tiruchinapalli	367.5	342.6	+24.90	620.01	+6.8	Medium positive
7. Thanjavur	448.7	403.1	+45.60	2079.36	+10.2	Medium positive
8. Madurai	420.5	414.4	+6.10	37.21	+1.5	Medium positive
9. Ramanatha Puram	287.7	359.6	–71.90	5169.61	–250	High negative
10. Tirunelveli	366.1	307.5	+58.6	3433.96	+16.0	Medium positive
11. Kanyakumari	596.9	547.4	+48.60	2361.96	+8.2	Medium positive

An important question at this point is, why for a given value of rainfall (*X*) the different districts do not show the same agricultural productivity? The most plausible answer is that rainfall is not the only determinant of agricultural productivity. There are several other variables also, operating positively as well as negatively. The agricultural productivity will be more than the average in districts where the positive factors dominate. Thus the residual $Y-\hat{Y}$ becomes a very meaningful indicator which shows the nature and intensity of operation of the factors in determining *Y* other than the independent variable already taken in the model.

Geographers often plot these residuals over the map to correlate the influence of left out positive or negative factors with other geographical features of the area. Hence, residual mapping can be used as tool to identify and regionalise the areas having negative and positive impact over agricultural productivity (*Y*), when the effect of rainfall (*X*) is removed. With the help of these maps a good geographer can easily find out the more effective spatial variables for further explanations of the variations in the dependent variable *Y*.

It is important to note that mean of these residuals as in Table 5.2 is :

$$\bar{u} = \frac{\Sigma\left(Y-\hat{Y}\right)}{n} = \frac{0.5}{11} = .045$$

Which is almost zero. Considering the mean equal to zero the standard deviation of the residuals (also known as standard error of estimates) is given by

$$\text{S.D. of Estimates} = \frac{\Sigma\left(Y - \hat{Y}\right)^2}{n-1} = \sqrt{\frac{4312.62}{10}} = 65.7$$

The standard error of estimate is used in classifying the residuals in different categories. Assuming the distribution of residuals as normal and using the properties of the normal distribution, residuals may be divided into six categories[1] as less than of –2 S.E., –2 S.E. to –S.E., –S.E. to Zero, Zero to + S.E. + S.E. to + 2. S.E., and + S.E. and above.

In the present example, because the number of observations are small, we may not get sufficient observations in each category. As the number of observations increase the puls and minus residuals are expected to be distributed equally such that a large number of observations will fall between 0 to –S.E. (medium negative) and 0 to +S.E. (medium positive). Relatively smaller number of observations will fall in between –S.E. to –2. S.E. (high negative) and + S.E. to + 2.S.E. negative) and there will be very few outliers in below –2 S.E. (very high negative) and above + 2 S.E. (very high positive). Extremely high residuals would be either below –3 S.E. or more than + 3 S.E. These residuals show the presence of some serious abnormality in that observation. Thus it is better to drop that particular observation. The lines parallel to the regression line but at a distance of one S.E. and 2 S.E. on either side may be drawn to show graphically the number of observations falling in each category[2] as shown in Fig. 5.1. A map of residuals, given in Table 5.2, is also prepared using the above classification and is given in Figure 5.2.

In case there are higher variations in the actual values of Y, the absolute residuals do not convey the correct impression. For example, suppose two actual values of 500 and 100 are estimated as 450 and 50. In both the cases we get a residual of 50 units, which is not as undesirable in the first case as it is in the second case. This problem can be handled by taking the relative values of the residuals. In relative terms the first residual is $\frac{50 \times 100}{500}$ = 10 per cent and second is 50 per cent. Table 5.2 gives the relative residuals also in column 6.

An explanation for the spatial distribution of positive and negative residuals may be found in terms of irrigation, nature of soil, consumption of fertilizers, topography and climatic conditions or some other variables.

The methods of incorporating these variables also in the model have been discussed in multiple regression given under the section of multivariate analysis.

1. Note that mean of Residuals is zero.
2. For further discussion on residuals and outliers please refer to : O. Rao and R. L. Miler, *Applied Econometric,* Prentice Hall, India (1972) pp. 112-126.

TAMIL NADU

Residuals from Regression of Agricultural Productivity on Rainfall

(1964 - 65)

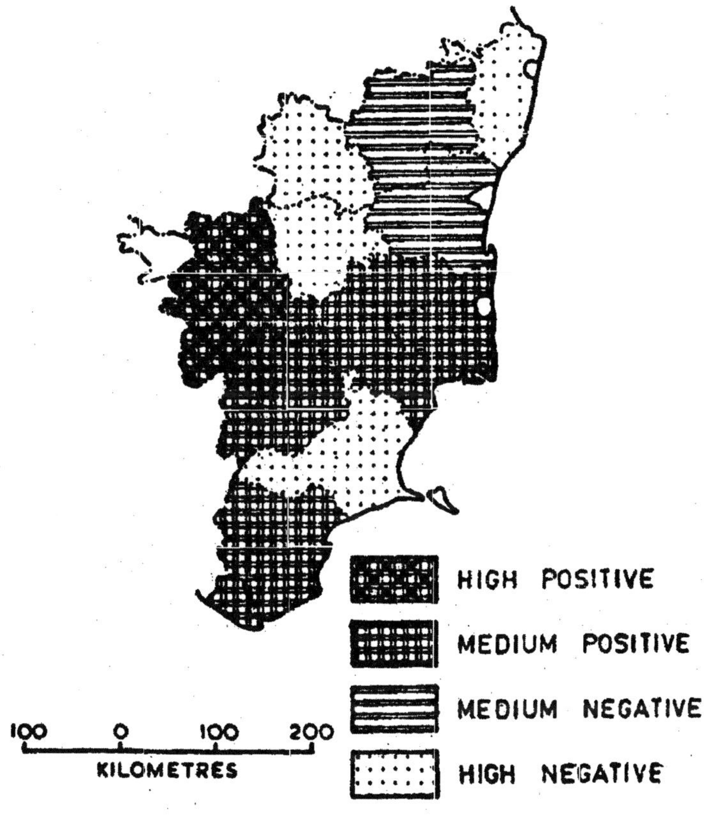

Fig. 5.2

EXERCISES

1. Fit a linear regression of Y on X, using the values given below. Find out the value of the coefficient of determination and test the significance of the regression cooefficient. With the help of this relationship also find out the estimated values of Y and their deviations from the actual values.

X=	10	10	18	25	28	33	34	39	42	43
Y=	15	22	21	35	36	27	33	40	41	47

2. The number of total workers and the number of literate persons among scheduled castes in urban areas of 10 districts of Bihar is given below for 1961. What percentage of variations

in literacy is being explained by employment (assuming a linear relationship). Calculate the residuals of literacy in each district and explain them.

	District	Total Workers (in 000)	Literate Person (in 000)
1.	Patna	22	11
2.	Gaya	12	4
3.	Shahbad	8	3
4.	Tiruth	21	8
5.	Saran	5	2
6.	Champaran	5	1
7.	Muzaffarpur	7	2
8.	Darbhanga	6	3
9.	Monghyr	14	6
10.	Bhagalpur	6	2

3. The yield of wheat and percentages of area of wheat under irrigation is given below for 10 randomly selected districts of Eastern Uttar Pradesh for 1972-73. Give the linear form of relationship showing yield function of irrigation. Does the data suggest that change in the yield associated with a unit change in the percentage of area under irrigation in the districtwise data for entire Eastern Uttar Pradesh is zero?

	District	Yield of Wheat (in Kgs/hect)	% of irrigated area of wheat
1.	Allahabad	991	69.8
2.	Varanasi	964	72.8
3.	Mirzapur	500	26.2
4.	Jaunpur	1529	99.7
5.	Gazipur	1085	78.1
6.	Balia	1378	7.82
7.	Gorakhpur	1055	89.2
8.	Deoria	1002	83.2
9.	Basti	1090	88.5
10.	Faizabad	1084	96.5

6
SPATIAL DISTRIBUTIONS AND INTERACTIONS

Near-Neighbour Analysis

The evolution of the settlement pattern of any area is governed by a number of forces which vary from one region to another and hence we get varying patterns in the spatial distribution of settlements. The conventional visual judgement of the settlement patterns as sparse, dispersed, agglomerated or dense has been replaced by more scientific judgements of their characterisation with the help of nearest neighbour index. Much of the pioneering work of this kind in Geography has been done by King and Dacey.[1]

Nearest neighbour analysis helps in distinguishing three kinds of basic distributions of points (settlements on an area) namely : (1) uniform, (2) random, and (3) clustered. The problem of the nearest neighbour analysis is that of finding a single index for any given pattern running on a continuous scale, i.e., from one extreme when all the points are clustered to the other extreme, a situation in which all the points are distributed uniformally.

Nearest Neighbour Index

The nearest neighbour index was originally devised by plant ecologists Clark and Evans.[2] It measures the deviation of any spatial pattern of the distribution of points from randomness. Assuming the distribution of points as random and the probability distribution of the distance between points and their first nearest neighbour as normal the expected mean nearest neighbour distance $\bar{D}_r$ between the points in a given area is given by :

$$\bar{D}_r = \frac{1}{2\sqrt{\frac{N}{A}}} \qquad ...(6.1)$$

where N is the number of settlements and A is the area of the place.

The nearest nighbour Index R is the ratio of the actual mean distance between nearest neighbour points in a given area ($\bar{D}_0$) to the mean expected distance of random distribution of the same number of points in the same area, *i.e.* $\bar{D}_r$ Thus :

---

1. Dacey, M.P. "Analysis of Central Place and Point Patterns by Nearest Neighbour Method". *Land Studies in Geography Series B, Human Geography* 24 (1962), 55-75 and L.J. King "A Quantitative Expression of the Pattern of Urban Settlements in the Selected Areas of United States". *Tijdschrifi voor Economische en Socilae Geografic*, Vol. 53, 1962 pp. 1-7.
2. For derivation of formula please refer J.P. Clark and F.C. Evans, Distance to Nearest Neighbour as a measure of Spatial Relationship" *Ecology*, 53 : 4445-53.

$$R = \frac{\bar{D}_0}{\bar{D}_r} = \frac{\bar{D}_0}{1/2\sqrt{\frac{N}{A}}} = 2\bar{D}_0\sqrt{\frac{N}{A}} \quad ...(6.2)$$

This ratio *R* ranges from *O*, when there is maximum aggregation of all the points at one location, throuth 1 which represents a random distribution, up to 2.15 which represent even distribution.

The standard error of the expected mean distance is given as :

$$\sigma\bar{D}_r = \frac{0.26126}{\sqrt{N^2 / A}} \quad ...(6.3)$$

If the value of R falls between 0–1 or 1–2.15 they may be explained as approaching cluster and approaching unform respectively, provided that the vaue of $\bar{D}_r$ is significantly different from $\bar{D}_0$, otherwise the pattern should be considered as random and the difference between $\bar{D}_0$ and $\bar{D}_r$ is attributed to the chance factors only. The Statistic

$$Z = \frac{\bar{D}_0 - \bar{D}_r}{\sigma\bar{D}_r} \quad ...(6.4)$$

is a standard normal variate[1] and is used to test the significance of the difference between $\bar{D}_0$ and $\bar{D}_r$

Points to note

1. It does not distinguish between a single and a multiclusterd pattern. For example, if pairs of tows are located on each side of a river, each pair at some distance from the other, the *R* value will come very close to zero, meaning thereby that towns are clustered around one point.

2. It averages out sub-patterns which may exist within the area, thus in any such case each sub-pattern should be studied separately.

3. The demarcation of boundaries of the areas under study is a difficult problem as it affects the value of *R*. The decision must lie with the researcher and can only be made in the light of the nature of the distribution and the particular factors that may affect it.

4. No point outside the boundary of the given area is included in the study, but if the nearest neighbour of any point in the given area lies outsides of its boundary this distance should be included in the computation.

---

1. The limit of which at 1% and 5% levels of significance are 2.58 and 1.96 respectively.

5. If the two points are the nearest neighbours of each other, the same distance should be measured twice.

Example 6.1

While studying the settlement pattern in Mewat region, the map of the region was divided into several grids of 10×10 sq. miles by Aziz.[1] Two such grids are given in Fig. 6.1 and 6.2 with the location of the rural settlement. In grid 1 (Fig. 6.1) the distance between each pair of nearest point is added together which is equal to 44.0 miles and is divided by 62 the number of such pairs to give $\bar{D}_0$ *i.e.*

$$\bar{D}_0 = \frac{44.0}{62} - 0.71$$

Also since $N = 62$ and $A = 10 \times 10 = 100$ sq. miles

$$\bar{D}_r = \frac{1}{2\sqrt{\frac{62}{100}}} = \frac{1}{2\sqrt{.62}} = 0.635$$

and so

$$R = \frac{\bar{D}_0}{\bar{D}_2} = \frac{0.71}{0.635} = 1.1176$$

Since the value of R is in between 1 to 2.15, it shows an approaching uniform distribution only when $\bar{D}_r$, is significantly different from $\bar{D}_0$. This test of significance is carried as below :

$$\text{Standard error } \sigma\bar{D}_{r1} = \frac{0.26136}{\sqrt{62\left(\frac{62}{100}\right)}} = \frac{.26136}{\sqrt{38.44}}$$

$$= \frac{.26136}{6.2} = 0.04215$$

and

$$Z = \frac{\bar{D}_0 - \bar{D}_r}{\sigma\bar{D}_{r1}}$$

$$= \frac{0.71 - .635}{0.04215} = 1.77935$$

Since the value is less than 2.58 it statistically insignificant even at 5% level of significance. Hence the value of R may be considered close to unity and shows a random distribution.

---

1. Abdul Aziz. "The Economy of Primary Production in Mewat : An Analysis of Spatial Patterns, Unpublished, M. Phil dissertation, Centre of the Study of Regional Development, Jawaharlal Nehru University, New Delhi, pp. 139-144, 1974.

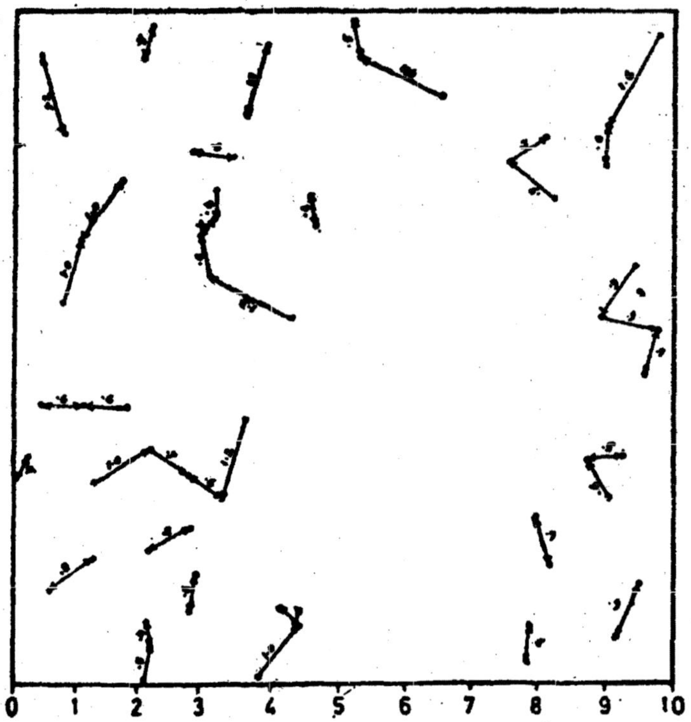

Fig. 6.1

Similarly in second grid (Fig. 6.2) distance between each pair of nearest point adds to 60 miles and is divided by 86, the total number of points in the grid to give $\bar{D}_0$ *i.e.*

$$\bar{D}_0 = \frac{60}{86} = 0.6977$$

Also

$$\bar{D}_{r2} = \frac{1}{2\sqrt{\frac{86}{100}}} = \frac{1}{2\sqrt{.86}} = \frac{1}{2\times.92736} = \frac{1}{1.8547} = 0.5392$$

$$\text{Standard error } \sigma\bar{D}_{r_2} = \frac{0.26136}{\sqrt{86\times.86}} = \frac{.26136}{8.6} = 0.03039$$

$$R = \frac{\bar{D}_0}{\bar{D}_{r_2}} = \frac{0.6977}{0.5392} = 1.2939$$

and $$Z = \frac{.6977 - .5392}{.03039} = 5.21553$$

which is statistically significant at 1% level of significance; so the distribution may be inferred as aproaching uniform. These results can be summarized as below :

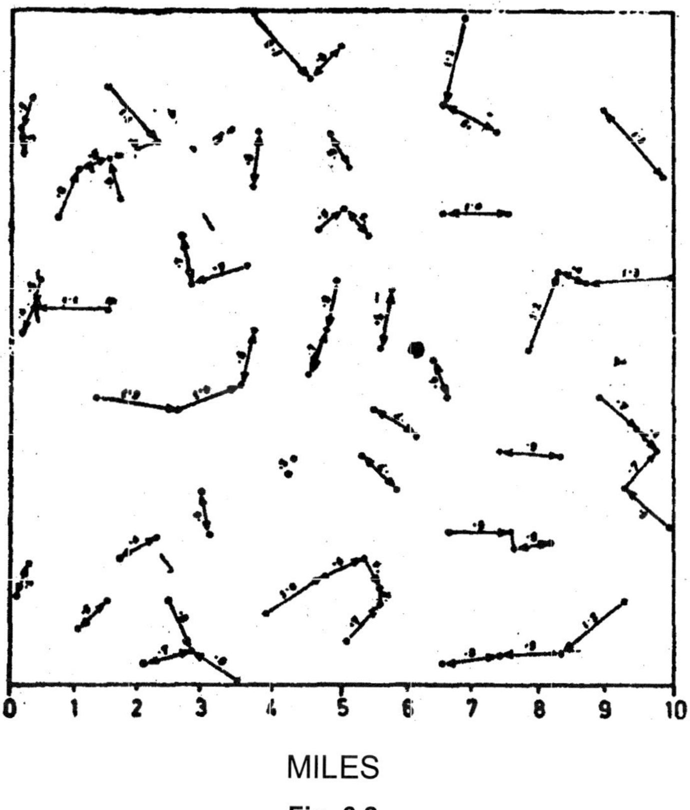

Fig. 6.2

Grid	$\bar{D}_0$	$\bar{D}_r$	R	S.E.	Z.	Remark
1.	0.71	0.635	1.1176	.04215	1.77935	Random
2.	0.6977	0.5392	1.2939	.03039	5.21553	Approaching Uniform

Rank Size Rule

The rank-size is an empirical regularity found in the urban system of many countries of the world. This regularity is more evident in many advanced countries and the countries which have an old urban tradition. According to this rule the population of a town is related with its rank in the following form of Pareto's distribution.

RANK SIZE RELATIONSHIP OF CITIES OF INDIA 1961

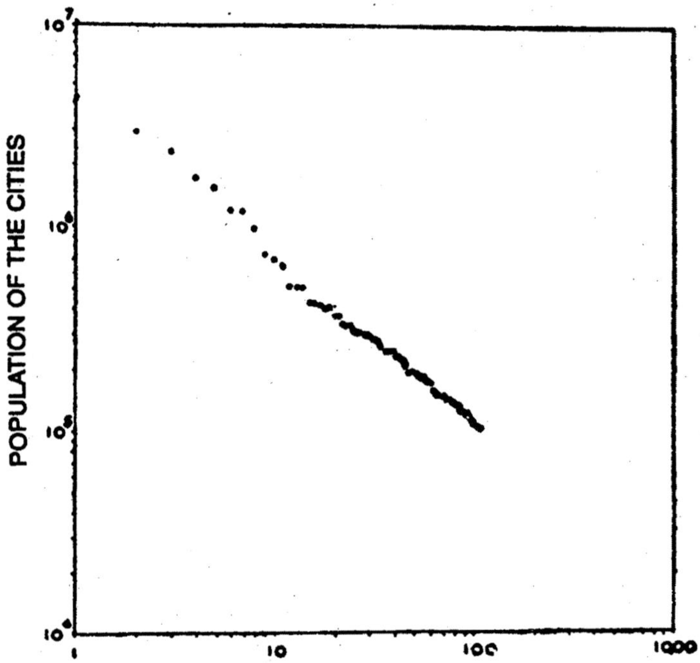

RANK OF THE CITIES

Fig. 6.3

$$P_r = KR^{-b} \qquad ...(6.5)$$

where P_r is the population of the town whose rank is R. K and b are the constants.

The above relationship gets transformed into the following linear form after taking the logarithm of both the sides.

$$Y = a - bX$$

where $Y = \log P_r$ ...(6.6)

$X = \log R$

and $a = \log K$

The regularity in the above relationship was originally observed by Zipf,[1] and later on Berry[2] also showed that this regularity prevails in many parts of the world.

1. G.K. Zipf ; *National Unity and Disunity* ; Bloomington, Ind : Principia Press 1941.
2. B. L. J. Berry : "City Size Distribution and Economic Development", *Economic Development and Cultural Change*, IX No. 4, July 1961, pp. 573-88.

RANK SIZE RELATIONSHIP OF CITIES OF INDIA 1951

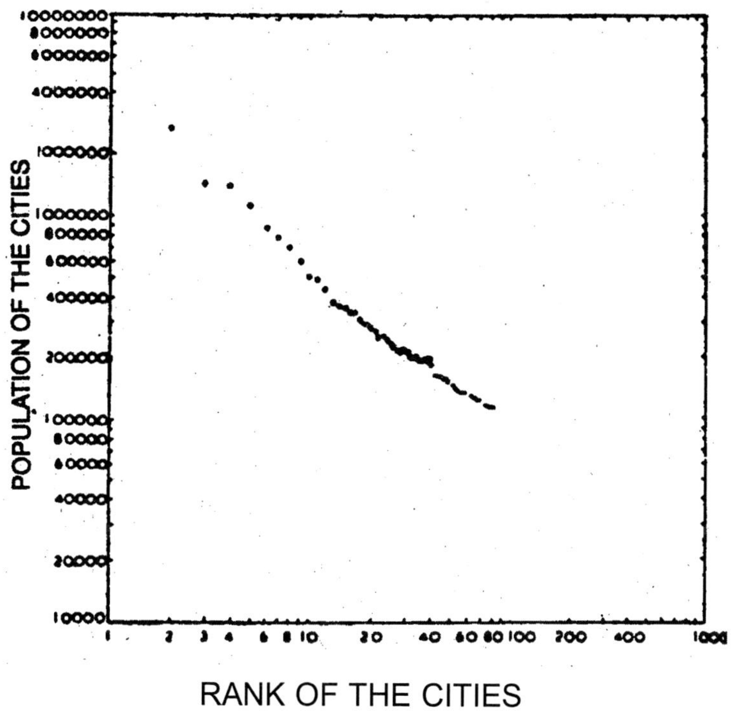

Fig. 6.4

Thus, if on a double log paper the population (P_r) of towns of an area are plotted on Y axis and their ranks (R) are plotted on X axis, we will get a scatter diagram which will closely form a straight line having a negative slope.

Such scatter diagrams of the population of Indian cities for 1961 and 1951 and their ranks on a double log paper are given in Figures 6.3 and 6.4. These figures show a close linear pattern in both the years.

Statistically this regularity can be examined by fitting a regression line of log P_r on log R. The regression coefficient of this line reflects the degree of primacy in the entire urban system and the coefficient of determination may be taken as a measurement of its goodness of fit to the system of rank-size regularity.

Table 6.1 gives the population of first 20 cities of India in 1961 with their ranks. These populations and their ranks have been converted into their logarithms and a regression line is fitted in the usual manner as given below.

Table 6.1

	Rank R	Population Pr	Log (R) =X	X^2	Log Pr =Y	Y^2	XY
G. Bombay	1	4152056	0	0	6.618	43.797924	0
Calcutta	2	2927289	.301	.090601	6.466	41.309156	1.946266
Delhi	3	2359403	.477	.227529	6.373	40.615129	3.039921
Madras	4	1729141	.602	.362404	6.238	38.912644	3.755276
Hyderabad	5	1607396	.700	.490000	6.206	38.514436	4.344200
Bangalore	6	1206961	.778	.620944	6.082	36.990724	4.731796
Ahmedabad	7	1206001	.845	.714025	6.081	36.978561	5.138445
Kanpur	8	971062	903	.815409	5.987	35.844169	5.405261
Poona	9	737426	.954	.910116	5.868	34.433424	5.598072
Nagpur	10	690302	1.000	1.000000	5.839	34.093921	5.839000
Lucknow	11	655673	1.041	1.083681	5.817	33.837489	6.055497
Howrah	12	512598	1.079	1.164241	5.710	32.604100	6.161090
Agra	13	508680	1.114	1.240996	5.706	32.558436	6.356484
Varanasi	14	489364	1.146	1.313316	5.690	32.376100	6.520740
Allahabad	15	430730	1.176	1.382976	5.634	31.741956	6.625584
Madurai	16	421810	1.204	1.449615	5.625	31.640625	6.772500
Jaipur	17	403444	1.230	1.512900	5.606	31.427236	6.895380
Amritsar	18	398047	1.255	1.575025	5.600	31.360000	7.028000
Indore	19	394941	1.279	1.635841	5.597	31.326409	7.158563
Jabalpur	20	367014	1.301	1.692601	5.565	30.969225	7.240065
Total			18.385	19.282221	118.308	701.831664	106.613140

$$b = \frac{\Sigma XY - \frac{\Sigma X \Sigma}{n}}{\Sigma X^2 - \frac{(\Sigma X)^2}{n}} = \frac{106.613140 - \frac{18.385 \times 118.301}{20}}{19.282221 - \frac{18.385 \times 18.385}{20}}$$

$$= -0.899102$$

$$a = \bar{Y} - b\bar{X} = \frac{118.308}{20}(-0.899102)\frac{(18.385)}{20}$$

$$= 6.7418995$$

Thus the equation in log P_r (Y) and log R (x) is

$$\log P_r = 6.7418995 - 0.899102 \log R$$

where $\log K = 6.7418995$ and $b = 0.899102$

The value of b here is a significant at .01% level of significance. The coefficient of determination of this equation was found to 0.9663 *i.e.* 96.63 per cent variations in log P_r are being explained by log R. This is a very high level of explanation which is rarely found in any bivariate case.[1]

The original equation from the values of the constants as found above can be written as

$$P_r = 5519497\, R^{-0.899102} \qquad ...(6.7)$$

where K = Antilog of 6.7418995 = 5519497.

If in equation (6.7) we substitute R=1, 2, 3, 4 and 5 etc., we get the population of cities ranking Ist, 2nd, 3rd, 4th and 5th etc., as per rank-size. Actual population of the cities may not be equal to these estimated values, as no city system fits completely into a rank size rule. At the same time if the coefficient of determination is large the difference between actual and estimated is not supposed to be very large. The population of first five cities are estimated according to the fitted rank-size relationship given in equation (6.7). These results are given in Table 6.2 with actual population and the deviations.

Table 6.2

City	Rank	Estimated population	Actual population	Difference	%Difference
G.Bombay	1	5519497	4152056	+1367441	+24.77
Calcutta	2	2959667	2927289	+32378	+1.09
Delhi	3	2055506	2359403	-303897	-14.78
Madras	4	1587034	1729141	-142107	-8.95
Hyderabad	5	1298536	1607396	-308833	-23.78
Total		13420240	12775285	644955	-5.05

Note that the deviation have been worked out here on the basis of the relationship between only 20 cities. These deviation may get reduced if larger number of cities are included in determining the relationship.

Though a perfect explanation for rank size regularity is missing, a wide range of partial explanations have been given by several authors.

At one point Khan and Wanmali[2] explain it in the following words :

"Population distribution patterns emerge in frameworks ranging from very simple to very

1. Methods for carrying out the test of significance and computations of coefficient of determinations are given of Chapter V.
2. Waheeduddin Khan and S. Wanmall, "Impact of Linguistic Reorganisation of States on city-size distribution," *Economic and Socio-Cultural Dimensions of Regionalization,* Office of the Registrar General India, 1972, p. 452.

complex forms of spatial economic organisation. In the first case, the resultant distribution tends to have greater degree of primacy and in latter the outcome approximates the rank-size rule and can be summed up in the from of a stochastic process. Movement from less complex to more complex economic organisation is also likely to be a movement towards rank-size regularity."

Berry and Garrison have also given an excellent discussion on explanation of the rank-size rule in the theoretical framework proposed by K. Zipf, W. Christaller and others.[1]

Gravity and Potential Models

Gravity Model as a measure of interaction has been derived from Newton's Law of Gravitation in Physics. As applied in Geography it states that the interaction between two places (i and j) is directly proportional to the product of their population and inversely proportional to the distance between them *i.e.*

$$I_{ij} = \frac{GM_iM_j}{d_{ij}} \qquad \text{...(6.8)}$$

Where I_{ij} = Interaction between i & j

M_i = Population of ith place

M_j = Population of jth place

d_{ij} = distance between i and j

G = Some constant

This is the most simple form of the Gravity Model. An accurate measurement of interaction may involve some exponent of d_{ij} and some appropriate weights may also be given to the populations of the two places.

Another important concept derived from equation (6.8) is the total interaction between a place i and all other places which is given by :

$$\sum_{j=1}^{n} I_{ij} = G\sum_{j=1}^{n} \frac{P_1P_j}{dij^b} \qquad \text{...(6.9)}$$

or

$$Vi = \frac{\sum^{n} Iij}{Pi} = G\sum \frac{P_1P_j}{dij^b} \qquad \text{...(6.10)}$$

(p_i can be taken out because summation is over j)

This V_i, the total interaction per unit of population is known as potential at area i.

1. B.L.J. Berry and W.L. Garrison : Alternate Explanations of Urban Rank Size Relationships, *Annals of Association of American Geographers.* XLVIII (March 1958). pp. 83-91.

The model becomes simpler if the value of *b* is taken as unity in the absence of any justification for some other value, as has been assumed by many researchers in India and abroad.[1] Stewart, while using the power of the distance equal to unity in the potential model, calls it a demographic potential which may be interpreted either (*i*) as a measure of proximity of people to that point, or (*ii*) as a measure of aggregate accessibility or more simply, (*iii*) as a measure of influence of people at a distance.[2]

An important point to note here is that

$$Vi = \frac{P_1}{d_{1i}} + \frac{P_2}{d_{2i}} + \dots + \frac{Pi}{dii} + \dots \frac{Pj}{dij}$$

involves $\frac{Pi}{dii}$ also, which is the potential of the *i*th city on itself. There is some problem in measuring *dii* which is the distance of *i*th area from itself. In practice the average distance from the centre to its periphery[3] is usd in place of d_{ii}. This could also be estimated as half of the distance from the nearest place.

Basic Issues

1. The population of different areas as a measure of their masses may be replaced by some other suitable proxy of mass in different situations. For example, if intermetropolitan migration is to be studied, it is apparent that employment or income of the areas tends to be a more significant index of mass than the population. In case the marketing problem of manufactured products is being examined, the total value of retail and wholesale tends to be a more significant measures. Thus the measure of mass to be employed depends on the studied, available data and related considerations.[4] The other possible measures of mass include total investment facilities, number of families, hospital beds, investment in farm equipment, value added in manufacturing, gross regional product, economic opportunities, school enrolment, etc.

2. The distance between the two areas can also be measured in different ways. Thus if a metropolitan traffic study it being conducted, distance along the rail road or highway or travel time is equally important. In case the industrial location is being analysed, transport cost distance is preferred. Thus like mass the measurement of distance also depends on the problem, the available data and related considerations.

3. Another basic issue relates to weights to be applied to the masses. In a study of luxury travel between the two areas, it is reasonable to expect that an area of high per capita income will generate a larger volume of such travel than the area of equal population but lower per capita income (other

---

1. Isard, W. : Methods of Regional Analysis M.I.T. 1960, p. 501
2. Garrothers G.A.P. : An Historical Review of the Gravity and Potential Concepts of Human Interaction *Journal of the American Institute of Planners 22* (Spring 1956) 94-102, reprinted in Embrose P.J. (ed) *Analytical Human Geography*, Longman, 1969, p. 230.
3. Yeats, M.H. : An Introduction to Quantitative Analysis in Economic Geography Mc-Graw-Hills, New York, p. 25.
4. Isard, W. : (1960), op. cit., pp. 505.

things being equal). One way to correct such a factor is to multiply the population of each area by its average per capita income *w*. Thus equation (6.8) can be written in the weighted from as :

$$Iij = G\frac{(WiPi)(WjPj)}{dij^{b}} \quad ...(6.11)$$

and the potential becomes

$$Vi = G\sum\frac{WjPj}{dij^{b}} \quad ...(6.12)$$

This kind of potential is known as income potential.

Among the other possible weights which might be a employed are occupational structure, sex ratio, age composition, percentage of population having own houses, literacy, urban-rural ratio, etc. Actually by weighting the population in some way we may derive other measures of the same masses as noted above in point No. 1.

4. The choice of exponent (*b*) to the distance used in equation (1) is a difficult problem. A number of investigators have proposed the value of *b* either unity or two.

5. The gravity model assumes that there is no legel or administrative barrier between the places under study.

Example 6.1

Taking all the towns of population 50000 and above in the National Capital Region (Delhi), Fig. 6.5, the computational problems of gravity model are explained as below :

Table 6.3 gives the straight line distance of each town from other town in brackets. The diagonal values of Table 6.3 are equal to half the least value given in each column. The population of each town is given below the name of each city.

The value in each column without the bracket are $\frac{Pi}{dij}$ and are obtained by dividing the population of different towns by their distances from that particular town. For example take column No. 2 which correspond to Meerut. The first town in the table is Delhi. Its population is 3647023 and the distance of Delhi from Meerut is 59 km., so $\frac{P_1}{d_{21}} = 3647023/59 = 61814$ person/km. Similarly, the second town in the table is Meerut itself. Its population is 367754 and the distance of the nearest town Hapur, is 29 km. Half of it, if rounded, is 15 km. So $\frac{P_2}{d_{22}} = \frac{367754}{15} = 24517$ person/km. The third town in the table is Gurgaon with a population of 57151 and its distance from Meerut is 82 km.

$$\text{So} \frac{P_3}{d_{23}} = \frac{57151}{82} = 697 \text{ persons/km.}$$

Likewise $\frac{P_4}{d_{2.4}} \frac{P_5}{d_{2.5}} \ldots\ldots \frac{P_{12}}{d_{5.12}}$ all are given in the second column. Thus the entries in each column show the potential of all those towns which have been taken into consideration on the particular town of that column. The sum of these potentials is given at the bottom of each column.

The potential values as given in Table 6.3 show a much larger potential at Delhi, which is the only huge urban complex in the region. The potential decreases as we move away from Delhi and the least potential is found at remote areas like Alwar, Panipat, Rohtak, Bulandshahar and Khurja etc. as is shown in Fig. 6.5.

The interaction between different places can also be worked out from Table 6.3. To illustrate, the intencity of interaction between Meerut and Delhi = (Population of Meerut × Population of Delhi) divided by distance between them.

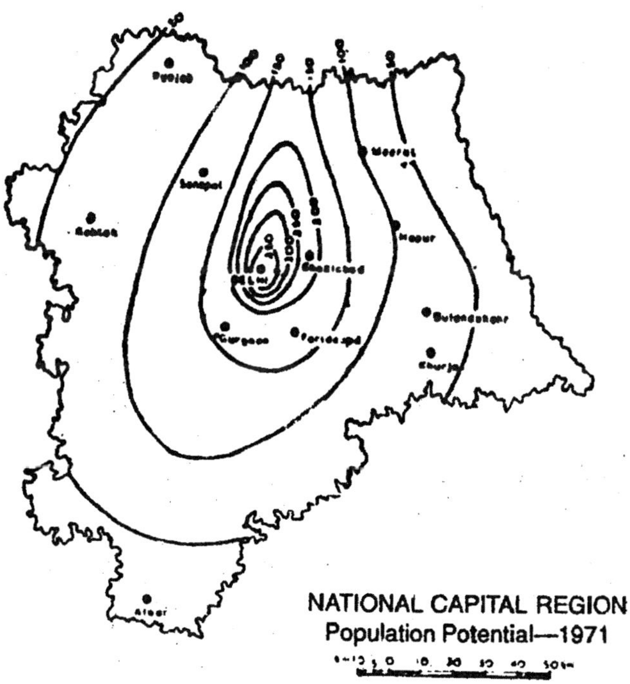

Fig. 6.5

Table 6.3
Consumption of Population Potential at the Towns of Population more than 50000 + in N.C.R. 1971.

S. No.	Towns	1	2	3	4	5	6	7	8	9	10	11	12
1	Delhi	(10)	(59)	(27)	(65)	(72)	(27)	(41)	(67)	(76)	(53)	(19)	(126)
	3647023	344702	61814	135075	56108	50653	135074	88952	54433	47987	68812	191948	28945
2	Meerut	(59)	(15)	(82)	(62)	(76)	(68)	(60)	(105)	(79)	(29)	(42)	(185)
	367754	6233	24517	4485	5932	4839	5408	6129	3374	4655	12681	8756	1988
3	Gugaon	(27)	(82)	(14)	(76)	(78)	(27)	(56)	(64)	(97)	(74)	(42)	(102)
	57151	2117	697	4082	752	733	2117	1021	893	589	772	1394	560
4	Bulandshahar	(65)	(62)	(76)	(8)	(15)	(51)	(97)	(131)	(132)	(32)	(49)	(149)
	59505	915	960	783	7438	3967	1167	613	454	451	1860	1214	399
5	Khurja	(72)	(76)	(78)	(15)	(8)	(52)	(108)	(136)	(144)	(47)	(59)	(140)
	50245	698	661	644	3350	8281	966	465	369	349	1069	852	359
6	Faridabad*	(27)	(58)	(27)	(51)	(52)	(14)	(67)	(86)	(109)	(54)	(28)	(113)
	105406	3904	1550	3904	2067	2027	7529	1573	1226	967	1952	3765	933
7	Sonepat	(41)	(60)	(56)	(97)	(108)	(67)	(20)	(47)	(40)	(76)	(51)	(156)
	62393	1522	1040	1114	643	578	931	3120	1328	1560	821	1233	400
8	Rohtak	(67)	(105)	(64)	(131)	(136)	(86)	(47)	(24)	(64)	(79)	(82)	(9138)
	124755	1862	1188	1949	952	917	1451	2654	5189	1949	1579	1521	1904
9	Panipat	(76)	(79)	(97)	(132)	(144)	(109)	(40)	(64)	(20)	(108)	(87)	(194)
	87981	1158	1114	907	667	611	807	2200	1375	3499	815	1011	454
10	Hapur	(53)	(29)	(74)	(32)	(47)	(54)	(76)	(79)	(104)	(15)	(35)	(165)
	71266	1345	2457	963	2227	1516	1320	938	902	685	4751	2036	432
11	Ghaziabad	(19)	(42)	(41)	(49)	(59)	(28)	(51)	(82)	(87)	(35)	(10)	(139)
	127700	6721	3040	3115	2606	2164	4561	2504	1557	1468	3649	12770	919
12	Alwar	(126)	(185)	(102)	(149)	(140)	(113)	(156)	(138)	(194)	(165)	(139)	(51)
	100379	797	543	984	674	717	888	643	727	517	608	722	1968
Potentials in Thousands													
Persons/km.		371	100	158	83	77	162	111	72	65	100	227	38

Including the township

$$\frac{3647023 \times 367754}{59} = 21610 \text{ million persons}^2/\text{km.}$$

Similarly, the interaction between Meerut and Ghaziabad is,

$$\frac{367754 \times 127700}{42} = 118 \text{ million persons}^2/\text{km.}$$

and between Meerut and Hapur is

$$\frac{367754 \times 71266}{29} = 904 \text{ million persons}^2/\text{km.}$$

Thus we see that though Hapur is closer to meerut than Ghaziabad but because population of Ghaziabad is large enough to out compete the distance effect, hence interaction between Meerut and Ghaziabad is greater than that between Meerut and Hapur.

REFERENCES

Near-Neighbour Analysis

1. Aziz, Abdul : "The economy of Primary Production in Mewat : An Analysis of Spatial Patterns" unpublished M. Phil. dissertation, *Jawaharlal Nehru University*, 1974.

2. Clark, P.J. and Evans, F.C. : "Distance to nearest neighbour as a measure of spatial relationships in populations", *Ecology*, 35 : 4 (1954), 445-53.

3. Dacey, M.F.: "A note on the derivation of the nearest neighbour distances," *Journal of Regional Science Association*, Vol. 2, (1960), pp. 81-87.

4. Dacey, M.F.: "Analysis of Central Place and point patterns by a nearest Neighbour Method", *Land Studies in Geography Series* B, Vol. 24, (1962) pp. 55-75.

5. Dacey, M.F.: "Other Nearest Neighbour Statistics for a class of Random Patterns in Multi-dimensional Space," *Annals of Association of American Geographers,* Vol. 53 (1963), pp. 505-515.

6. Getis, A. : "Temporal Land-use Patterns Analysis with the use of Nearest Neighbour and Quadrant Methods", A.A.A. Vol. (1964) 54, pp. 891-99.

7. King, L.J. : "A Quantitative expression of the pattern of urban settlement in selected areas of U.S." *Tijdschrift Voor Economische en Sociale Geografic*, Vol. 53, pp. 1-7.

8. Medvedkov, Y.V. : "Application of Mathematics to some problems in Economic Geography", *Soviet-Geography,* Vol. 5, (1964) pp. 36-53.

9. Warntz, W. Neft, D. : "Contribution to a Statistical Methodology for Areal Distributions". *Journal of Regional Science* Vol. 2, (1960), pp. 47-66.

Rank-Size Rule

1. Berry, B.J.L. : "City-size Distribution and Economic Development". *Economic Development and Cultural Change,* Vol. IX, No. 4, 1961, pp. 573-588.

2. Berry, B.J.L. : "Cities as Systems within systems of Cities, "Regional Science Association

(1964) 13, pp. 147-163.

3. Khan, W. and Wanmali, S. : "Impact of Linguistic Reorganisation of states on city-size Distribution," Economic and Socio-cultural Dimensions of Regionalisation, Office of the Registrar General of India 1972, p. 452.

4. Mark Jefferson : "The Law of Primate City," *The Geographical Review*, XXIX No. 2, April 1939 (pp. 226-32).

5. Martin Beekmen: "City Hierarchies and the distribution of City-Size," *Economic Development and Cultural Changes*, VI, April 1958, pp. 243-48.

6. Stewart. J.Q. : "Empirical Mathematical Rules concerning the Distribution and Equilibrium of Population", *The Geographical Review,* Vol. XXXVII No. 3, 1947, pp. 451-485.

7. Stewart, Charles T.Jr. : "The Size and Spacing of Cities." *The Geographical Review,* 1958, pp. 222-245.

8. Sovani, N.V. : "Trend of Urbanization in India" Paper read at the 39th Annual Confernce of the Indian Economic Association (1958 Bombay), pp. 107-114.

9. Sadasyuk Galina : "Urbanization and the Spatial Structure of Indian Economy", *Economic and Socio-Cultural Dimensions of Regionalization,* Office of the Registrar General India, 1972, p. 452.

10. Ullman, E.L. : "Theory of Location of Cities ", *American Journal of Sociology.* Vol. XLVI No. 6 (May 1941), pp. 853-64.

11. Zipf, G.K. : *National Unity and Disunity, Bloomington,* Ind. Principia Press, 1941.

12. Zipf, G.K. : *Human Behaviour and Principle of Least Efforts* Readings, Mass : Addison - Wesley, 1949.

Gravity and Potential Model

1. Anderson, Theodore : "Potential Model and Spatial Distribution of Population", Papers and Proceedings of Regional Science Association Vol. 2. (1956).

2. Carrother, "An Historical Review of the Gravity and Potential Concepts of Human Interaction", Concepts in Analytical Human Geography ed. by Peter Embrose Longman, pp. 226-242.

3. Dunn Edgar S. : "The Market Patential Concept and the Analysis of Location", Papers and Proceedings of Regional Science Association, Vol. 2, (1956).

4. Isard, W. : *Methods of Regional Analysis* : M.I.T. Press, 1960.

5. Stewart Q. : "Demographic Gravitation : Evidence and Applications" Sociometry Vol. II (Feb. and May 1948).

6. Stewart, J.Q. and William Warantz : "Physics of Population Distribution", *Journal of Regional Science Association*, Vol. I (Summer 1958).

7. Zip George K. : "The Pi P2/D Hypothesis on the Inter-city Movement of Persons", *American Social Review*, Vol. II (Oct. 1946).

7
MEASUREMENTS OF DISPARITIES

In most of the regionalisation problems no single variable is sufficient enough to portray some of the complex characteristics which are not directly observable. As these characteristics are only partially reflected by several variables we have to measure them through these related variables. A composite picture from properly chosen variables may be extracted by working out a composite index from them.

Theoretically such a composite index I from variables X_1, X_2....................X_n is obtained by their weighted sum, as:

$$I = W_1X_1 + W_2X_2 + \ldots\ldots\ldots\ldots + W_nX_n$$

where W_1, W_2.............W_n are the weights of the corresponding variables.

Construction of a composite index, in the above manner, poses two serious problems: (a) removing the biasness of scale and (b) determining the weights of the variables.

Biasness of Scale : Under any weightage system, the values of any composite index are highly sensitive to the units of measurement of the original variables. To illustrate, suppose we want to measure the statewise transport development by a weighted index of (1) the number of railway stations per 100 square km. and (2) the average capacity of transactions per station in tonnes for a certain years. In the above example the number of stations will be very small in comparison to the yearly tonnage per station. The variations in tonnage are also expected to be much higher than the number of stations. If the two variables are added together, under any system of weightages, the state having a higher level of tonnage but mainly concentrated in fewer numbers of huge transport junctions may rank higher than the state having fairly balanced distribution of railway stations, but may not have a tonnage turnover comparable with the first state. A planner more interested in the balanced regional development may not agree with this kind of ranking. The basic reason, apart from the weightages, lies in the fact that the two variables have different scales of measurement. Thus it is necessary to eliminate the biasness of scale before evolving any system of weightages. The biasness of scale may be eliminated by the following methods :

(1) Ranking Method

(2) Division by some suitable value

(3) Standardization

The choice of any of the above methods depends on the objective of the study and the researcher's own value system. A brief discussion on them will help the researcher in choosing the proper method.

Ranking Method : In this method we rank the observations and their ranks become new variables. Following points should be noted while using the ranking method.

(1) The rank variable is discrete and has no dimension.

(2) The values of two consecutive ranks do not have an equal amount of difference in their original values.

(3) Mean, standard deviation and coefficient of variation of all the variables after ranking become equal.

(4) The larger the number of variables, the smaller will be the distortion in composite index due to ranking.

Division by some suitable value

If the original values of a variable are divided by some of its parameters like mean, standard deviation or coefficient of variation, the scale effect gets neutralized because these parameters are also affected by the same scale of measurement.

When we divide the observations by its mean, the mean of the new variable equals unity and the standard deviation equals the coefficient of variations of the original series. The coefficient of variations of both the original and the transformed series remain same. (Thus new transformation retains the relative variability of the original variable).

When we divied the original observations by their standard deviation, the variance of the variables becomes unity.

An individual researcher may use some other divisor as well to eliminate the biasness of scale. Such a transformation will affect the variables according to the stablished statistical properties of which the two important properties are (*a*) if a constant a is subtracted from the values of a variable X with mean $\overline{X}$, the mean of new values would be $X - a$ and this transformation is known as change of origin. (*b*) if the values of a variable are divided by a constant, say h, the standard deviation of the new values will be $1/h$ times of the values of the original standard deviation and is known as change of scale.

Standardization : In this method the mean of each variable is subtracted from its different values and this difference is then divided by its S.D. Standardization changes simultaneously the origin as well as the scale of measurment. Means of all the standardized variables are equal to zero and the standard deviations equal to unity. This is a very popular form of transformation used by the professional statisticians. Under this method the matrix of the sums of squares and cross products becomes the correlation matrix of the original variables.

Thus the choice of the methods of removing the biasness of scale should be made carefully in the light of the properties of the different methods discussed above and the objective of the study.[1]

Determinig the Weights of Different Variables :

After identifying the variables and eliminating the biasness of scale from their measurement, the crucial problem in preparing a composite index from them is that of assigning weights to them. The weights are generally of two kinds : (*a*) subjective and (*b*) mathematical. The subjective weightage system is purely arbitrary and depends on the ability of the person (*s*) to determine the weights. A highly skilled reasearcher may derived some very useful conclusions with this simple method of determining the weights. Subjective weighting, however, can not be justified in the absence of strong favourable arguments relating the weights with the objective of the study. There is greater scope of manipulation of the results with the subjective scheme of weights than in any other method. The advantage of this method is that being a very simple method this expedites the work and saves labour.

Mathematical Weights :

The weights of different variables can also be determined with the help of their mathematical properties, minimizing the subjectivity in it. Any such weightage system will be evolved through the theoretical framework of the problem and its mathematical logic. Hence, mathematical weights are also subjective in a restricted sense. Few important method using different kinds of weights in different cases are discussed below :

Kendall's Method

While measuring the agricultural efficiency in England and Wales, the noted statistician M.G. Kendall[2] took the countrywise data on per acre production of different crops. The scale effect was eliminated by converting the production per acre of each crop into ranks and the weightage problem was handled by assigning equal weights to each crop.The composite index of agricultural efficiency was constructed by adding the rank of different crops in each area. Thus if Rij is the rank of the ith crop in the jth area, its composite index of agricultural efficiency Ij is given by

$$Ij = \sum_{i=1}^{n} Rij$$

where n is the number of selected crops.

The rationale of using this subjective scheme of weightage in the words of Kendall is as below:

> "Such a procedure in fact, maximizes the average Spearman correlation between the ranking so reached and the ranking according to the p-variates. The Rank-vector therefore gets as close to p rank-vectors as it can, so to speak, and will approximate to the first principal component."[3]

1. For further discussion readers may refer to A. Kundu : "Construction of Composite Indices for Regionalization - An Enquiry itno the Methods of Analysis", *Geographical Review of India* Vol. 37, No. 1, March 1975. pp. 19-29.
2. Kendall, M.G. : "The geographical distribution of crop productivity in England" ; *Journal of Royal Statistical Society* 102, 21 (1939).
3. Kendall, M.G. : *A Course in Multivariate Analysis* Charles Griffin Co. London, 1968, p. 35.

The same method has also been used by Mitra[1] in classifying the Indian Districts into four quartiles of development using 35 indicators of regional development.

This ranking method of constructing a composite imdex is illustrated in the following example.

Example : The production (in M.T.) per hectare of six important crops in Rajasthan is given below for 1970-71. Construct the composite index of agricultural productivity using the ranking method.

Yield in M.T. per Hactare in Rajasthan 1970-71

District	Maize	Wheat	Bajra	Jowar	Barley	Gram
1. Ajmer	.850	1.136	.667	.343	1.378	.551
2. Alwar	.905	2.249	.567	.611	1.640	.991
3. Banswara	1.309	1.475	—	.436	1.543	.053
4. Barmer	—	1.330	.496	.413	1.333	.500
5. Bharatpur	1.000	1.679	1.107	.403	1.020	.658
6. Bhilwara	1.008	1.273	.518	.196	1.295	.470
7. Bikaner	—	1.333	.156	.500	—	1.000
8. Chittorgarh	1.801	1.507	—	.632	1.577	.482
9. Churu	—	1.200	.251	.500	—	.418
10. Dungurpur	.868	1.476	.500	.434	1.568	.316
11. Ganganagar	1.307	1.279	.951	.405	.756	.692
12. Jaipur	3.397	1.497	.679	.444	1.767	1.248
13. Jaisalmer	—	1.315	.180	.400	—	.666
14. Jhalawar	1.303	.775	.509	.583	1.500	.406
15. Jhunjhunu	—	1.433	.520	.500	1.516	.314
16. Jodhpur	1.000	1.488	.527	.292	1.133	.552
17. Kota	1.443	.932	.521	.624	1.456	.581
18. Nagaur	1.42	1.039	.307	.275	1.204	.554
19. Pali	.806	5.331	.851	.512	1.199	.558
20. Sawai Madhopur	.910	1.284	.880	.799	1.435	.825
21. Sikar	—	1.438	.480	.500	1.973	.814
22. Sirohi	1.830	1.534	.530	.393	1.950	.553
23. Tonk	1.004	.812	.668	.355	1.395	.736
24. Udaipur	1.320	1.637	.500	.365	1.824	.775
25. Bundi	1.387	1.256	.571	.576	1.464	.594
26. Jolare	2.000	1.511	.081	.419	1.190	.558

Solution : Using Kendall's method the productivity of all the 26 districts has to be ranked seperately for each crop. Thus every district will have six ranks one for a each crop. The sum of the six ranks of a district will give the composite scores reflecting agricultural productivity of the district. In Table 7.1 the districs have been ranked six times according to their yield per acre in each crop. The district having the highest yield has been assigned the first rank, the next highest has been assigned the 2nd rank and so on.

---

1. Asok Mitra : "Levels of Regional Development, Census of India, 1961.

Problem of Ties : In some cases the yields of a few districts are equal in certain crops. This problem of ties is a common problem in any ranking procedure. The convention to avoid this complication is to give them a rank value equal to the average of the successive ranks given to them. For example, the yield of Jowar is 0.500 in districts Bikaner, Sikar, Jhunjhunu and Churu. The last highest value is 0.512 whose rank is 7. We assign the successive ranks to the next four values, which are equal to 0.500 as 8, 9, 10, 11. The average of them is 9.5 so each of these 4 values has been assigned 9.5 as its rank. The next higher value 0.485 in Ganganagar has been ranked 12. The ranking of all other value is done in the usual way. The same rule will apply to any number of districts having equal yield.

After ranking the districts for each crop, these ranks are added row-wise. The sum of these ranks is given in the last column of Table 7.1.

Table 7.1
Computation for working out the composite index of Agricultural Productivity using Ranking Method

	Yield Ranks of						
District	Maize	Wheat	Bajra	Jowar	Barley	Groundnut	Total
Ajmer	19	22	7	23	15	15	104
Alwar	14	2	9	4	5	3	37
Banswara	8	11	25.5	14	8	26	92.5
Barmer	23.5	15	18	17	16	19	108.5
Bharatpur	15.5	3	1	18	23	10	70.5
Bhilwara	12	19	14	26	17	21	109
Bikaner	23.5	14	23	9.5	25	2	98
Chittorgarh	2	7	25.5	2	6	20	64.5
Churu	23.5	21	21	9.5	25	22	122
Dungurpur	18	10	16.5	15	7	24	90.5
Ganganagar	9	18	2	12	3	8	53.0
Jaipur	1	8	8	13	3	1	31
Jaisalmer	23.5	16	22	19	25	9	114.5
Jhalawar	10	26	5	5	10	23	89
Jhunjhunu	23.5	13	12	9.5	9	25	93.5
Jodhpur	15.5	9	11	24	22	17	98.5
Kota	5	24	12	3	12	12	68.0
Nagaur	11	23	20	25	18	15	111
Pali	20	1	4	7	19	13.5	64.5
Sawai Madhopur	17	17	3	1	13	4	55.0
Sikar	23.5	12	19	9.5	2	5	71.0
Sirohi	3	5	10	20	20	16	74.0
Tonk	13	25	6	22	14	7	87.0
Udaipur	7	5	16.5	21	1	6	55.5
Bundi	6	20	8	6	11	11	62.0
Jolare	2	6	24	16	21	13.5	82.5

Thus the composite score of ranks given in the last column show the overall agricultural productivity of all the districts based on these six crops. According to this exercise Jaipur is agriculturally the most productive district because the value of its composite score is the least. Alwar is the next agriculturally productive district followed by Ganganagar and so on. The least agriculturally productive district according to its productivity in the six major crops given above is Churu whose composite score is the highest. This composite index has also been plotted on a map to show the spatial variation in the agricultural productivity (Fig. 7.1).

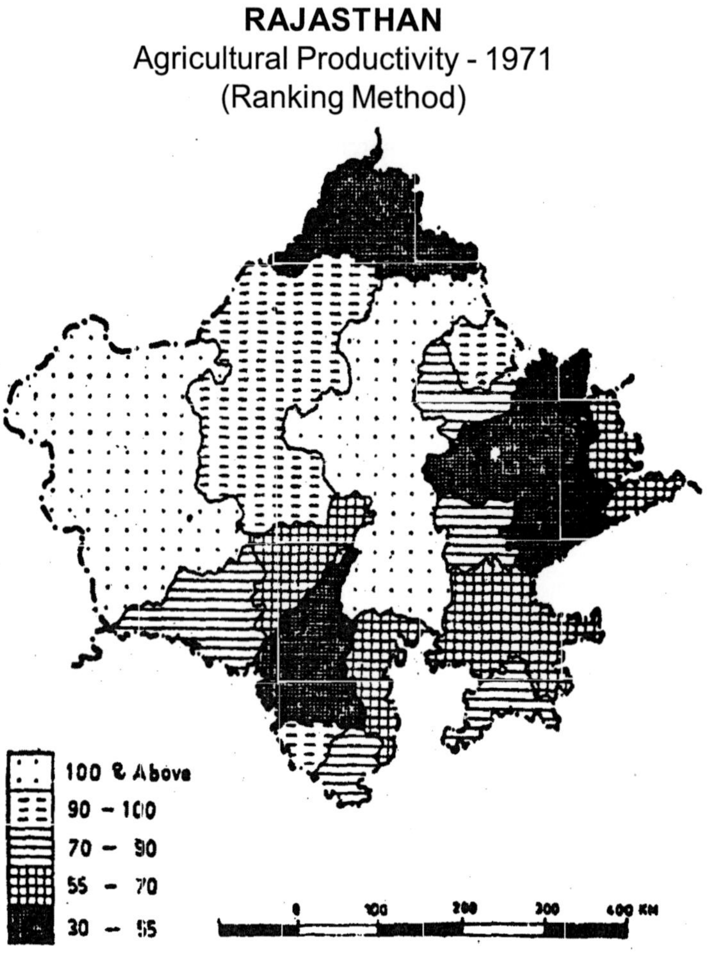

Fig. 7.1

Bhatia's Method : Ranking method, besides having the advantage of simple in computation, has some serious disadvantages also. When we rank the districts according to their yield of a crop, the absolute differences are ignored. For example, if the highest value of the yield of a crop is 0.95, the next highest is 0.90 and the third highest value is 0.70, we will rank them as 1, 2, and 3. Here the difference of 0.05 units in the first two districts adds one rank to the second district, whereas the difference of 0.20 units in the 2nd and 3rd districts also adds one rank in the 3rd district.

Another serious drawback of this method is that the ranks of all the crops have been treated as equally important irrespective of the area under each crop.

Taking into account the above two shortcomings of Kendall's Method, Bhatia[1] suggested a method of compositing the yield per acre of different crops as the weighted mean of the ratio's of the yields of different crops in a district to the yields of the respective crops in the region. The weights as suggested by Bhatia are the proportions of the area under each crop to the cropped area. The formula for Bhatia's method is given as :

$$Ij = \frac{\Sigma Yij\, Cij}{\Sigma Cij}$$

where Ij is the composite index of districts j, Cij is the proportion of area under ith crop to the total cropped area in the jth district and

$\text{Yij} = \frac{Eij}{Ei}$, where Eij is the yield of the jth district and Ei is the yield of the ith crop in the region as a whole.

The divison of the yield of each crop in the districts by the yield of the same crop in the region, eliminates the biasness of scale but retains its absolute differences.

Thus in order to apply Bhatia's method, the values required are the districtwise production of different crops and their acreage. The districtwise yield of each crop (E) can be obtained by dividing the production of each crop in the district by its area. The proportion of area under each crop (Cij) may also be obtained by dividing the area under each crop to the total cropped area in the district. The yield of each crop in the region is obtained by dividing the total production of each crop in the region by the total area under that crop in the region.

The procedure is explained below by taking the same six crops as given in the previous example.

Example : Taking the area and production figures of maize, wheat, bajra, jowar, barley and groundnut for all the districts of Rajasthan (1970-71) work out a composite index of their agricultural productivity for each district using Bhatia's method.

Solution : The Production per hectare (E) of the given six crops are given in Table 7.2. The proportion of area under each of them to the total cropped area (c) has been worked out and given in column C of Table 7.2. Each E value is then divided by the corresponding productivity per acre in the state as a whole given in the bottom row of the Table 7.2 and is put under the column Y of each crop. For each crop the Y values have been multiplied by corresponding C values and the sum of six such values is given in column (13) of Table 7.2. All the six C values for each district also have been added and given in column (14). Index Ij is obtained by dividing column 13 by column 14 and is

1. S.S. Bhatia : "Patterns of Crop Concentration and Diversification in India", Economic Geography, Vol. XL, 1965, pp. 38-56.

given in column 15. This composite index has also been mapped and is given in Fig. 7.2. It should be noted that Fig. 7.1 and 7.2 have a close correspondence.

RAJASTHAN

AGRICULTURAL PROUCTIVITY - 1971

(Bhatia's Method)

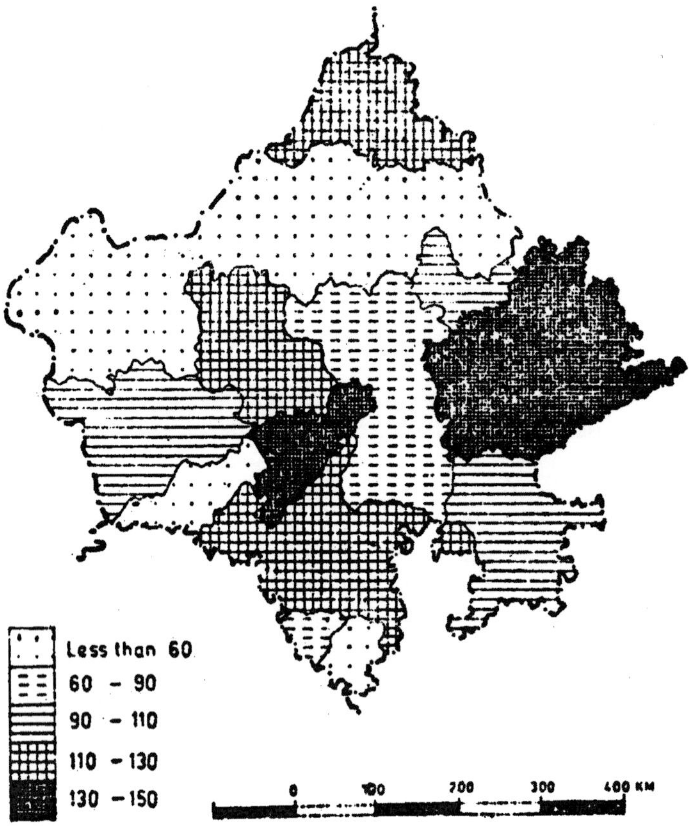

Fig. 7.2

The correspondence between the results of the two methods can also be established by working out the coefficient of correlation between them. The Spearman's coefficient of rank correlation was found to be 0.687 which is significant at .01% level of significance.

Note that the yield per acre used in both the above example is for one point of time, which may not be a normal year. Thus in order to avoid the effects of the random factors on productivity, the

Table 7.2
Computations for Working out the Composite Index of Agricultural Productivity using Bhatia's Method.

District	Maize		Wheat		Bajra		Jowar		Barley		Gram				
	Y	C	Y	C	Y	C	Y	C	Y	C	Y	C	ΣYC	$\Sigma CI=$	$\frac{\Sigma YC}{\Sigma C}\times 10C$
	(1)	(2)	(3)	(4)	(5)	(6)	(7)	(8)	(9)	(10)	(11)	(12)	(13)	(14)	(15)
Ajmer	.697	8.385	.864	11.73	1.426	15.89	.694	28.04	.950	9.16	.750	10.45	77.177	87.30	86.132
Alwar	.746	1.91	1.705	11.05	1.213	29.48	1.245	5.19	1.123	6.34	1.36	30.69	111.408	84.65	131.61
Banswara	1.074	12.77	1.121	3.29	–	–	.878	1.43	1.120	–	.068	61.86	22.864	79.35	28.810
Barmer	–	0	1.008	1.24	1.064	96.8	–	–	.910	–	.660	–	104.245	99.37	104.406
Bharatpur	–	0	1.273	18.70	2.362	23.49	.816	6.02	.700	3.19	.904	29.50	113.102	80.90	139.803
Bhilwara	.828	30.24	.962	16.59	1.106	–	.408	11.53	.890	11.88	.644	6.40	60.398	74.64	80.908
Bikaner	–	0	1.008	–	.34	97.49	–	–	–	–	–	–	33.147	98.82	33.543
Bundi	1.139	9.2	.955	31.14	–	–	1.184	23.97	.990	3.56	.808	17.69	86.416	85.56	101.000
Chittorgarh	1.475	23.85	1.144	22.79	–	–	1.286	16.66	1.080	1.94	.658	6.29	88.909	71.53	124.296
Churu	–	0	.909	–	.532	85.95	–	–	–	–	.575	13.24	53.334	98.24	54.289
Dungerpur	.713	37.69	1.121	13.49	–	–	.886	1.60	1.080	3.07	.438	19.44	55.243	75.29	73.374
Ganganagar	1.074	–	.970	17.18	.021	15.04	1.000	0.67	.520	4.49	.95	48.29	95.941	85.67	111.989
Jaipur	2.787	1.05	1.136	11.62	1.447	44.04	.898	6.33	1.210	14.78	1.710	12.41	124.640	90.23	138.136

Contd....

	(1)	(2)	(3)	(4)	(5)	(6)	(7)	(8)	(9)	(10)	(11)	(12)	(13)	(14)	(15)
Jaisalmer	–	–	1.000	1.71	.383	94.86	.816	3.15	–	–	–	–	40.612	99.71	40.279
Jallore	–	–	1.144	8.13	.170	80.89	–	–	.820	–	–	–	23.052	89.02	25.895
Jhalawa	1.066	11.55	.591	16.06	1.085	1.89	1.184	42.82	1.030	–	.562	7.94	77.834	78.26	99.456
Jhunjhunu	–	–	1.083	8.56	1.106	3.39	–	–	1.040	9.69	.425	65.26	50.834	86.90	58.597
Jodhpur	–	–	1.129	4.37	1.28	80.41	.592	3.48	.770	–	–	–	97.696	88.26	110.691
Kota	1.180	3.64	.705	34.42	–	–	1.270	37.31	1.000	1.00	.808	16.91	90.608	93.28	99.136
Nagaur	–	–	.788	4.22	.660	74.21	.570	9.21	.820	1.18	.753	2.10	60.102	90.92	66.104
Pali	.664	5.30	4.038	3.57	1.810	35.90	1.040	21.58	.820	5.95	.767	4.38	113.608	76.69	148.139
Sawai-Madhopur	.746	0.96	.970	14.93	1.872	26.65	1.630	12.32	.980	5.35	1.137	19.11	110.14	79.32	138.855
Sikar	–	–	.091	3.17	1.021	80.49	1.020	–	1.210	5.19	1.110	8.60	101.461	97.45	105.115
Sirohi	1.50	12.12	1.159	22.41	1.128	38.12	.800	2.32	0.820	3.24	.753	3.94	94.633	82.16	114.181
Tonk	820	5.53	.614	20.94	1.426	9.22	.73	29.61	0.960	10.19	1.014	16.89	83.063	92.38	89.914
Udaipur	1.082	42.32	1.242	16.35	–	–	.76	7.66	1.230	12.50	1.068	8.47	96.340	87.30	110.355
Yield in the State (MT/ Hectare)	1.22		1.32		0.47		0.49		1.46		0.73				

average yield of the crops for few years may also be used in the examples and will give more reliable results.

Method of First Principal Component :

Bhatia's method is more suitable, particularly, for measuring the agricultural efficiency, provided that the data is available in the required form. Another useful and versatile method of construction of a composite index, applicable in many problems of different nature, is the method using first principal component as used by Dasgupta[1] and Pal[2]. The composite index obtained by this method is characterized as having the maximum sum of squares of correlation with the selected variables. Because of this property it may be considered as the best representative of all the selected variables. The first principal component should not be considered as a suitable method in problems where maximization of sum of squares of correlation is not desirable.

The first principal component is a linear combination (weighted sum) of the standard scores of the given variables.

The weights used in this case are the elements of the eigen vector[3] corresponding to the highest eigen value of the correlation matrix R of the selected varables[4]. The eigen vector used here is also normalised to the highest eigen value used. The efficiency with which the first principal component reflects the combined picture of the given n variable is measured by the ratio of the highest eigen value of R to n.

Example

For working out a composite index of development (non-agricultural) for different districts of Assam, Meghalaya and Mizoram following variables are used[5].

(1) Number of workers in registered factories per 10,000 of total workers (x_1)

(2) Urban population per 10,000 of total population (x_2)

(3) Number of workers in trade and commerce to 10,000 total workers (x_3)

Table 7.3 contains data on these variables with its means and standard deviations as well as the composite index.

1. Biplab Dasgupta, "Socio-Economic Classification of Indian Districts— A Statistical Approach" : *Economic and Political Weekly*, August 14, 1971.
2. M.N. Pal : "Regional Disparities in the Levels of Development in India", *Indian Journal of Regional Science*, Vol. II, No. 1, 1975, pp. 12-35.
3. A discussion on eigen values and vectors is given in Chapter XI on Matrix algebra.
4. A correlation matrix, R, of the variables X_1, X_2.......X_1, is a matrix whose element's Rij show the coefficients of Correlation between the variable Xi and Xj.
5. Author is thankful to Mr. J.K. Gogoi, Research Scholar of Jawaharlal Nehru University for providing these intermediate results from his M. Phil. project.

Table 7.3

	District	x_1	x_2	x_3	Composite Index
	(1)	(2)	(3)	(4)	(5)
1.	Golpara	67	775	593	.3699
2.	Kamrup	91	1174	675	1.1617
3.	Darrang	197	598	495	.6491
4.	Nowgong	71	708	511	–.0502
5.	Sibsagar	308	842	493	1.5362
6.	Lakhimpur	455	1191	694	3.6982
7.	Cachar	120	792	485	.1942
8.	Mikir Hills	52	269	311	1.4191
9.	North Cachar	13	683	287	–1.5666
10.	Mizo Hills	2	1136	108	–2.2849
11.	Garo Hills	5	380	151	–1.4711
12.	Khasi & Jaintia Hills	48	2470	387	.1008
	Mean	119.08	920.66	432.49	
	S.D.	131.63	542.64	180.73	

The correlation matrix R for x_1, x_2 and x_3 is

$$R = \begin{Bmatrix} 1.0000 & & \\ .0725 & 1.000 & \\ .6380 & .1592 & 1.0000 \end{Bmatrix}$$

(Because R is a symmetric matrix, only half portion of it is conventionally written)

The eigen values of R are

1.6778, 0.9562 and 0.3558.

the eigen vector W, corresponding to highest eigen value 1.6778 and normalised to 1.6778 is

$$W = \begin{bmatrix} 0.87995 & 0.30563 & 0.90008 \end{bmatrix}$$

Thus using 0.87995, 0.30563 and 0.90008 as weights for standardised values of x_1, x_2 and x_3 a weighted sum for each district is worked out and is given in column 5 of Table 7.3. To illustrate the computation, the composite index for Golpara, Lakhimpur and North Cachar is worked out as below:

1. Golpara $\dfrac{67-119.08}{131.62}(.87995)+\dfrac{775-920.66}{542.67}(.30567)+$

$$\frac{593-432.49}{180.73}(.90008) = 0.3699$$

ASSAM MEGHALAYA AND MIZORAM
INDEX OF DEVELOPMENT
(First Principal Component Method)

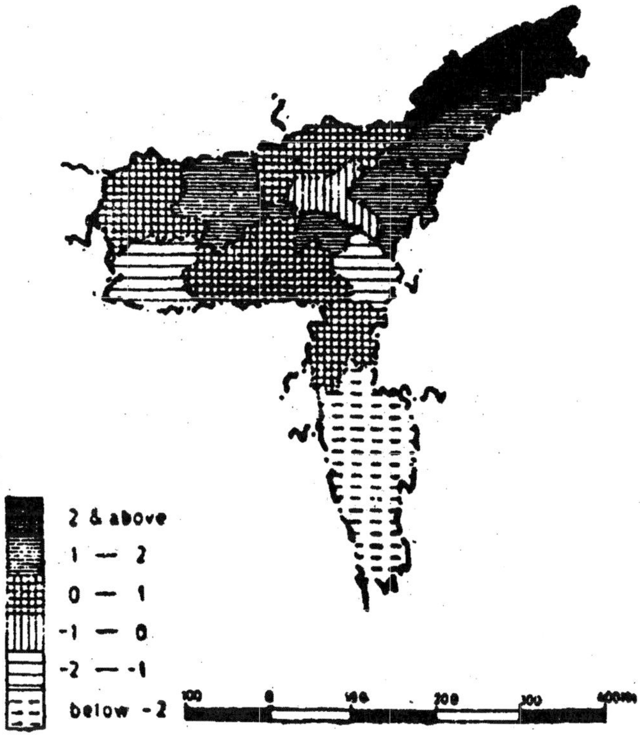

Fig. 7.3

2. Lakhimpur $\frac{455-119.08}{131.62}(.87995)+\frac{1191-920.66}{542.67}(.30567)+$

$$\frac{694-432.49}{180.73}(.90008)=3.6997$$

3. North Cachar $\frac{13-119.08}{131.62}(.87995)+\frac{683-920.66}{542.67}(.30567)+$

$$\frac{287-432.49}{180.73}(.90008)=1.5666$$

The efficiency of the composite index is worked out by the ratio $\frac{1.6778}{3}$ = 55.93, as $n = 3$ in present case, which shows that the composite index reflects only 55.93 per cent variations of the given three variables. As the maximum limit of this ratio is unity (100 per cent), the composite index does not give a complete combined picture of the given variables.

The index of development has also been plotted on a map and is given in Fig. 7.3.

This method gives good results only when all the given variables are highly correlated and there by showing a undimensionality in the data. In case some of the values of the correlation matrix are higher and some of them are lower, the data shows a multi-dimensionality in the structure of the variables. In such cases standard method of Factor Analysis should be used for working out more than one composite index. These composite indices are also known as factors or principal components and describe the underlying structure of a set of a large number of variables by a smaller number of factors. A more elaborate discussion on factor analysis is given in the multivariate analysis section of this book.

The above four methods have been given here because they have been frequently used by Indian scholars in tackling different problems. However, a good discussion on the same lines is also given Shafi (1960), Pal (1971), Jain (1972), Subbiah (1975), Sharma (1975) and Gogai (1975).

REFERENCES

1. Bhatia, S.S., : Pattern of Crop Concentration and Diversification in India", *Economic Geography* Vol. XL (1965) pp. 38-56.

2. Dasgupta B., "Socio-Economic Classifications of Indian Districts - A Statistical Approach" *Economic and Political Weekly*, 14 Aug., 1971.

3. Jain, A., "Tribal Territories in India - A Regional Analysis" unpublished M. Phil dissertation, Centre for the Study of Regional Development, Jawaharlal Nehru University 1972.

4. Kundu, A., "Construction of Composite Indices for Regionalisation - An Enquiry into the methods of Analysis", *Geographical Review of India,* Vol. 37, No 1March 1975, pp. 19-29.

5. Kandall, M.G. "The Geographical Distribution of Crop Productivity in England" *Journal of Royal Statistical Society* 102, 21(1939).

6. Kandall, M.G. *A Course in Multivariate Analysis*, Charles and Griffin Co. London, (1968) p. 35.

7. Mitra, A., *Levels of Regional Development, Census of India* (1961).

8. Pal, M.N., "Quantitative Techniques for Regional Planning" *Indian Journal of Regional Science,* Vol, III No. 1, 1971 pp. 1-33.

9. Pal, M.N., "Regional Disparities in the Levels of Development", *Indian Journal of Regional Science,* Vol. II No. 1, 1975 pp. 12-35.

10. Shafi, M. "Measurement of Agricultural Efficiency in Uttar Pradesh", *Economic Geography*, Vol. 36. 1960 pp. 296-305.

11. Sharma, K.L., "Spatial Disparities in Rajasthan" *Indian Journal of Regional Science* Vol. VII No. 1, 1975 pp. 70-88.

12. Subhiah, S., "Environmental, Techological and Institutional Determinants of Agricultural Productivity in Tamil Nadu, 1954-55 to 1969-70", unpublished M.Phil. Dissertation of Centre for the Study of Regional Development, Jawaharlal Nehru University, New Delhi 1975.

8

MEASURES OF INEQUALITY

The spatial distribution of a particular attribute is a result of multi-dimensional interactions of its determinants. As this process is dynamic and varies in space as well, we observe concentration and dispersion in many of the spatial distributions.

This concentration or dispersal of any phenomenon can be studied in several different ways which are discussed below :

1. Location Quotient :

When the proportion of any characteristic in an area is studied in relation to its proportion in the region, the ration used is known as the Location Quotient. This relative way of studying the proportions is important because a simple proportion of any characterstic like, proportion of urban population to total population, proportion of workers in manufacturing or proportion of scheduled castes etc. of an area are related to the local picture only. They do not tell us anything about its position in the region or in the country. For example, in a less urbanised region a pocket of 20% urban population may be considered as a higher concentration of urban population than its counter-part in a more urbanised region. Location quotient which gives us the relative picture of such proportions is defined as the ratio of the proportion of a particular characteristic in an area to the same proportion in the region, symbolically it can be defined as

$$\text{LQi} = \frac{Pij / Pi}{Pj / P}$$

where Pij = number of person in jth (=1, 2.........m) category of area i (= 1, 2,......n)

$Pi = \sum_{j=1}^{m} Pij$ = total population in all the categories of area i

$Pj = \sum_{j=1}^{m} Pij$ = Sum of persons of category j in all the n areas *i.e.* population of region under category j

$\text{P} = \sum_{i=1}^{n} \sum_{i=1}^{m} Pij$ = Sum of pi in all the areas *i.e.*, total population of the region in each category.

Note that in place of persons any other characteristic as value added in different sectors and area under different crops etc. may also be used in the same way.

While seeking interpretation for the values of L.Q., one should note the following points :

1. If the L.Q. of an area is unity, the share of that category in the area and in the region is the same. The proportional share of the particular activity in the area would be more than or less than its value in the region, according to the value of L.Q. being more than or less than unity.

2. Location quotients are ratios of the ratios and hence have no dimension.

3. Because they are ratios, the LQs. of one region are comparable with the LQs. of another region.

Keeping the above points in view, the L.Q. as a tool of regional analysis may by interpreted as below.

"In a regional context a higher or lower value of the L.Q. indicates relative concentration or dispersion of the concerned attribute. This information is of limited use in exploratory work, but can be of considerable use in conjunction with other tools and techniques of analysis which fully recognize and incorporate in their framework the broader prospects of regional analysis".[1]

The advantage of L.Q. is that it does not require extensive data collection and is easily understood.

Example :

The districtwise total population of scheduled castes and tribes in Assam, Meghalaya and Mizoram is given below for 1971. Find out the areas of relative concentration of tribal population and of scheduled caste population.

District	Total Population	Population of Scheduled Caste	Population of Scheduled Tribe
Goalpara	2225103	120006	308287
Kamrup	2854183	164762	298090
Darrang	1736181	77104	185640
Nowgong	1580995	167263	125115
Sibsagar	1837389	86920	125311
Lakhimpur	2922719	77789	286300
Mikir Hills	379310	9820	210039
North Cachar Hills	76047	826	52583
Cachar	1713318	208867	15283
Mizo Hills	332390	82	313299

1. Readers are referred to P.S. Florence : *Investment, Location and Size of Plants* ; Cambridge University Press, 1948. For a detailed discussion also refer to Walter Isard, *Methods of Regional Analysis* M.I.T. Press, pp. 123-126.

Table 8.1

	District	% of S.T. to Total Population	% of S.C. to Total Population	L.Q. for S.T.	L.Q. for S.C.
	(1)	(2)	(3)	(4)	(5)
1.	Goalpara	13.85	5.39	1.08	0.88
2.	Kamrup	10.44	5.77	0.81	0.95
3.	Darrang	10.69	4.44	0.81	0.73
4.	Nowgong	8.44	9.95	0.58	1.63
5.	Sibsagar	6.82	4.69	0.53	0.77
6.	Lakhimpur	13.45	3.67	1.05	0.60
7.	Mikir Hills	55.37	2.59	4.31	0.42
8.	North Cachar Hills	69.15	1.22	5.30	0.20
9.	Cachar	0.89	12.19	0.07	2.00
10.	Mizo Hills	94.26	0.03	7.34	0.004
	Region	12.84	6.10		

Solution

The percentages of Scheduled Castes and Scheduled Tribes to the total population have been worked out for each district and also for the whole region and are given in columns 2 and 3 of Table 8.1 To get the location quotients these districtwise percentages have been divided by the same percentage in the region, and the resultant values are also given in column 4 and 5 Table 8.1.

The values of the location quotient show a higher concentration of Scheduled tribes in Mizo Hills, North Cachar Hills and in Mikir Hills (as L.Q. > 1 in these districts). In Goalpara and Lakhimpur it is quite balanced. In all other districts the population of Scheduled tribes is much dispersed (as the value of L.Q. < 1).

Similarly the population of Scheduled Castes is found to be highly dispersed in the whole of Assam except in Cachar and Nowgong districts where it has a higher concentration (as the value of L.Q. is greater than unity in these districts).

Sometimes we may be interested in knowing the overall level of inequality caused by the concentration in any distribution, instead of going in for the spatial units of concentration or dispersion. The index of dissimilarity and Ginni's coefficient are powerful summary indices for measuring the inequality in any distribution and Lorenz's curve is a commonly used graph to show it visually.

Index of Dissimilarity

It is devised to measure the net deviation in the percentage distribution of one attribute in relation to the other. It is computed from a set of percentage point differences (of one sign, either positive or negative) of the two distributions. The accuracy of this computation is easily checked by summing up the positive and negative differences separately which should be equal. Since it gives the percentage of one group which would need to be redistributed in order to make it exactly match the other group, it is also known as the measure of displacement. The range of this index is from zero to hundred, indicating the total agreement to disagreement in the percentage distribution of the two groups. The following examples will make the concept clearer.

Example

The marital status by age of males are given below in Table 8.2 for Tamil Nadu in 1961. In order to see the dissimilarity or similarity in the age composition of the persons with different marital status, first the age structure of each group is converted into percentage distributions a given in Table 8.3. The index of dissimilarity between any two marital status, say between never-married and married, is worked out by taking the sum of the differences of their percentage age distributions. The index of dissimilarity between widowed and divorced are also computed in the same manner. These results are given in Table 8.4.

Table 8.2
Distribution of Marital Status by Age (15-55) of Males in Tamilnadu 1961

Age Group	Never-Married	Married	Widowed	Divorced
15-20	14160360	4328306	55110	40881
20-25	7978330	936502	163792	103305
25-30	3282684	14772271	310596	158264
30-35	1239335	14188429	418559	133915
35-40	624965	12369228	499614	104126
40-45	472558	10795933	723548	89184
45-50	320426	8543469	802841	65657
Total	28078658	65934138	2974060	595332

Table 8.3
Percentage Distribution of Marital Status of Males in Tamilnadu 1961 by Age

Age Group	Never-Married	Married	Widowed	Divorced
15-20	50.43	6.56	1.85	5.88
20-25	28.41	1.42	5.51	14.86
25-30	11.69	22.40	10.44	22.76
30-35	4.42	21.52	14.07	19.26
35-40	2.23	18.76	16.80	14.97
40-45	1.68	16.38	24.34	12.82
45-50	1.14	12.96	26.99	9.45
Total	100.00	100.00	100.00	100.00

Table 8.4
Percentage Point Differences between the Age Distribution of Different Marital Status Given in Table D.

Age Group	Between never married and married	Between Widowed and Divorced
15-20	43.87	–4.03
20-25	26.99	–9.35
25-30	–10.71	–12.32
30-35	–17.10	–5.19
35-40	–16.53	+1.83
40-45	–14.70	+11.52
45-50	–11.82	+17.56
Index of Dissimilarity $\Delta = 70.86$		30.89
Index of Similarity $= 100 - \Delta = 29.14$		69.11

Thus with the help of above indices we find that the age composition of married and never married is less similar than the age structure of the widowed and divorced. In other words, it can also be concluded that the difference in the married and unmarried is more a function of age than the difference in widowed and divorced.

Points to note :

1. A detailed cross classification will give a higher value of Δ than the more aggregated classification.
2. Index of dissmilarity (Δ) may be converted into an index of similarity also given by 100–Δ
3. The sum of the plus deviations are equal to the sum of minus deviations.
4. It does not compare with the absolute composition.
5. When the distribution of a characteristic is studied in relation to the space it is known as coefficient of geographic association also.

Lorenz Curve :

The Lorenz Curve, first expounded in 1905, has long been used to measure the inequality in the distribution of wealth or income.[1] It has also been used to depict the state of concentration of population and other demographic attributes.

It basically deals with the cumulative percentage distributions of the two attributes at different points. The cumulative percentages of one variable upto certain points plotted on a graph against the cumulative percentage to the other variable up to the same points. The different points so obtained are then joined by a smooth freehand curve. For comparison a diagonal line is also drawn, joining the last point and the origin, showing the line of equal distributions. The deviations of any curve from this diagonal is in proportion to the level of inequality in the distribution of one attribute in relation to the other.

1. M.O. Lorenz, "Methods of Measuring the Concentration of Wealth", *Quarterly Publication of the American Statistical Association* 9 (70) : 209-219 June 1905.

Example :

The statewise total population, population of scheduled castes and tribes of India in 1971 are given in Table 8.5 below. The concentration of Scheduled Castes and tribes in relation to the total population is shown by the Lorenz Curve, give in Fig. 8.1.

The steps involved in preporation of the Lorenz Curve for Schedule tribes are given as :

Step I : First arrange the states according to the ascending (or descending) order of their percentage of Scheduled tribe population to total population.

Step II : Take the percentage of the total population of each state to the total population of the country as given in column 3 of Table 8.6.

Step III : Similarly, note the percentage of the tribal population of each state to the total tribal population of the country, given in column 4 of Table 8.6.

Step IV : Accumulte the percentages obtained in step II and step III such that the last cumulative percentage of each column is 100.00. These values are also given in column 5 and 6 of Table 8.6.

Step V : Plot each of the values in column 5 on the x - axis and the corresponding value in column 6 on the y - axis.

Step VI : Join the origin and other points in succession and also the last point and the origin.

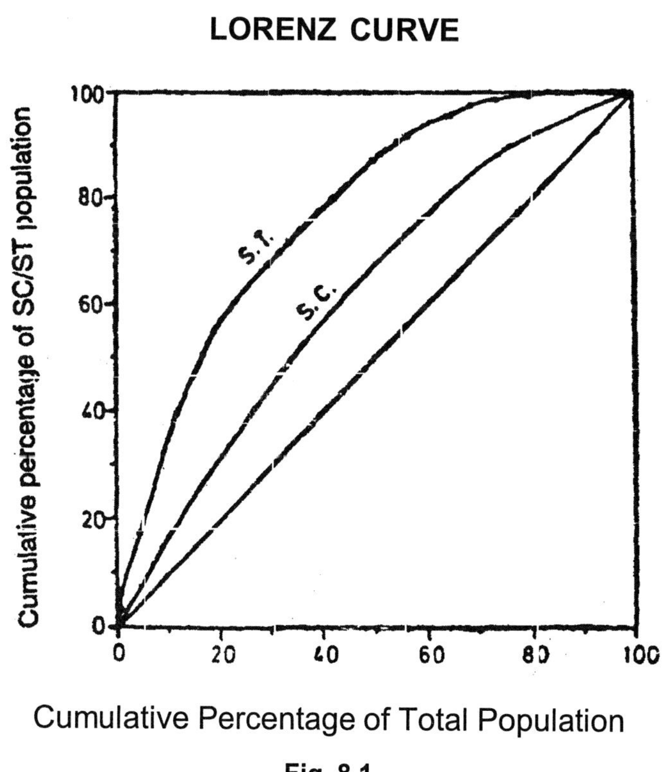

Fig. 8.1

Similarly, we can prepare the Lorenz Curve for Scheduled Caste also. The two curves so obtained are given Figure 8.1. An examination of the two curves reveals that the distribution of Scheduled Tribes is relatively more concentrated than that of Scheduled Castes. A careful inspection of Table 8.6 or Figure 8.1 would also reveal that about 91 per cent of the tribal population is living with 53.67 per cent of the total population and the rest of the tribal population (which is nearly 9 per cent) is living with 47.33 per cent of the total population. The curve for Scheduled Castes on the other hand, does not show such a high degree of concentration.

Table 8.5

(in thousands)

State	Total Population	Population of S.C.	Population of S.T.
Andhra Pradesh	43503	5775	1658
Assam	14958	911	1920
Bihar	56353	7951	4933
Gujarat	26697	1825	3734
Haryana	10037	1896	0
Himachal	3460	770	142
Jammu & Kashmir	4617	381	0
Kerala	21347	1772	269
Madhya Pradesh	41654	5454	8387
Maharashtra	50412	3026	2954
Manipur	1073	16	334
Meghalaya	11012	4	814
Mysore	29300	3850	231
Nagaland	516	0	458
Orissa	21945	3311	5072
Punjab	13551	3348	0
Tamilnadu	41299	7316	2126
Rajasthan	25766	4076	312
Tripura	1556	193	451
Uttar Pradesh	88341	18548	199
West Bengal	44312	8816	2533
Others	6341	756	489
Total	558050	79996	37016

Source : Census of India 1571, Part II-A (II) Union Primary Census Abstract.

Table 8.6

	State	% of S.T. Pop. to Total Population	% distribution of total Population	% distribution of tribal Population	Cumulative % distribution of total Population *Xi*	Cumulative % distribution of total Population *Yi*
	(1)	(2)	(3)	(4)	(5)	(6)
1.	Nagaland	88.76	.09	1.24	.09	1.24
2.	Manipur	31.13	.19	.90	.28	2.14
3.	Tripura	28.98	.27	1.22	.55	3.36
4.	Orissa	23.11	3.94	13.70	4.49	17.06
5.	Madhya Pradesh	20.13	7.47	22.66	11.96	39.72
6.	Gujarat	13.99	4.78	10.09	16.74	49.81
7.	Assam	12.84	2.68	5.05	19.42	55.00
8.	Bihar	8.75	10.09	13.33	29.51	68.33
9.	Others	7.71	1.14	1.32	30.65	69.65
10.	Meghalaya	7.93	1.98	2.20	32.63	71.85
11.	Maharashtra	5.86	9.03	7.98	41.66	79.83
12.	West Bengal	5.72	7.94	6.84	49.60	86.67
13.	Tamil Nadu	5.15	7.41	5.74	57.01	92.41
14.	Himachal Pradesh	4.10	0.62	0.38	57.63	92.79
15.	Andhra Pradesh	3.81	7.80	4.48	65.43	97.27
16.	Kerala	1.26	3.82	0.73	69.25	98.00
17.	Rajasthan	1.21	4.62	0.84	73.87	98.84
18.	Mysore	0.79	5.25	0.62	79.12	99.46
19.	Uttar Pradesh	0.23	15.83	0.54	94.95	100.00
20.	Haryana	0	1.80	–	96.75	100.00
21.	Jammu & Kashmir	0	0.80	–	97.57	100.00
22.	Punjab	0	2.43	–	100.00	100.00

The differences in the two concentration curves may be explained in terms of the underlying socio-economic, geographical and historical processes.

Gini's Cofficient

The overall concentration found in any such curve may also be measured numerically in terms of the ratio of the area under the curve and the line of equal distribution to the area of the triangle formed by the x-axis, the y-axis and the line of equal distribution. In case the tribal population is uniformally distributed, the curve will fall on the line and the area between the curve and the line would be zero, whereas the area of the triangle would be $\frac{100 \times 100}{2} = 5000$, the ratio in this case would be $\frac{0}{5000} = 0$. In case of highest concentration, *i.e.* when all the tribals are concentrated only at one place, the curve will move along the y-axis and then along the x-axis, such that the area between the curve and the line would be very close to the area of the traingle and the ratio would be nearly unity. This ratio, hence, varies between zero and one.

The ratio mentioned above is known as Gini's coefficient (G) and can be numerically worked out by using the following formula.

$$G = \frac{1}{100 \times 100}\left(\sum_{i=1}^{n} XiYi + 1\right) - \left(\sum Xi + 1Yi\right)$$

Table 8.7

	State (1)	*XiYi+1* (2)	*Xi+1 Yi* (3)
1.	Nagaland	01926	0.348
2.	Manipur	0.9408	1.177
3.	Tripura	9.383	15.086
4.	Orisa	178.342	204.037
5.	Madhya Pradesh	595.7727	664.912
6.	Gujarat	920.700	967.310
7.	Assam	1326.968	1623.050
8.	Bihar	2055.371	2094.314
9.	Others	2202.202	2272.679
10.	Meghalaya	2604.852	2993.271
11.	Maharashtra	3610.672	3959.568
12.	West Bengal	4583.536	4941.056
13.	Tamil Nadu	5289.957	5325.588
14.	Himachal Pradesh	5605.670	6071.249
15.	Andhra Pradesh	6412.140	6735.947
16.	Kerala	6844.670	7239.260
17.	Rajasthan	7347.110	7820.220
18.	Mysore	7912.00	9443.727
19.	Uttar Pradesh	9495.00	9675.00
20.	Haryana	9675.00	9757.00
21.	Jammu & Kashmir	9757.00	10000.00
22.	Punjab		
	Total	86427.4334	91804.798

Where *Xi* and *Yi* are the cumulative percentage distributions of the two attributes (in the present case total population and population of Scheduled Tribe) in ith State. Its computation requires all the columns of Table 8.6 and two more columns which are given in Table 8.7. The values of column 2 of Table 8.7 are obtained by multiplying first elements of column 5 by the second element of column 6 of Table 8.6, the second element of column 5 with the third element of column 6 and so on. Third column of Table 8.7 is obtained by multiplaying the 1st element of column 6 with the second element of column 5 of Table 8.6, the second element of column 6 with the third element of column 5 and so on. The sum of column (5) of Table 8.7 gives $\Sigma XiYi+1$ and that of column (6) gives $\Sigma YiXi+1$.

Using the values from Table 8.7, the Gini's co-efficient is found as below :

$$G = \frac{1}{100 \times 100} 86427.43 - 91804.80 = 0.537$$

Similarly the value for Scheduled Caste was found to be $G = 0.537$.

The above two values also show a relatively higher concentration of tribal population than the Scheduled Caste population in relation to the total population.[1]

REFERENCES

1. Duncan, O.D., : "The Measurement of Population Distribution", *Population Studies*, July 1957 p. 40.

2. Florence, P.S. : *Investment, Location and Size of Plants*, Cambridge University Press 1948.

3. Isard, W. : *Methods of Regional Analysis*, M.I.T. Press 1960.

4. Lorenz, M.O. : "Methods of Measuring the concentration of Wealth" *Quarterly Publication of American Statistical Association* 9 (70) : 209-219 June 1905.

---

1. For a good dicussion on Index of dissimilarity, Lorenz Curve and Gini's Coefficient, refer to Otis Dudley Duncan, "The Measurement of Population Distribution", *Population Studies* July 1957 p. 40.

9
COMBINATIONAL ANALYSIS

Any process of development has an inherited property of pushing the economic system from simpler to more complex. This complexity as manifested by diversification of places in terms of their economic activities can be measured by the different combination of their activities. Geographers are, therefore, particularly interested in classifying the places into different combinations of dominent activities.

An intuitive classification based on subjective judgements like commercial towns, industrial towns or wheat zones, rice zones, etc. have no statistical basis. Places, in fact, have multiple functions, but all of them may not be equally important at every places. Some of them may be very significant, while others might be quite inconsequential. A statistical basis is therefore necessary for identifying the group of significant functions, which also represent the functional personality of an area.

The first attemt towards indentification of the dominant characteristics of an area was made by Harris[1]. While classifying the cities of United States into different functional types, Harris used the proportion of the labour force in a particular occupation as the basic criterion for determining the intensity of its specialization. The combination of the percentages of different occupations, in each of the well recognised types of the cities in U.S.A., have been used as standards for classification of other cities. These threshold percentage may vary from country to country.

Nelson[2] used almost similar method with a threshold which could be worked out from the mean and standard deviation of the occupational structure of the given cities itself. According to Nelson's method first percentages of each occupation to the total labour force of the city are worked out for each city. The mean and standard deviation (SD) of these percentages among all the cities are then calculated seperately for each occupation. The cities are then classified according to their percentages of each occupation being more than or equal to; mean + S.D., mean + 2SD and mean + 3SD. The percentage of a function less than its mean + S.D. is not consideres as significant. The Nelson's method is not mutually exclusive, i.e. a city may provide more than one type of services in outstanding proportions. The cities which do not rank high in any occupation are considered as diversified or as not specializing in any service.

1. C.D. Harris : "A Functional Classification of Cities in the United States" : Geographical Review XXXIII January 1943, pp. 86-99.
2. H.J. Nelson, : "A Service Classification of American Cities", Economic Geography, Vol. XXXI No. 3 (1955), pp. 189-210.

Table 9.1

Census Industrial Classification of Workers in Selected Cities 1971

City	Total working Popu-lation	As Culti vators (CL)	As Agri-cultural Labour ers (AL)	Live stock, Fisheries, Hunting, Plantation Forestry Orchard & allied activi-ties (LS)	Mining & Quar-rying (MQ)	Manufacturing Processing Servicing and Repair: in house hold industry (M fh)	Manufacturing Processing Servicing and Repair: in other than house hold indus-try (Mf)	Const-ruction (CN)	Trade & Com-merce (TC)	Trans-Port, Stor-age & comun-ication (TS)	Others (O)	Fun-ctional Types
		I	II	III	IV	Va	Vb	VI	VII	VIII	IX	
Bombay	2198098	2672	2958	20088	1944	29142	900361	670125	491515	236894	445507	
		(.12)	(–13)	(.91)	(.08)	(1.32)	(40.96)	(3.04)	(2.36)	(10.77)	(20.26)	MFI
Calcutta	1165542	225	556	4411	554	7710	316149	28121	337845	158103	311868	TCI
		(.01)	(.04)	(.37)	(.04)	(.66)	(27.12)	(2.41)	(28.28)	(13.56)	(26.76)	
Jamshedpur	131599	1784	2818	798	229	1527	74046	5413	16323	9787	18874	
		(1.36)	(2.14)	(.61)	(.17)	(1.16)	(56.34)	(4.13)	(12.40)	(7.44)	(14.34)	Mf3
Saharanpur	61117	867	895	583	19	2749	16403	1602	13844	10465	13690	
		(1.41)	(1.46)	(0.95)	(4.03)	(4.49)	(26.83)	(2.62)	(22.65)	(17.12)	(27.39)	
Durgapur	56734	2115	3721	454	6232	2073	19332	2716	5238	2782	12061	MQ2
		(3.72)	(6.55)	(0.8)	(10.98)	(3.65)	(34.07)	(4.78)	(9.23)	(4.90)	(21.27)	MFI
...	...	...	...	...	...	...	...	...	...	...	...	
Mean of (m) Percentages		2.81	3.29	1.34	0.64	5.81	23.21	4.33	20.60	11.65	2739	
S.D.		2.24	2.84	1.58	4.48	9.11	10.75	4.56	4.95	5.86	8.53	
m + SD		5.05	6.13	3.38	5.12	14.92	33.96	8.89	25.55	17.51	35.92	
m + 2SD		7.29	8.97	4.96	9.60	24.03	44.71	13.45	30.50	23.37	44.45	
m + 3SD		9.53	11.81	6.54	14.08	33.14	55.46	18.01	35.45	29.23	52.98	

Example

Using the 1971 Census industrial classification of the workers in Indian cities, their functional types by Nelson's method have been worked out by Kaur[1]. Some of her results are given below.

Table 9.1 gives the industrial classification of workers in a few Indian cities for 1971. The percentage distribution of industrial categories is given in the brackets. The mean and S.D. of these percentages are calculated from all the cities and are given at the bottom of each column along with the mean + SD, mean + 2 SD and mean + 3 SD values. In each city the percentages of each occupation are then compared with given 3 values and accordingly the functional types are given in the last column of Table 9.1, where subscript 1, 2 or 3 with different functions means that the percentage of that function in a city is more than the mean by 1 SD, 2 SD or 3 SD.

Weaver's Method

Functional specialization of a town is a relative notion and is determined in relation to the percentage distribution of different activities in all the other cities. However, in agricultural studies where in some cases only the nature of croping pattern of an area is studied, one need not to relate it with cropping pattern to other areas. A simple and convenient method of finding out the combination of crops, having significant share in the total cropped area has been suggested by Weaver.[2] He compared the actual percentage area under each crop with an hypothetical percentage. This theoretical percentage share of a crop is different in different hypothetical situations. For example in a hypothetical monoculture area, the theoretical percentage share of a crop is 100 per cent. For a two crop combination region it is 50 per cent for each crop. For a three-crop combination it is $33\frac{1}{2}$ per cent for each and so on. The actual percentage of the area under different crops in a region are compared with these different theoretical percentages. It starts from the assumptions of one-Crop combination, then two-crop combination, three-crop combination and so on. Each time we work out an index σ^2 as given below. The minimum of σ^2 gives the best fit.

$$\sigma^2 = \frac{\Sigma\left(x_i - \overline{X}\right)^2}{N}$$

where $\overline{X}$ is the theoretical percentage, Xi is actual percentage and N is the number of crops we include in the test.

Thus ; first we convert the area under different crops as percentage to the total cropped area. Its highest percentage is then compared with the assumed value of one crop region *i.e.* 100. In the next step we take first two highest percentage and compare them with the assumed values of a two-crop combination region *i.e.* 50 and 50. Similarly we compare three highest percentage with $33\frac{1}{2}$, $33\frac{1}{3}$

1. Satwant Kaur : "Functional Classification of Ist Class Cities in India", unpublished M.A. (Geog.), Project Jawaharlal Nehru University, New Delhi 1974.
2. Weaver, J.C. : "Crop Combination Region in the Middle West", *Geographical Review* Vol. XLIV No. 2, April 1954, pp. 173-200.

and $33\frac{1}{3}$ and four highest percentages with 25, 25 and 25 so on. In each step we will get some value of σ^2. The theoretical percentage which give the minimum value of σ^2 is considered to be matching best with the reality and hence, the area is identified with it.

Example

Percentage distribution of the average area for three years (1970-73) under 8 different crops in Mehsana district of Gujrat is given below, using Weaver's method identify the significant crops of the district.

Crop	Bajra	Jowar	Cotton	Wheat	Rape & Mustard	Castor Seed	Ground Nut	Tur
% Area	35.9	23.7	15.2	11.4	4.7	2.6	2.4	1.2

Solution

One Crop

		Summation
Hypothetical	% 100	
Observed	% 35.9	
Difference	64.1	
d^2	4108.81	
$\frac{d^2}{n}$	4108.8	4108.8

Two Crops

Hypothetical %	50	50	
Observed %	35.9	23.7	
Difference, d	14.1	26.3	
Σd^2	198.81	+691.63	=890.5
$\frac{\Sigma d^2}{n}$			445.25

Three Crops

Hypothetical %	33.3	33.3	33.3	
Observed %	35.9	23.7	15.2	
Difference, d	2.6	–9.6	–18.1	
Σd^2	6.76	+92.16	+327.61	=426.53
$\frac{\Sigma d^2}{n}$				142.18

Four Crops

Hypothetical %	25	25	25	25	
Observed %	35.9	23.7	15.2	11.4	
Difference, d	10.9	–1.3	–9.8	–13.6	
Σd^2	116.81	+1.69	+96.04	+184.94	401.50
$\frac{\Sigma d^2}{n}$					100.38

Similarly further values of Weaver's index for five, six, seven and eight Crops are 169.5, 131.798, 133.71 and 136.05 respectively.

The district may therefore be identified as a four crops region (as the value of the index is least for four crops) having Bajra as the most dominating crop followed by jowar, cotton and wheat respectively.

Thomas[1] modified Weaver's method by including the crops with zero% theoretical values also in each step of the comparison. As this method involves all the crops in each step, there is no need of dividing Σd^2 by n.

Example

As an example the crop combination of Mehsana district has been again identified using the modification suggested by Thomas.

One Crop

Hypothetical %	100	0	0	0	0	0	0	0	Sum
Observed %	35.9	22.7	15.2	11.4	4.7	2.6	2.4	1.2	
Difference, d		23.7	15.2	11.4	4.7	2.6	2.4	1.2	
d^2	4108.81	561.69	231.04	129.96	22.09	6.75	5.76	1.44	5067.55 × 8

Two Crops

Hypothetical %	50	50	0	0	0	0	0	0	Sum
Observed %	35.9	23.7	15.2	11.4	4.7	2.6	2.4	1.2	
Difference, d	14.1	26.3	15.2	11.4	4.7	2.6	2.4	1.2	
d^2	198.81	691.69	231.04	129.96	22.09	6.76	5.76	1.44	643.77 × 8

Three Crops

Hypothetical %	33.33	33.33	33.33	0	0	0	0	0	Sum
Observed %	35.9	23.7	15.2	11.4	4.7	2.6	2.4	1.2	
Difference, d	–2.57	9.63	18.13	11.4	4.7	2.6	2.4	1.2	
d^2	6.6	92.74	328.70	129.96	22.09	6.76	5.76	1.44	198.01 × 8

1. D. Thomas : Agriculture in Wales during the Napoleonic Wars, Wales University Press 1963.

Four Crops

Hypothetical %	25	25	25	25	0	0	0	0	
Observed %	35.9	23.7	15.2	11.4	4.7	2.6	2.4	1.2	
Difference, d	–10.9	1.3	9.8	13.6	4.7	2.6	2.4	1.2	
d^2	118.81	1.69	96.04	184.96	22.09	6.76	5.76	1.44	109.38×8

Proceeding in the same manner we will get the value of the index as 611.55, 797.59, 1186.54 and 1070.05 for five, six, seven and eight crop combinations respectively.

The four crops by this method also are found to be significant.

Weaver's method (even after modification), however, in cases of one or two functions are predominantly significant and all other functions are equally insignificant, gives undue importance to the functions of very low significance. In many empirical problems, therefore, Weaver's method does not give intuitively correct results. The basic reason of this fallacy in Weaver's method as pointed out by Rafiullah[1] is that :

(a) it ignores the signs of the deviations, and

(b) for a higher number of crops or functions the theoretical percentages go down and so the deviations caused by last values are under - estimated.

While applying Weaver's method for functional classification of towns, Rafiullah suggested another modification in it. His modified index σ is given as :

$$\sigma = \frac{\Sigma D_P^2 - \Sigma D_N^2}{N^2}$$

Where ΣD^2_P and ΣD^2_N are the sum of squares of positive and negetive deviations from the middle of the theoretical values.

Here the maximum values of σ gives the critical combination.

Example

Find out the functional type of Ambala city on the basis of the Census industrial classification of its workers as given below for 1971.

Occupational Category	I	II	III	IV	Va	Vb	VI	VII	VIII	IX
% of workers	2.2	1.7	0.4	0.3	1.8	14.8	2.8	27.1	10.7	38.2

(The detailed description of Categories is same as given in Table 9.1).

1. S.M. Rafiullah : "A New Approach to Functional Classification of Towns". *The Geographer,* Volume XII 1965, pp. 40-53.

Solution

Mono Function		2 Functions		3 Functions		
Function	IX	IX	VIII	IX	VII	Vb
Percentage of the function	38.2	38.2	27.1	38.2	27.1	14.8
Middle value of Theoritical basecurve	50	25	25	16.7	16.7	16.7
Difference	–11.8	+13.2	+2.1	+21.5	+10.4	–1.9
Difference Square	(–) 139.24	+174.24	+4.41	+462.25	+108.76	(–) 3.61
Net Sum of Squared Differences	(–) 139.24	+178.65			566.89	
Sum divided by the square of Number of functions	(–) 139.24	$\frac{178.65}{2\times 2}$	=44.66	$\frac{566.89}{3\times 3}$	=62.98	

	4 Function				5 Functions				
Functions	IX	VII	Vb	VII	IX	VII	Vb	VIII	VI
% of Functions	38.2	27.1	14.8	10.7	38.2	27.1	14.8	10.7	2.8
Middle of Theo-retical value	12.5	12.5	12.5	12.5	10	10	10	10	10
Differences D	+25.7	+14.6	+2.3	(-) 1.8	+28.2	+17.1	+4.8	+0.7	-7.2
Differences D^2	+660.49	+213.16	+5.29	(-) 3.24	795.24	+292.41	23.04	+0.49	(-) 51.84
Net Sum of (D^2) Squared differences		875.70							
$=\frac{D^2}{N^2}$	$\frac{875.70}{4\times 4}=54.82$				$\frac{1059.34}{5\times 5}=42.37$				

The values of σ for six, seven and eight function are similarly worked out as 34.1, 27.81 and 23.12 respectively. Thus according to Rafiullah's formula the city Ambala may be classified as a City of two Predominant functions *e.g.* service (IX) and Trade and Transport (VII).

The Ternary Diagram

All the methods of classification discussed above, in fact, require considerable computational labour. A ternary diagram was, however, found the most suitable device for classification of large number of India towns in 1961 Census. Ternary diagram is a triangle showing the influence of three variables. The diagram consists of an equilateral triangle, the sides of which form three scales graduated 0 to 100 per cent, so that each apex forms zero on two scales and 100 per cent on the third. It can be used whenever information concerning three variables can be converted into percentages totalling 100. Any such set of three percentages can be represented by a point on the diagram, the position of which within the triangle reflects the relative dominance of each component.

Mitra[1] for the first time used the ternary diagram for functional classification of towns in 1961 Census. His method of classification is based on the concept of dominant functions of a city. The seven Census categories of workers were grouped into three broad non-agricultural categories as given below :

Group		Census Industrial Categories
A	Industry Trade	III, IV, V and VI
B	and Transport	VII and VIII
C	Services	IX

Categories of agricultural workers and labourers (I & II) have been excluded.

The three percentages of A, B and C of towns were than ploted on a Ternary diagram and their position in the triangle was taken as the main determinant of their functional classification.

Mitra also divided the triangle into six sub-triangles, representing different combinations as given in Table 9.2. These sub-triangles were further divided into four parts by three circles with centre at the middle of the triangle (representing 33.3 per cent of each group) and radius equal to $6\frac{2}{3}$, $11\frac{2}{3}$, and $16\frac{2}{3}$. Any point within first circle was supposed to be representing highly balanced composition of A, B and C. The points of any sub-triangle within the second circle were classified as showing the first ranking function moderately balanced and the remaining two functions as moderate. The points of any sub-triangle within the third circle were, however, classified as showing the first ranking functions as moderately accentuated and the other two functions as low. Finally, the points of any sub-triangle outside the third circle the first ranking function highly accentuated and the remaining two function as low. These categories are given in Table 9.2.

1. Asok Mitra : *Internal Migration and Urbanization in India*, Office of the Registrar General, India 1967, pp. 35-81.

Table 9.2
Degree of Intensity of Functions according to the position of towns in any of the sub - triangle of triangular coordinates

Predominat	Sub-triangle	Secondary Functions
Service Towns	I	Low Industry Medium Trade and Transport High Service
	II	Low Trade and Transport Medium Industry High Service
Industrial Towns	III	Low Trade and Transport Medium Service High Industry
	IV	Low Service Medium Trade and Transport High Industry
Trade and Transport Towns	V	Low Service Medium Industry High Trade and Transport
	VI	Low Industry Medium Service High Trade and Transport

Example

To illustrate the classification procedure as laid down above, consider the values A, B and C of four towns as given below in 1961 :

Town	Percentage Value of		
	A	B	C
1. Mainpuri	20	34	46
2. Baraut	27	38	35
3. Sardhana	42	25	33
4. Firozabad	64	23	31

These points have been plotted on the above ternary diagram (Fig. 9.1) and are denoted by 1, 2, 3 and 4.

The point No. 1 is in sub - triangel I which shows high service and because it falls in the third circle, service is moderately accentuated. The town Mainpuri is therefore classified as having moderately accentuated service, medium trade and transport and low industry.

TERNARY DIAGRAM

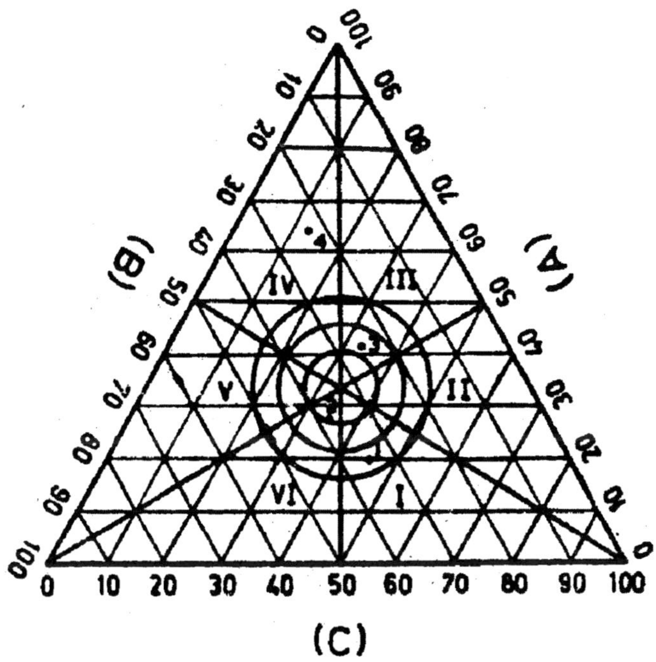

Fig. 9.1

Similarly, the other towns are also classified as given below :

Towns	Group
1. Mainpuri	Moderately accentuated Service Medium Trade and Transport and low industry
2. Baraut	Highly balanced
3. Sardhana	Moderately balanced industry, medium service and low trade and transport
4. Firozabad	Highly accentuated industry, medium trade and transport and low service

Exercise

The percentage values of four towns are given below as in 1961. Find out their functional types.

Town	Percentage Value of		
	A	B	C
1. Shikohabad	26	33	31
2. Jalpaiguri	21	33	46
3. Cooch Behar	19	37	44
4. Nowgong	20	37	43

REFERENCES

1. Harris, C.D. : "A Functional Classification of Cities in the United States" *Geographical Review XXXIII*, January 1943, pp. 86-99.

2. Mitra, Asok. *Internal Migration and Urbanisation in India*, Registrar General's Office, New Delhi 1967, pp. 35-81.

3. Nelson, H.J. "A Service Classification of American Cities", *Economic Geography* Vol. XXXI 1955, pp. 189-210.

4. Rafiullah S.M. : "A New Approach to Functional Classification of Town", *The Geographer* Vol. XII 1965 pp. 40-53.

5. Thomas, D. : *Agriculture in Wales During the Nepoleonic Wars*, Wales University Press 1963.

6. Weaver, J.C. : Crop Combination Region in the Middle West. *Geographical Review* Vol. XLIV No. 2 April 1954, pp. 173-200.

10
NETWORK ANALYSIS

Networks are important concern of geographers. The may comprise roads, railways, airlines or telephone links etc. Whatever may be the form of a network it can be transformed into graphs and can be portrayed as a connectivity matrix. Garrison (1960) used topological properties of the graphs and used graph theory in his study. Later Kansky (1963) further developed these concepts.

Any network for the sake of simplicity can be converted into a graph. For example the network given in fig. 10.1a can be converted into the graph given in fig. 10.1b.

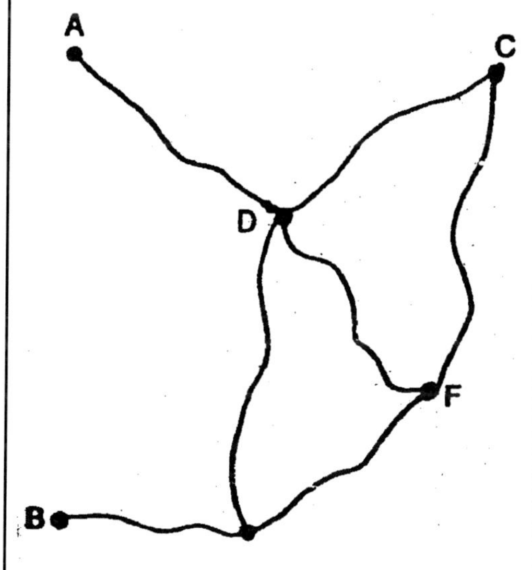

Fig. 10.1a

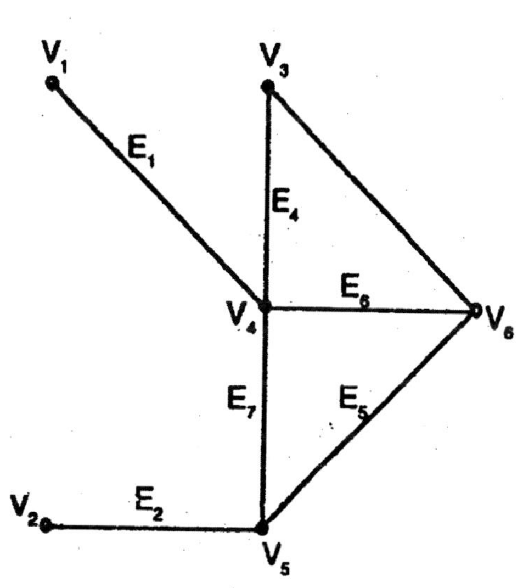

Fig. 10.1b

Any ordinary graph representing a network will consist of the followings :

1. Vertex (V) : Where more than on route meet or a road terminates. It could be a crossing or a terminus. In fig. 10.1b there are six vertieies VI to V6.

2. Edge (E) : The route joining two verticies is called an edge. In fig. 10.1b there are seven edges, E1 to E7.

3. Sub-Graph (P) : The number of subsidiary graphs. In fig. 10.1b there is only one graph, so P=1.

4. Circuils : It is a path starting from a particular Vertex and comes back to the same Vertex without crossing any of the edges more than once.

The connection of a network can also be shown by a connectivity matrix whose elements aij are either 0 or 1. In a connectivity matrix aij corresponds to connection between Vertex i and j. The value of aij=0 shows that there is no direct connection or link between vertex i and vertex j. The value of aij=1, however, shows a direct connection between vertex i and vertex j. Thus the network connections given in fig. 10.1b can be shown in a connectivity matrix given in Table 1.

Table 10.1
Connectivity matrix of the graph given in figure 1B

Vertex	V1	V2	V3	V4	V5	V6
V1	0	0	0	1	0	0
V2	0	0	0	0	1	0
V3	0	0	0	1	0	1
V4	1	0	1	0	1	1
V5	0	1	0	1	0	1
V6	0	0	1	1	1	0

Note that all the diagonal elements of the connectivity matrix *i.e.* aij i.e. all, a22, a33, a44................ are all *zero*, as a place does not require a connection to itself.

As more and more verticies are connected with each other, the number of edges and circuits will increase. With the help of some of the topological characteristics - derived from graph theory - we can measure the efficieny with which the network is connected as a whole and each individual vertex is connected with every other vertex. These topological measures are as given below :

1. Cyclometic number (μ)
2. Alpha index (α)
3. Beta index (β)
4. Gama index (γ)
5. Eta index (η)
6. Theta index (θ)
7. Road density (Dn)

1. Cyclometic number :
It is a simple index and indicate the number of circuits in a network. It is given by :

$$\eta = E - V + \rho$$

where E is the number of edges and V is the number of vertex of the given network and P is the number of graph. As mentioned earlier, a circuit is a path starting froma a perticular vertex and comes back to the same vertex without crossing any of the edges more than once.
Example : As in figure 1B, there are six verticies (V=6) and seven edges (E=7) and only one graph (P=1), the value of the cyclometic number η will be :

$$\eta = E - V + 1 = 7 - 6 + 1 = 2$$

Example

Find the cyclometic number of the network given below in fig. 2

Nobal structure of the matrix shown in Table 10.2

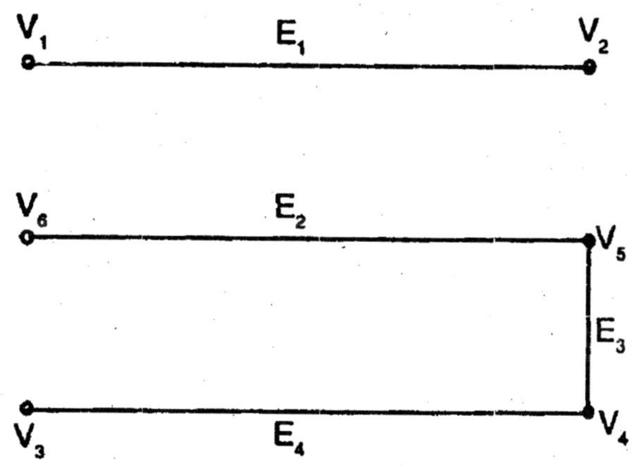

Fig. 10.2

Since in fig. 2, V = 6 , E = 4 and P = 2

$\eta = 4 - 6 + 2 = 0$, thus there is no circuit in the network shown in fig. 2.

It should be noted that cyclometic number increases with the completness of the connection and the complexity of the network. In that case there will be more number of edges lesser number of verticies. Cyclometic number would bear a direct relationship with the levels of development of a region (Garivision & Marble 1974).

2. **Alpha index (α) :**

In a network with V number of verticies, the maximum number of possible circuits are given by ½ (V^2–V) – (V–1). The index alpha α in fact is the ratio of actual number of circuits and the maximum number of possible circuits. Thus,

$$\alpha = \frac{E - v + 1}{\frac{1}{2}(V^2 - V) - (V - 1)}$$

The value of α varies from 0 to 1. The value of $\alpha = 1$, shows that the network is completely interconnected as the number of edges decrease the connectivity value also decrease.

One of the important advantage of this index is that two networks of inequal graphs can also be compared.

Example

The value of alpha for the network given in fig. 10.1a is :

$$\alpha = \frac{7-6+1}{\frac{1}{2}(6\times6-6)-(6-1)} = \frac{2}{15-5} = \frac{2}{10} = 0.2$$

Example

The alpha index for the network given in fig. 2 is

$$\alpha = \frac{4-6+2}{\frac{1}{2}(6\times6-6)-(6-1)} = 0$$

3. Beta index (β) :

The index Beta (β) is the ratio edges to vertex i.e.

$$\beta = \frac{E}{V}$$

β is the simplest measure at the same time it is a very useful index also. Disconnected graphs and those in the form of trees with several branches but no circuits will have a β values less than 1.0. the value of $\beta = 1$ will correspond to a network with only one circuit. A value of $\beta>1$, however, will correspond to more complex networks with an increase number of edges in relation to verticies.

Example :

The value of Beta index (β) for the network given in fig. 1A & B is :

$$\beta = \frac{7}{6} = 1.17$$

The value of the Beta index (β) for the network given in fig. 2 is :

$$\beta = \frac{4}{6} = 0.67$$

4. Gama index (γ) :

The Gama index (γ) is the ratio of the actual number of edges (E) or route connections to the maximum possible number of route connections or edges. In a network with number of edges as E and number of verticies as V, the maximum number of possible route connections are ½ (V^2-V). The Gama index (γ) is thus given as :

$$\gamma = \frac{E}{\frac{1}{2}\left(V^2 - V\right)}$$

The value of the Gama index (γ) also varies between 0 to 1. When $\gamma = 0$ it means $E = 0$ *i.e.* there is no edge or connection in the network. The value of $\gamma = 1$ shows the maximum number of connection between verticies in the network.

Example :

The value of Gama index of the network given in fig. 1A and B is :

$$\gamma = \frac{7}{\frac{1}{2}\left(6 \times 6 - 6\right)} = 0.267$$

Also for network given in fig. 2

$$\gamma = \frac{4}{\frac{1}{2}\left(6 \times 6 - 6\right)} = 0.267$$

5. Eta Index (η) :

The index Eta (η) represent the average length of the edges and is thus given as the ratio of the total length of all the edges (m) *i.e.* total road mileage of an area and the number of edges (E) in that area. Thus the index is given as :

$$\eta = \frac{m}{E}$$

Higher value of Eta index indicate lower development of transport network and vice versa.

6. Theta Index (θ) :

The index Theta (θ) represent the average length of edges (m) per vertex (V) and is given by

$$\theta = \frac{m}{V}$$

The index takes care of lenght, structure and also the degree of connectivity simultaneously.

7. Road Density (Dn) :

Road density is difined as length of road per unit area and is one of the most traditional indicator of transport development.

Ibrahim (1984) has used all these seven indicators of network development to analyse Regional Development in Delhi - Jaipur - Agra triangle.

Nodal Structure :

Physical networks provide information about connectivity between nodes (or places). It does not give any information about the magnitude or the direction of flows. Magnitudes and the directions of flow are, however, important aspects of networks. To portray the magnitude and the direction of flows the matrix of observed flows is used instead of connectivity matrix. Each element of the flow matrix shows the magnitude of flow from an origion to a destination. Thus the element aij of the flow matrix shows the magnitude of flow from origion i to destination j.

To the flow matrix, mentioned above, a particular technique developed by Nystuen and Dacey and based on graph theory may be applied. This technique gives the hierachical nodal structure of the region in terms of distinct clusters (sub - graphs). Nystuen and Dacey (1961) have shown that for a given set of cities in an area and a measure of association between them, a regional hierarchy may be built up.

The method is also discussed by Haggett (1965 pp. 252-3) and is explained with he help of a hypothetical matrix of intercity flow of telephonic messages among 12 cities as given in Table 10.2. The sum of all incoming messages is found for all cities and are given a rank order - r.

Table 10.2
Matrix of flow between pairs of centres*

To centre / From centre	*r*	*a*	*b*	*c*	*d*	*e*	*f*	*g*	*h*	*i*	*j*	*k*	*l*
a	8	00	**75**	15	20	28	02	03	02	01	20	01	00
b	1	**69**	00	45	50	58	12	20	03	06	35	04	02
c	5	05	**51**	00	12	40	00	06	01	03	15	00	01
d	6	19	**57**	14	00	30	07	06	02	11	18	05	01
e	3	07	40	**48**	26	00	07	10	02	37	39	12	06
f	10	01	06	01	01	10	00	**27**	01	03	04	02	00
g	7	02	16	03	03	13	**31**	00	03	18	08	03	01
h	11	00	04	00	01	03	03	06	00	12	**38**	04	00
i	4	02	28	03	06	43	04	16	12	00	**98**	13	01
j	2	07	40	10	08	40	05	17	34	**98**	00	35	12
k	9	01	08	02	01	18	00	06	05	12	**30**	00	15
l	12	00	02	00	00	07	00	01	00	01	06	**12**	00
Total		113	337	141	128	290	071	118	065	202	311	091	039
Rank order, r :		8	1	5	6	3	10	7	11	4	2	9	12

Source : Nystuen and Dacey, 1961, p. 35.
* Hypothetical data.

The system of flow is considered as independent when it is centred on a place whose greatest outflow is to an area of lower rank order *i.e.* with a smaller number of incoming flow (Christopher Board, 1971 p. 206). For each city, therefore, the greatest out-flow is identified and is given in bold figures of Table 10.2.

Examination of matrix of intercity flow of messages as given in Table 10.2 , however, reveals that for four of the cities (b, e, g and j) the largest flow is to a lower order city, (In case of rank order, however, their rank is lower and the rank of their respective highest flow destination is higher). These cities, therefore, will form the terminal points of the graph, as mentioned above. Each of these terminal points or dominant nodes will have its own sub-graph, with the place subordinate to it connected by lines. Beginning with the four terminal points (b, e, g and j) as given above, the other eight cities can be linked directly or indirectly with these terminal points according to the nodal flows from each city. The resulting hierarchical graph is given in Figure 10.2. The figure very clearly shows the nodal structure of the area in terms of the flow of telephonic messages among the cities of the region. It gives four distinct clusters or sub-graphs.

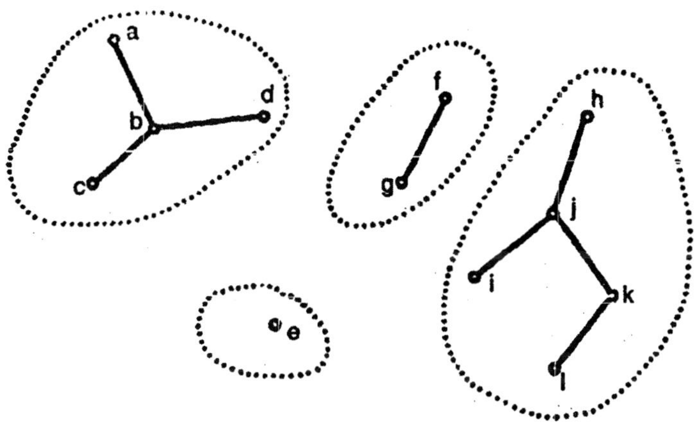

Fig. 10.2

Nodal structure of the matrix shown in Table 10.2

The city K, though defined as dominant, should be regarded as a secondary node as it is itself subordinate to city j. The isolated city e may also have a secondary status.

REFERENCES

1. Christopher Board (1971) " Movements in the African Population of the Republic of South Africa" in Shafi M. and Mehdi Raza (ed), *Studies in Applied and Regional Geography,* Aligarh, Deptt. of Geography, Aligarh Muslim University p. 206.

2. Haggett, P. (1965) *Locational Analysis in Human Geography* London, Edward Arnold Ltd. pp. 237 & 251-253.

3. Ibrahim R. (1984) Market - Centres and Regional Development : A Case Study of Delhi - Jaipur - Agra Triangle, Bhir Delhi, B.R. Publishing Corporation.

4. Garrison William L. (1960) "Connectivity of the Inter - State Highway System", *Regional Service Association, Papers and Proceedings* Vol. 6 pp. 121-137.

5. Kansky K.J. (1963) "*Structure of Transportation Networks, Relationships Between Network Geometry and Regional Characteristics*" University of Chicago, Geography Research Paper, 84.

6. Garrison W.L. and DF Marble (1974) "Graph Theoratic Concepts" in Eliot Hurst and E. Michel (ed) *Transportation Geography - Comments and Readings* New York McGraw Hill p. 64.

7. Simith D.M. (1975) *Patterns in Human Geography* Penguin Books pp. 279-303.

8. Nystuen J.D. and M.F. Dacey (1961) "A Graph Theory Interprelation of nodal regions" Regional Science Association, Papers and Proceedings Vol. 7 pp. 29-42.

11
MATRICES

Any set of equations consisting of several variables over large number of observations will appear fairly complex, in ordinary algebra. Through matrix algebra, however, these equations can be represented in a compact form. Data manipulations through Computers are also much faster when it is given in matrix form. Before going into techniques of multivariate analysis, therefore, it will be useful to have some basic understanding of matrices.

Any rectangular arrangement of arrays arranged in columns or rows is known as a matrix. It can also be defined as a system of *m.n* numbers arranged in the form of an ordered set of *m* rows, each row consisting of an ordered set of *n* numbers. Such a matrix is called an *m*x*n* matrix (to be read as *m* by *n* matrix).

Consider the equations

$$2X+3Y+Z+2U=0$$
$$X+5Y+9Z+5U=0$$
$$3X+Y+4Z+U=0$$

The system of coefficients in this set of equations written in order of their occurrence, give a 3x4 matrix

$$\begin{bmatrix} 2 & 3 & 1 & 2 \\ 1 & 5 & 9 & 5 \\ 3 & 1 & 4 & 1 \end{bmatrix}$$

It has 3 rows and 4 columns. The general form of any *m*x*n* matinx A, is written as :

$$\underset{m\times n}{A} = \begin{bmatrix} a_{11} & a_{12}\ldots\ldots & a_{1n} \\ a_{21} & a_{22}\ldots\ldots & a_{2n} \\ \ldots\ldots & \ldots\ldots & \ldots\ldots \\ a_{m1} & a_{m2} & a_{mn} \end{bmatrix} \qquad = \left[a_{ij}\right]$$

$i = 12\ldots\ldots\ldots\ldots m$
$j = 12\ldots\ldots\ldots\ldots n$

The first suffix is invariant for each row and the second suffix is invariant for each column. Thus a_{ij} means the element of *i*th row and *j*th column. The number of rows and the number of column in any matrix are known as its dimension.

Equal Matrices

The two matrices A and B are said to be equal if; (a) they have equal number of rows and equal number of columns and (b) their corresponding elements are equal.

Square Matrix

The matrix whose number of columns are equal to the number of rows is known as square matrix, otherwise it is known as a rectangular matrix.

Row and column Matrix

Any 1xn matrix, which has only one row is known as a row matrix or a row vector. Similarly a mx1 matrix which has only one column is known as a column matrix or a column vector.

Diagonal of a Square Matrix

The elements of a square matrix which correspond to same number of column and row are known as its diagonal elements. Thus in a square matrix a_{11}, a_{22}, a_{33}......... a_{nn}, are the diagonal elements.

Any square matrix whose all off diagnall elements are zero is known as diagonal matrix. For example, the matrix A given below is a 3x3 diagonal matrix.

$$A = \begin{bmatrix} 3 & 0 & 0 \\ 0 & 2 & 0 \\ 0 & 0 & 7 \end{bmatrix}$$

Trace of a Matrix

The sum of the diagonal terms of a square matrix is known as its trace.

Null Matrix

A matrix *B*, whose all the elements are zero is known as a null matrix or zero matrix and is written as *B*=0.

Scalar Matrix

Any square matrix whose all the diagonal elements are equal but all the off diagonal elements are zero is known as scalar matrix. For example, the matrices *A* and *B* given below are the scalar matrices.

$$A = \begin{bmatrix} 3 & 0 \\ 0 & 3 \end{bmatrix} \qquad B = \begin{bmatrix} 5 & 0 & 0 \\ 0 & 5 & 0 \\ 0 & 0 & 5 \end{bmatrix}$$

Identity or Unit Matrix

Any scalar matrix whose diagonal elements are unity is known as identity or unit matrix. These matrices are denoted by ***I***. The Matrices I_{3x3}, I_{4x4}, as given below, are 3x3 and 4x4 identity matrices.

$$I_{3\times3}=\begin{bmatrix}1&0&0\\0&1&0\\0&0&1\end{bmatrix}\qquad I_{4\times4}=\begin{bmatrix}1&0&0&0\\0&1&0&0\\0&0&1&0\\0&0&0&1\end{bmatrix}$$

Matrix Addition

The addition (difference) of the two matrices A and B of same order is the matrix C whose order will be the same as that of A or B. Each element of C is the sum (difference) of the corresponding elements of A and B. If the two matrices are not of the same order, their addition (difference) is not possible.

Example

$$\text{If A}=\begin{bmatrix}2&1&5\\7&3&2\end{bmatrix}\qquad \text{B}=\begin{bmatrix}5&2&1\\5&2&0\end{bmatrix}$$

$$\text{A+B}=\begin{bmatrix}2+5&1+2&5+1\\7+5&3+2&2+0\end{bmatrix}=\begin{bmatrix}7&3&6\\12&5&2\end{bmatrix}=B+A$$

$$\text{A–B}=\begin{bmatrix}2-5&1-2&5-1\\7-5&3-2&2-0\end{bmatrix}=\begin{bmatrix}-3&-1&4\\2&1&2\end{bmatrix}$$

Matrix Multiplication

If the matrix A is of order m x n and B is of order n x p, their product AB is defined by a matrix C=[Cij] which will have m rows and n columns. Each element of (Cij) is obtained by the multiplication of corresponding terms of ith row of A and jth column of B, as explained below :

$$\text{A}=\begin{bmatrix}2&5\\3&1\end{bmatrix}\qquad \text{B}=\begin{bmatrix}6&8\\7&4\end{bmatrix}$$

$$\text{C}=A\times B=\begin{bmatrix}2&5\\3&1\end{bmatrix}\times\begin{bmatrix}6&8\\7&4\end{bmatrix}$$

$$=\begin{bmatrix}2\times6+5\times7&2\times8+5\times4\\3\times6+1\times7&3\times8+1\times4\end{bmatrix}=\begin{bmatrix}47&36\\25&28\end{bmatrix}$$

$$\text{B}\times\text{A}=\begin{bmatrix}6&8\\7&4\end{bmatrix}\times\begin{bmatrix}2&5\\3&1\end{bmatrix}=\begin{bmatrix}6\times2+8\times3&6\times5+8\times1\\7\times2+4\times3&7\times5+4\times1\end{bmatrix}$$

$$=\begin{bmatrix}36&38\\26&39\end{bmatrix}$$

Thus, the necessary condition for a matrix multiplication is that the number of the columns of the first matrix should be equal to the number of the rows of the second matrix. It is important to note that in matrix algebra $AB\neq BA$ (except in some special cases).

Example

If $A = \begin{bmatrix} 3 & 2 & 7 \\ 1 & 2 & 3 \end{bmatrix}_{2\times3}$ $B = \begin{bmatrix} 1 & 3 & 2 \\ 5 & 4 & 1 \\ 2 & 5 & 7 \end{bmatrix} 3\times3$

$$A \times B = \begin{bmatrix} 3\times1+2\times5+7\times2 & 3\times3+2\times4+7\times5 & 3\times2+2\times1+7\times7 \\ 1\times1+2\times5+3\times2 & 1\times3+2\times4+3\times5 & 1\times2+2\times1+3\times7 \end{bmatrix}$$

$$AB = \begin{bmatrix} 27 & 52 & 57 & \\ 17 & 26 & 25 & 2\times3 \end{bmatrix}$$

In this case $B \times A$ is not possible because columns of B are not equal to rows of A.

It is important to note that in matrix multiplication the change in the order of multiplication changes the whole meaning.

In any matrix multiplication the term which comes first is known as prefactor and the other as postfactor. For example in $A \times B$, A is prefactor and B is postfactor. We may also say that B is premultipled by A or A is postmultipled by B.

Scalar Multiplication

If λ is a scalar (some fixed number) then multiplication of λ with matrix A is not a matrix multiplication but is called as scalar multiplication. In this case each element of A will get multiplied by λ.

Example

(i)

$$A = \begin{bmatrix} 2 & 5 & 3 \\ 1 & 2 & 9 \\ 3 & 2 & 4 \end{bmatrix}, \lambda = 5$$

$$\lambda A = 5x \begin{bmatrix} 2 & 5 & 3 \\ 1 & 2 & 9 \\ 3 & 2 & 4 \end{bmatrix} = \begin{bmatrix} 10 & 25 & 15 \\ 5 & 10 & 45 \\ 15 & 10 & 20 \end{bmatrix}$$

(ii)

$$5I_{3x3} = 5 \times \begin{bmatrix} 1 & 0 & 0 \\ 0 & 1 & 0 \\ 0 & 0 & 1 \end{bmatrix} = \begin{bmatrix} 5 & 0 & 0 \\ 0 & 5 & 0 \\ 0 & 0 & 5 \end{bmatrix}$$

Exercises

If $A = \begin{bmatrix} 2 & 3 & 4 \\ 1 & 2 & 3 \\ 5 & 6 & 1 \end{bmatrix}$ $B = \begin{bmatrix} 1 & 4 & 3 \\ 2 & 7 & 8 \\ 5 & 3 & 2 \end{bmatrix}$

and $C = \begin{bmatrix} 4 & 1 & 2 \\ 3 & 7 & 3 \\ 5 & 3 & 1 \end{bmatrix}$

verify :

(1) A (B+C) = AB+AC
(2) 1 (A+B) = 1A+1B
(3) A (B×C) = (A×B)×C
(4) IA = AI = A

Transpose of a Matrix

The transpose of matrix A is defined by a matrix A' such that the rows of A become the columns of A and the columns of A' becomes the rows of A. For example if

$$A = \begin{bmatrix} 3 & 2 & 5 \\ 7 & 3 & 9 \\ 1 & 2 & 4 \end{bmatrix}, \quad A' = \begin{bmatrix} 3 & 7 & 1 \\ 2 & 3 & 2 \\ 5 & 9 & 4 \end{bmatrix}$$

$$B = \begin{bmatrix} 3 & 2 & 1 \\ 5 & 7 & 4 \end{bmatrix}, \quad B' = \begin{bmatrix} 3 & 5 \\ 2 & 7 \\ 1 & 4 \end{bmatrix}$$

Theorams :

$(A')' = A$

$(AB') = B'A'$

$(A+B)' = A'+B'$

Symmetric Matrix

If the transpose of a square matrix is same as the given matrix, i.e, $ai_{ij} = a_{ji}$ the matrix is known as symmetric matrix,

Example

if $A = \begin{bmatrix} 1 & 2 & 3 \\ 2 & 4 & 5 \\ 3 & 5 & 6 \end{bmatrix}$ $A' = \begin{bmatrix} 1 & 2 & 3 \\ 2 & 4 & 5 \\ 3 & 5 & 6 \end{bmatrix}$

As A' = A we say that A is a symmetrical matrix

Idompotent

If a matrix A is matrix such that $A^2=A$ the matrix is called the idempotent matrix, *i.e.* $A=A^2=A^2$.................A^n

Example

$$A = \begin{bmatrix} 2 & -2 & -4 \\ -1 & 3 & 4 \\ 1 & -2 & -3 \end{bmatrix}$$

$$A^2 = \begin{bmatrix} 2 & -2 & -4 \\ -1 & 3 & 4 \\ 1 & -2 & -3 \end{bmatrix} \times \begin{bmatrix} 2 & -2 & -4 \\ -1 & 3 & 4 \\ 1 & -2 & -3 \end{bmatrix}$$

$$= \begin{bmatrix} 4+2-4 & -4-6+8 & -8-8+12 \\ -2-3+4 & 2+9-8 & 4+12-12 \\ 2+2-3 & -2-6+6 & -4-8+9 \end{bmatrix} = \begin{bmatrix} 2 & -2 & -4 \\ -1 & 3 & 4 \\ 1 & -2 & -3 \end{bmatrix} = A$$

Thus matrix A is idompotent matrix.

Minors and Cofactors

Consider any square matrix $A = [a_{ij}]$, i=12......n, j=12........n.

Take its any element a_{ij} and remove the ith row and jth column from A, the determinant of remaining (n–1)(xn–1) square matrix, Mij, is called one of the 1st minors of A. More precisely, it is called the minor of aij. The minor of aij when multiplied by $(-1)^{i+j}$ is called the cofactor of aij and is denoted by Aij.

The algebric signs attached with the minors Mij to obtain the corresponding cofactors are (+) if (i+j) is even and (–) if (i+j) is odd as indicated below for a 4×4 matrix.

$$\begin{array}{cccc} + & & + & - \\ - & + & - & + \\ + & - & + & - \\ - & + & - & + \end{array}$$

Determinant of a Square Matrix

Associated with any square matrix A, there is a scalar quantity, known as the determinant of A and is denoted by $|A|$. The determinant of a 2×2 and 3×3 matrix is worked out as below :

If $$A = \begin{bmatrix} a_{11} & a_{12} \\ a_{21} & a_{22} \end{bmatrix}, \quad |A| = (a_{11}, a_{22} - a_{12}a_{21})$$

and if $A = \begin{bmatrix} a_{11} & a_{12} & a_{13} \\ a_{21} & a_{22} & a_{23} \\ a_{31} & a_{32} & a_{33} \end{bmatrix}$

$$|A| = a_{11} \times \begin{bmatrix} a_{22} & a_{23} \\ a_{32} & a_{33} \end{bmatrix} - a_{12} \begin{bmatrix} a_{21} & a_{23} \\ a_{31} & a_{33} \end{bmatrix} + a_{13} \begin{bmatrix} a_{21} & a_{22} \\ a_{31} & a_{32} \end{bmatrix}$$

$$= a_{11} (a_{22}. a_{33} - a_{23}. a_{32}) - a_{12} (a_{21}. a_{33} - a_{23}. a_{31}) + a_{13} (a_{21}. a_{32} - a_{22}. a_{31})$$

This can also be written in terms and cofactors as

$$|A| = a_{11} \times M_{11} - a_{12} \times M_{12} + a_{13} \times M_{13}$$

OR

$$= a_{11} \times A_{11} + a_{13} \times A_{12} + a_{13} \times A_{13}$$

Example

(i) $A = \begin{bmatrix} 1 & 2 \\ 3 & 4 \end{bmatrix}, |A| = (1 \times 4 - 2 \times 2) = -2$

(ii) $A = \begin{bmatrix} 2 & 3 & 5 \\ 1 & 0 & -2 \\ 0 & -5 & -6 \end{bmatrix}$

$$|A| = 2\begin{vmatrix} 0 & -2 \\ -5 & -6 \end{vmatrix} - 3\begin{vmatrix} 1 & -2 \\ 0 & -6 \end{vmatrix} + 5\begin{vmatrix} 1 & 0 \\ 0 & -5 \end{vmatrix}$$

$$= 2(0-10) - 3(-6-0) + 5(-5-0)$$

$$= -20 + 18 - 18 - 25 = -27$$

Singular Matrix

A square matrix is said to be singular if its determinant is zero. Otherwise it is called as non-singular.

Properties of Determinant

In Any square matrix

1. Interchanging of rows and columns will not change the value of the determinant.
2. If each element of any row or column is zero, the determinant will be zero.
3. Interchanging any two rows (or column) will reverse the sign of the determinant.
4. If two rows or column of a determinant are identical, the value of the determinant will be zero.

5. If each of the elements in a row (or column) is multiplied by the same number p, the value of the determinant will also get multiplied by p.

6. If to each element of a row (or column) is added m times the corresponding elements of any other row (or column) the value of the determinant is not changed.

Adjoint of a Square Matrix

Let A = (a_{ij}) be $a_{n \times n}$ square matrix and A_{ij} be the cofactor of the element a_{ij}, then the matrix

$$\begin{bmatrix} A_{11} & A_{21} \ldots A_{n1} \\ A_{12} & A_{22} \ldots A_{n2} \\ A_{1n} & A_{2n} \ldots A_{n \times n} \end{bmatrix}$$

is called as the adjoint of the matrix A. Note carefuly that it is transpose of the matrix obtained by putting cofactors of a_{ij} in place of a_{ji}.

Example

Find the adj. A if, $A = \begin{bmatrix} 3 & 2 \\ 4 & 3 \end{bmatrix}$

A11 = 3, A12 = 4, A21 = 2, A22 = 3

$$\text{Adj. A} = \begin{bmatrix} 3 & -4 \\ -2 & 3 \end{bmatrix} = \begin{bmatrix} 3 & -2 \\ -4 & 3 \end{bmatrix}$$

Find the Adj A, if $A = \begin{bmatrix} 2 & 3 & 1 \\ 1 & 5 & 3 \\ 4 & 2 & 1 \end{bmatrix}$

$$A_{11} = -1, \quad A_{12} = +11, \quad A_{13} = -18$$
$$A_{21} = -1, \quad A_{22} = -2, \quad A_{23} = +8$$
$$A_{31} = 4, \quad A_{32} = -5, \quad A_{33} = 7$$

$$\text{Adj} = A = \begin{bmatrix} -1 & +11 & -18 \\ -1 & -2 & 8 \\ 4 & -5 & 7 \end{bmatrix} = \begin{bmatrix} -1 & -1 & 4 \\ +11 & -2 & -5 \\ -18 & 8 & 7 \end{bmatrix}$$

Inverse of a Square Matrix

If A and B are square matrices of the same order such that $AB=BA=I$, than B is called the inverse of A (*i.e.* $B=A^{-1}$) and A is called the inverse of B (*i.e.* $A=B^{-1}$). The necessary condition for A to have its inverse is that A should be non-singular *i.e.* $|A| \neq 0$

Example

$$(i)\quad \text{If } A=\begin{bmatrix}2 & 3\\ 1 & 4\end{bmatrix}, B=\begin{bmatrix}\frac{4}{5} & -\frac{3}{5}\\ -\frac{1}{5} & \frac{2}{5}\end{bmatrix}$$

$$AB=\begin{bmatrix}2 & 3\\ 1 & 4\end{bmatrix}\times\begin{bmatrix}\frac{4}{5} & -\frac{3}{5}\\ -\frac{1}{5} & \frac{2}{5}\end{bmatrix}=\begin{bmatrix}\frac{8}{5}-\frac{3}{5} & \frac{6}{5}+\frac{6}{5}\\ \frac{4}{5}-\frac{4}{5} & \frac{3}{5}+\frac{8}{5}\end{bmatrix}$$

$$=\begin{bmatrix}1 & 0\\ 0 & 1\end{bmatrix}=I, \text{ So } A=B^{-1}$$

$$(ii)\quad \text{If } A=\begin{bmatrix}2 & 3 & 1\\ 1 & 2 & 3\\ 3 & 1 & 2\end{bmatrix}\quad B=\begin{bmatrix}\frac{1}{18} & -\frac{5}{18} & \frac{7}{18}\\ \frac{7}{18} & \frac{1}{18} & \frac{5}{18}\\ -\frac{5}{18} & \frac{7}{18} & \frac{1}{18}\end{bmatrix}$$

$$AB=\begin{bmatrix}\frac{2}{18}+\frac{21}{18}-\frac{5}{18} & -\frac{10}{18}+\frac{3}{18}+\frac{7}{18} & \frac{14}{18}-\frac{15}{18}+\frac{1}{18}\\ \frac{1}{18}+\frac{14}{8}-\frac{15}{18} & -\frac{5}{18}+\frac{2}{18}+\frac{21}{18} & \frac{7}{18}-\frac{10}{18}+\frac{3}{18}\\ \frac{3}{18}+\frac{7}{18}-\frac{10}{18} & -\frac{15}{18}+\frac{1}{18}+\frac{14}{18} & \frac{21}{18}-\frac{5}{18}+\frac{2}{18}\end{bmatrix}$$

$$=\begin{bmatrix}1 & 0 & 0\\ 0 & 1 & 0\\ 0 & 0 & 1\end{bmatrix}$$

So, $A=B^{-1}$

Thus in each case one is the inverse of the other.

Computation of the Inverse

The inverse of a matrix is worked out by using the relationship.

$$A^{-1}=\frac{1}{|A|}(adj\,A)=\frac{1}{|A|}\times\begin{bmatrix}A_{11} & A_{21}\ldots\ldots A_{n1}\\ A_{12} & A_{22}\ldots\ldots A_{n2}\\ A_{1n} & A_{2n}\ldots\ldots A_{nm}\end{bmatrix}$$

Example

Find of the inverse of A = $\begin{bmatrix} 2 & 3 \\ 4 & -1 \end{bmatrix}$

Since $|A| = (-2-12) = -14$,
the inverse exist, also

$$A_{11} = -1, \qquad A_{12} = -4$$
$$A_{21} = -3, \qquad A_{22} = 2$$

$$adj\ A = \begin{bmatrix} -1 & -4 \\ -3 & 2 \end{bmatrix} = \begin{bmatrix} -1 & -3 \\ -4 & 2 \end{bmatrix}$$

It is easy to verify that :

$$A\,A^{-1} = \begin{bmatrix} 1 & 0 \\ 0 & 1 \end{bmatrix} = I$$

Example :

Find the inverse of $A = \begin{bmatrix} 1 & 2 & 3 \\ 2 & 5 & 7 \\ -2 & -4 & -5 \end{bmatrix}$

$$|A| = 1(5{\times}5-7{\times}4){\times}2(-5{\times}2-7{\times}-2)+3(-4{\times}2-5{\times}-2)$$

$$=(-25+28)-2(-10+14)+3(-8+10)$$

$$=3-8+6=1$$

$$A_{11} = 3, \qquad A_{12} = -4 \qquad A_{13} = 2$$
$$A_{21} = -2 \qquad A_{22} = 1 \qquad A_{23} = 0$$
$$A_{31} = -1 \qquad A_{32} = -1 \qquad A_{33} = 1$$

So $Adj\ A = \begin{bmatrix} 3 & -2 & -1 \\ -4 & 1 & -1 \\ 2 & 0 & 1 \end{bmatrix}$

$$A^{-1} = \frac{1}{|A|}\,adj\ A = \frac{1}{1} \times \begin{bmatrix} 3 & -2 & -1 \\ -4 & 1 & -1 \\ 2 & 0 & 1 \end{bmatrix} = \begin{bmatrix} 3 & -2 & -1 \\ -4 & 1 & -1 \\ 2 & 0 & 1 \end{bmatrix}$$

Exercises :

1. Find the inverse of

$$A=\begin{bmatrix}1 & 2 & 3\\ 2 & 5 & 7\\ -2 & -4 & -5\end{bmatrix}, \qquad \text{Ans. } A^{-1}=\begin{bmatrix}3 & -2 & -1\\ -4 & 1 & -1\\ 2 & 0 & 1\end{bmatrix}$$

2. Find the inverse of A when :

$$A=\begin{bmatrix}1 & 2 & 3\\ 4 & 5 & 6\\ 6 & 7 & 9\end{bmatrix}, \qquad \text{Ans } A^{-1}=\begin{bmatrix}-1 & -1 & 1\\ 0 & 3 & -1\\ \frac{2}{3} & -\frac{5}{3} & 1\end{bmatrix}$$

Properties of the Inverse

1. $(AB)^{-1}=B^{-1}\times A^{-1}$ and $(ABC)^{-1}=C^{-1}B^{-1}A^{-1}$
2. $AA^{-1}=1$
3. $(A')^{-1}=(A^{-1})'$

Matrix Representation of Equation and Their Solution

Suppose we have a set of n non-homogeneous equations in n unknown as :

$$a_{11}x_1+a_{12}x_2+\ldots\ldots\ldots\ldots+a_{1n}x_n=C_1$$
$$a_{21}x_1+a_{22}x_2+\ldots\ldots\ldots\ldots+a_{2n}x_n=C_2$$
$$a_{31}x_1+a_{32}+x_2+\ldots\ldots\ldots\ldots+a_{3n}x_n=C_3$$
$$\ldots\ldots\ldots\ldots\ldots\ldots\ldots\ldots\ldots\ldots\ldots\ldots$$
$$a_{n1}x_1+a_{n2}x_2\ldots\ldots\ldots\ldots\ldots+a_{3n}x_n=C_n$$

This set of equations can also be written in matrix form as :

$$\begin{bmatrix}a_{11} & a_{12\ldots\ldots} & a_{1n}\\ a_{21} & a_{22\ldots\ldots} & a_{2n}\\ a_{n2} & a_{n2\ldots\ldots} & a_{nn}\end{bmatrix}\begin{bmatrix}x_1\\ x_2\\ \vdots\\ x_n\end{bmatrix} \text{ and } C=\begin{bmatrix}C_1\\ C_2\\ \vdots\\ C_n\end{bmatrix}$$

or $\qquad AX=C$

Where

$$A=\begin{bmatrix}a_{11} & a_{12\ldots\ldots} & a_{1n}\\ a_{21} & a_{13\ldots\ldots} & a_{2n}\\ a_{n1} & a_{1n\ldots\ldots} & a_{nn}\end{bmatrix}, X=\begin{bmatrix}x_1\\ x_2\\ \vdots\\ x_n\end{bmatrix} \text{ and } C=\begin{bmatrix}C_1\\ C_2\\ \vdots\\ C_n\end{bmatrix}$$

The Solution, when A is non-singular[1]

Consider $AX = C$,

pre-multiplying both the sides by A^{-1}

$$A^{-1}AX = A^{-1}C \qquad \text{or} \qquad IX = A^{-1}C$$

or $$X = A^{-1}C$$

Thus the elements of the vector $A^{-1}C$ will corresponed to the values of the elements of vector X.

Example

Solve the equations :

$$x_1 + 2x_2 + 3x_3 = 14$$
$$4x_1 + 5x_2 + 6x_3 = 32$$
$$6x_1 + 7x_2 + 9x_3 = 47$$

writing it in usual matrix notation AX=C

$$\begin{bmatrix} 1 & 2 & 3 \\ 4 & 5 & 6 \\ 6 & 7 & 9 \end{bmatrix} \begin{bmatrix} x_1 \\ x_1 \\ x_3 \end{bmatrix} = \begin{bmatrix} 14 \\ 32 \\ 47 \end{bmatrix}$$

working out the inverse of the coefficient matrix A we get

$$A^{-1} = \begin{bmatrix} -1 & -1 & 1 \\ 0 & 3 & -2 \\ \frac{2}{3} & -\frac{5}{3} & 1 \end{bmatrix}$$

Using the solution equation

$$X = A^{-1}C$$

$$\begin{bmatrix} X_1 \\ X_2 \\ X_3 \end{bmatrix} = \begin{bmatrix} -1 & -1 & 1 \\ 0 & 3 & -2 \\ \frac{2}{3} & -\frac{5}{3} & 1 \end{bmatrix} \times \begin{bmatrix} 14 \\ 32 \\ 47 \end{bmatrix} = \begin{bmatrix} 1 \\ 2 \\ 3 \end{bmatrix}$$

Hence, $x_1 = 1$, $x_2 = 2$, and $x_3 = 3$

---

1. For several other methods used in different cases, please refer to G. Hadley, Linear Algebra, Addison-Wesley Publishing Company, pp. 162-187.

Exercises

Solve the following equations with the help of matrix methods :

(1) $2x_1 + 3x_2 = 13$ **Ans.** 2, 3

$4x_1 - x_2 = 5$

(2) $x_1 + 2x_2 + 3x_3 = 32$

$2x_1 + 5x_2 + 7x_3 = 75$

$-2x_1 - 4x_2 - 5x_3 = -58$ **Ans.** 4, 5, 6.

Length of a Vector

If the n element of a row vector or of a column vector are considered as co-ordinates of a point P in n-dimensional space, the length of the vector is the distance of point P from the origin. In case of a vector $X' = (x_1 x_2 .....x_n)$, the length is given by:

$$|X| = \sqrt{x^2{}_1 + x^2{}_2 + ...x^2{}_n}$$

If, $|X| = 1$, X is known as a vector normalised to unity.

Angle between two vectors

If X and Y are two vectors of n elements, the angle q between them is obtained by the following relation :

$$X'Y = |X| . |Y| \cos q \qquad ...(11.1)$$

The Projection of vector X on Y is given by :

$$P_{xy} = \frac{X'Y}{|Y|} \qquad ...(11.2)$$

where $X'Y = \Sigma x_i y_i$

If the angle between the two vectors, q, is 90°, Cos $q = 0$ and from (11.1) $X'Y = \Sigma xy = 0$, since length of vector X or Y cannot be zero. Such vectors are known as orthogonal vectors.

Linear Dependence of Vectors

Let A be a $m \times n$ matrix whose columns are denoted by vectors $a_1 a_2 .....a_n$ Consider a linear combination of the columns of A as :

$$X_1 a_1 + X_2 a_2 + ... + X_n a_n = 0 \qquad ...(11.3)$$

Where $X_1 X_2 ......X_n$ are some unknowns. If equation (11.3) is satisfied only when $X_1 = X_2 = ... = X_n = 0$ (trivial solution), the vectors $a_1 a_2 ....$and a_n are said to be linearly independent. If, however, there exist a non-trival solution of (11.3), the set of the vectors is said to be linearly dependent.

Example

If
$$A = \begin{bmatrix} 1 & 2 & 3 \\ 2 & 3 & 5 \\ 3 & 4 & 7 \end{bmatrix}$$

$$a_1 = \begin{bmatrix} 1 \\ 1 \\ 3 \end{bmatrix}, \quad a_2 = \begin{bmatrix} 2 \\ 3 \\ 4 \end{bmatrix} \quad \text{and } a_3 = \begin{bmatrix} 3 \\ 5 \\ 7 \end{bmatrix}$$

For $X_1 = 1, X_2 = 1$ and $X_3 = -1$

$$X_1 a_1 + X_2 a_2 + X_3 a_3 = \begin{bmatrix} 1+2-3 \\ 2+3-5 \\ 3+4-7 \end{bmatrix} = \begin{bmatrix} 0 \\ 0 \\ 0 \end{bmatrix} = 0$$

As the equation (11.3) is satisfied for non-zero values of X, the theree vectors are linearly dependent. Note that the determinant of the matrices whose vectors are linearly dependent is zero. The determinant of matrix A in the above example is zero. Thus a non-singular matrix has linearly independent vectors.

Rank of Matrix

Rank of a matrix is defined as the maximum number of its linearly independent vectors. In the previous example if all the three column vectors of A are taken together they are linearly dependent. Thus the rank of A is not 3. When each pair is taken separately, we find

$$X_1 a_1 + X_2 a_2 \neq 0. \qquad X_1 a_1 + X_2 a_2 \neq 0, \qquad \text{and } X_2 a_2 + X_3 a_3 \neq 0$$

[for any values of $X_1 X_2$ and X_3]

As the maximum number of linearly independent vectors is 2, the rank of A is 2,

In case of a $n \times n$ non-singular matrix A (*i.e.* .$|A| \neq 0$) the rank is the number of columns (rows) of the matrix and is said to be of full rank. In case A is singular (*i.e.* $|A| = 0$) rank of A is less than n.

Orthogonal Matrices

A square matrix is said to be orthogonal if

$$A'A = I$$

i.e.
$$A' = A^{-1}$$

Example

$$A = \begin{bmatrix} \sqrt{\frac{2}{3}} & -\frac{1}{\sqrt{3}} \\ \frac{1}{\sqrt{3}} & \sqrt{\frac{2}{3}} \end{bmatrix}$$

$$A'A = \begin{bmatrix} \sqrt{\frac{2}{3}} & \frac{1}{\sqrt{3}} \\ \frac{-1}{\sqrt{3}} & \sqrt{\frac{2}{3}} \end{bmatrix} \times \begin{bmatrix} \sqrt{\frac{2}{3}} & \frac{-1}{\sqrt{3}} \\ \frac{1}{\sqrt{3}} & \sqrt{\frac{2}{3}} \end{bmatrix} = \begin{bmatrix} 1 & 0 \\ 0 & 1 \end{bmatrix}$$

Thus A is orthogonal.

It may be noted that in an orthogonal matrix :

1. The vectors are orthogonal to each other :
2. The determinant is $= \pm 1$

Eigen Values and Eigen Vectors

For a given $n \times n$ symmetric matrix A any $n \times 1$ vector X, which satisfies the equation.

$$AX = \lambda X \text{ or } (A - \lambda I)X = 0, X \neq 0 \qquad \text{......(11.4)}$$

is known as the eigen vector and λ the scalar is known as the eigen value of A. Their other names are characteristic vector and characteristics root or latent vector and letent root also. As an example, consider the matrix ;

$$A = \begin{bmatrix} 4 & 2 \\ 2 & 1 \end{bmatrix} \text{ and } X = \begin{bmatrix} \frac{2}{\sqrt{5}} \\ \frac{1}{\sqrt{5}} \end{bmatrix}$$

Here,

$$\begin{bmatrix} 4 & 2 \\ 2 & 1 \end{bmatrix} \times \begin{bmatrix} \frac{2}{\sqrt{5}} \\ \frac{1}{\sqrt{5}} \end{bmatrix} = \begin{bmatrix} \frac{10}{\sqrt{5}} \\ \frac{5}{\sqrt{5}} \end{bmatrix} = 5 \begin{bmatrix} \frac{2}{\sqrt{5}} \\ \frac{1}{\sqrt{5}} \end{bmatrix}$$

which can be written as $AX = 5X$

Thus vector X is said to be the eigen vector of A corresponding to the eigen value equal to 5.

Equation (11.4) will have non-trivial solution (other than X being a null vector) only if the determinant of $(A - \lambda I)$ is zero, *i.e.*

$$|A - \lambda I| = 0 \qquad \text{.......(11.5)}$$

Equation (11.5) yields a nth degree polynomial in λ, which may be solved and consequently by putting the numerical values of λ in (11.4) corresponding eigen vectors can also be worked out.

Example

Find the eigen values and eigen vectors of

$$A = \begin{bmatrix} 2 & \sqrt{2} \\ \sqrt{2} & 1 \end{bmatrix}$$

Solution

$$[A-\lambda I]\begin{bmatrix} 2 & \sqrt{2} \\ \sqrt{2} & 1 \end{bmatrix}-\lambda\begin{bmatrix} 1 & 0 \\ 0 & 1 \end{bmatrix}=\begin{bmatrix} 2-\lambda & \sqrt{2} \\ \sqrt{2} & 1-\lambda \end{bmatrix}$$

$$|A-\lambda I| = (2-\lambda)\times(1-\lambda)-\sqrt{2}\times\sqrt{2} = 0$$

$$= 2-3\lambda+\lambda^2-2 = 0$$

or $\quad \lambda^2-3\lambda=0$

or $\quad \lambda(\lambda-3)=0$

or $\quad \lambda=3 \text{ or } \lambda=0$

Thus there will be two eigen vectors of A, one corresponding to $\lambda = 3$ and another corresponding to $\lambda=0$.

To determine the eigen vector when eigen value is 3, from (11.4) we get

$$[A-3I]X=\begin{bmatrix} 2-3 & \sqrt{2} \\ \sqrt{2} & 1-3 \end{bmatrix}\begin{bmatrix} x_1 \\ x_2 \end{bmatrix}=0$$

or
$$\begin{bmatrix} -1 & \sqrt{2} \\ \sqrt{2} & -2 \end{bmatrix}\begin{bmatrix} x_1 \\ x_2 \end{bmatrix}=0$$

$$-x_1+\sqrt{2}\ x_2=0$$

or $\quad \sqrt{2}.x_1-2\ x_2=0$

We observe that the two equations are nothing but one and give

$$x_1=\sqrt{2}\ x_2$$

If there is no other restriction to vector X, we can give any value to x_2 and get the corresponding value of x_1. For example if $x_2=1$

$x_1=\sqrt{2}(1)=\sqrt{2}$ and the eigen vector would be $X_1=\left(\sqrt{2},\ 1\right)$ similarly when we put $\lambda=0$ we get

$$\begin{bmatrix} 2-0 & \sqrt{2} \\ \sqrt{2} & 1-0 \end{bmatrix}\begin{bmatrix} x_1 \\ x_2 \end{bmatrix}=0 \text{ or}$$

$$2x_1+\sqrt{2}x_2=0$$

$$\sqrt{2}x_1+x_2=0$$

solving them we get

$$x_1 = \frac{-1}{\sqrt{2}} x_2$$

Giving again an arbitary value, say $x_2 = 1$, we get

$$x_1 = \frac{-1}{\sqrt{2}}$$

So the second eigen vector is

$$x_2 = \left(\frac{-1}{\sqrt{2}}, 1 \right)$$

It is important to note that : (*a*) the $X'_1 X_2 = 0$, meaning thereby that the two eigen vector are orthogonal to each other and (*b*) sum of the eigen values is equal to the trace of A.

In some cases the length of the eigen vectors is made constant. The solution of any such case would require the following equations :

$$|A - \lambda I| X = 0$$

and $\quad X'X = \text{Constant}$

For example, in the above example, if the length of the eigen vector is predetermined as unity, the equations which we get for $\lambda = 3$ are

$$\begin{bmatrix} -1 & \sqrt{2} \\ \sqrt{2} & -2 \end{bmatrix} \begin{bmatrix} x_1 \\ x_2 \end{bmatrix} = 0$$

and $\quad X_1^2 + x_2^2 = 1 \qquad$ Note that $(X'X = X_1^2 + x_2^2 .....)$

or $\quad -x_1 + \sqrt{2} x_2 = 0 \qquad$ ...(11.6)

$$\sqrt{2} x_1 - 2x_2 = 0 \qquad ...(11.7)$$

and $\quad X_1^2 + x_2^2 = 1 \qquad$ ...(11.8)

from (11.6) or (11.7) we get $x_1 = \sqrt{2} x_2$

Putting $\sqrt{2} x_2$ in place of x_1 in (11.8)

$$\left(\sqrt{2} x_2\right)^2 + x_2^2 = 1$$

$$\text{or } 3x^2_2 = 1 \quad \text{or} \quad x_2 = \frac{1}{\sqrt{3}}$$

and so $$x_1 = \sqrt{2}x_2 = \frac{\sqrt{2}}{\sqrt{3}}$$

similarly for $\lambda = 0$

The three equations we have are

$$2x_1 + \sqrt{2}x_2 = 0 \qquad ...(11.9)$$

$$\sqrt{2}x_1 + x_1 = 0 \qquad ...(11.10)$$

and $$x^2_1 + x^2_2 = 1 \qquad ...(11.11)$$

From equation (11.9) or (11.10)

we get $x_1 = \frac{-1}{\sqrt{2}}x_2$

Substituting this value in (11.11).

$$\left(\frac{-1}{\sqrt{2}}x_2\right)^2 + x_2^2 = 1$$

or $$\frac{1}{2}x^2{}_2 + x^2{}_2 = 1$$

or $$x_2 = \frac{\sqrt{2}}{\sqrt{3}}$$

and $$x_1 = \frac{-1}{\sqrt{2}} \times \frac{\sqrt{2}}{\sqrt{3}} = -\frac{1}{\sqrt{3}}$$

so the two characteristics vectors are

$$X_1 = \begin{bmatrix} \frac{\sqrt{2}}{\sqrt{3}} \\ \frac{1}{\sqrt{3}} \end{bmatrix} \qquad X_2 = \begin{bmatrix} -\frac{1}{\sqrt{3}} \\ \frac{\sqrt{2}}{\sqrt{3}} \end{bmatrix}$$

One can verify that both the vectors have unit length that $X'_1X_2 = O$ *i.e.*, the two vectors are still orthogonal to each other.

The characteristic roots and vectors have an important bearing on multivariate analysis, where at several times we get the final equation in the form of $AX = \lambda X$. Thus whenever in any exercise we reach at this step we can immediately apply the known properties and theorems of characteristics roots and vectors.

An important point to note here is that working out of the characteristics root and vectors for a symmetric matrix whose order is more than 2×2 matrix is only given above. The same principle is being applied for working out the characteristic roots and vectors for a matrix whose order is more than 2×2. A good number of such exercises are found in most of the good books on matrices.[1]

The important properties and theorems related to the characteristics roots and vectors are given below without their proof.

1. The number of characteristics roots and vectors of a symmetric matrix are equal to the number of rows or columns of the matrix. For example if we have a 5×5 matrix, it will have five different characteristic roots and vectors.

2. Sum of all the different values of the characteristic of the root of symmetric matrix is equal to the sum of the diagonal terms (trace) of the matrix.

3. All the characteristic vectors of a matrix are orthogonal.

4. If the characteristic root of a $n \times n$ matrix A has k equal values, there will be exactly k characteristic vectors, with the same characteristic value in any set of n orthogonal characteristic vectors.

5. The characteristic roots of a correlation matrix (which is a semi-positive definite matrix) are never negative.

6. The characteristic roots of a diagonal matrix are the element of its diagonal.

7. If the rank of a $n \times n$ symmetric matrix A is k, then at least n-k characteristic roots are zero.

8. Determinant of a $n \times n$ symmetric matrix is equal to the product of its eigen values.

1. Readers may refers to G, hadley : Op. cit. pp. 236-272.

12
MULTIVARIATE ANALYSIS

Multiple Linear Regression Analysis :

In Chapter V we have discussed the simple linear relationships between the two variables. As in Social Sciences any dependent variable is rarely explained by only one independent variable, the bivariate model has a limited scope. Thus, in order to have a better explanation of any dependent phenomenon, it is necessary to explain it by all of its possible explanatory variables for which the data is available.

Multiple linear regression analysis is an extension of the simple linear regression model. Its theoretical framework is discussed below in matrix notation.

Let there exist a linear relationship between a dependent variable Y and K-1 independent variables $X_2 X_3 \ldots X_k$ and a disturbance term U. This relationship between a set of such values can be written as

$$Y_i = \beta_1 + \beta_2 X_{2i} + \beta_3 X_{3i} + \ldots\ldots \beta_{ki} + U_i, \; i = 1, 2, \ldots\ldots n \qquad \ldots(12.1)$$

All these n equations can be written compactly in matrix notations as:

$$Y = X\beta + U \qquad \ldots(12.2)$$

$$\text{where } Y = \begin{bmatrix} Y_1 \\ Y_2 \\ \vdots \\ Y_n \end{bmatrix}, X = \begin{bmatrix} 1 & X_{21} & X_{31\ldots} & X_{k1} \\ 1 & X_{22} & X_{32} & X_{k2} \\ & \vdots & \vdots & \vdots \\ 1 & X_{2n} & X_{3n} & X_{kn} \end{bmatrix}, \beta = \begin{bmatrix} \beta_1 \\ \beta_2 \\ \vdots \\ \beta_k \end{bmatrix} \text{ and } U = \begin{bmatrix} U_1 \\ U_2 \\ \vdots \\ U_k \end{bmatrix} \qquad \ldots(12.3)$$

Note that because β_1, the intercept has no variable units are inserted in the first column of X, All other columns of X show the n values of K–i independent variables.

The true values of these β coefficients are not possible to work out because; (a) we do not know the disturbance term U, and (b) our data have several kinds of limitations. If we apply the principle of least squares to estimate the β coefficient of (12.1), we get

$$\hat{\beta} = (X'X)^{-1} X'Y \qquad (12.4)$$

Where $\hat{\beta}$ is a column vector of estimates of β. These estimates are the best linear unbiased estimates[1] of β, provided that the random element U fulfils the following assumptions. These assumptions have also been discussed in chapter V on simple linear regression analysis.

Assumption :

1. Mean of random term, $\bar{U} = 0$
2. Any random term U_i is independent of any other random term U_j.
3. Varience of U is constant (also know as condition of homoscedasticity)
4. The independent variable have no exact linear relationship among them - selves *i.e.* rank of X is k.

Once the values of β are estimated, its significance can be tested provided that the random term is normally distributed. The standard errors of β required in significance test are given by :

Var $\left(\hat{\beta}\right) = \sigma u^2 (X'X)^{-1}$, and so $t_i = \dfrac{\beta_i}{S.E.\ (\beta_i)}$ will follow the 't' distribution with $(n - k)$ degress of freedom. Here σu is a constant which, when multiplied by the first diagonal terms of $\sqrt{(X'X)^{-1}}$ gives the square of S.E. of $\hat{\beta}_1$, second diagonal term will give the square of S.E. of $\hat{\beta}_2$ and third diagonal term will correspond to square of S.E. of $\hat{\beta}_3$ and so on.

Also, unbiased estimate of σu^2 is $\dfrac{Y'Y - \hat{\beta} X'Y}{n-k}$

Example

Given

Y	X_1	X_2
3	2	1
2	2	2
9	6	3
5	4	4
1	1	2

Fit a regression line of Y on X_1 and X_2 and carry out the test of significance of the regression coefficients.

---

1. These are the statistical properties of a good estimate for a detailed discussion on them lease refer to Hoel, P.G. Introduction to Mathematical Statistics, John Wiley and Sons, 1954 pp. 228-240 and J.J Johnston, Econometric Methods, Mc-Graw-Hill, New York, 1960, pp. 121-169.

Solution :

$$X'X = \begin{bmatrix} 1 & 1 & 1 & 1 & 1 \\ 2 & 2 & 6 & 4 & 1 \\ 1 & 2 & 3 & 4 & 2 \end{bmatrix} \times \begin{bmatrix} 1 & 2 & 1 \\ 1 & 2 & 2 \\ 1 & 6 & 3 \\ 1 & 4 & 4 \\ 1 & 1 & 2 \end{bmatrix} = \begin{bmatrix} 5 & 15 & 12 \\ 15 & 61 & 42 \\ 12 & 42 & 34 \end{bmatrix}$$

$$(X'X)^{-1} = \begin{bmatrix} 1.3135 & -.0254 & -.4322 \\ -.0254 & .1101 & -.1271 \\ -.4322 & -.1271 & .3389 \end{bmatrix}$$

$$X'Y = \begin{bmatrix} 1 & 1 & 1 & 1 & 1 \\ 2 & 2 & 6 & 4 & 1 \\ 1 & 2 & 3 & 4 & 2 \end{bmatrix} \times \begin{bmatrix} 3 \\ 2 \\ 9 \\ 5 \\ 1 \end{bmatrix} = \begin{bmatrix} 20 \\ 85 \\ 56 \end{bmatrix}$$

$$\hat{\beta} = (X'X)^{-1} X'Y = \begin{bmatrix} 1.3135 & -.0254 & -.4322 \\ -.0254 & .1101 & -.1271 \\ -.4322 & -.1271 & .3389 \end{bmatrix} \begin{bmatrix} 20 \\ 85 \\ 56 \end{bmatrix} = \begin{bmatrix} -.0922 \\ 1.7329 \\ -.4690 \end{bmatrix}$$

Thus the equation of the regression line of Y on X_1 and X_2 is

$$Y = -.0922 + 1.7329X_1 - .4690X_2$$

For working out the standard erros of β values we need σu^2 as given below :

$$\sigma u^2 = \frac{Y'Y - \hat{\beta} X'Y}{n-k}$$

$$Y'Y = \begin{bmatrix} 3 & 2 & 9 & 5 & 1 \end{bmatrix} \begin{bmatrix} 3 \\ 2 \\ 9 \\ 5 \\ 1 \end{bmatrix} = 120$$

$$\hat{\beta} X'Y = \begin{bmatrix} -.0922 & 1.7329 & -.4690 \end{bmatrix} \begin{bmatrix} 20 \\ 85 \\ 56 \end{bmatrix} = 119.1885$$

Thus $\quad \sigma u^2 = \dfrac{120 - 119.1885}{5-3} = \dfrac{.8115}{2} = 0.4057$

$$S.E.\left(\hat{\beta}\right) = \sqrt{3.4057\left(X'X\right)^{-1}}$$

$$\text{S.E.}\left(\hat{\beta}_1\right) = \sqrt{0.4057 \times 1.3135} = 0.73, \qquad t = \frac{\beta_1}{\text{S.E.}\left(\hat{\beta}_1\right)} = \frac{.0922}{0.73} = -0.1263$$

$$\text{S.E.}\left(\hat{\beta}_2\right) = \sqrt{0.4057 \times .1101} = 0.2114, \qquad t_2 = \frac{\beta_2}{\text{S.E.}\left(\hat{\beta}_2\right)} = \frac{1.7329}{0.2114} = 8.197$$

$$\text{S.E.}\left(\hat{\beta}_3\right) = \sqrt{0.4057 \times 0.3389} = 0.3708, \qquad t_3 = \frac{\beta_3}{\text{S.E.}\left(\hat{\beta}_3\right)} = \frac{-.4690}{03.708} = -1.2648$$

The tabulated value of t for $(n\text{-}k)$ *i.e.* 2 degrees of freedom at 1% level of significance is 6.965, and at 5% level of significance is 2.920. Thus $\hat{\beta}_2$ is statistically significant even at 1% level of significance. Other values of $\hat{\beta}$ are statistically insignificant *i.e.* the population values of $\hat{\beta}_1$ (the intercept) and $\hat{\beta}_3$ may be considered as zero.

A summary statistic R^2, the coefficient of determination, measuring the proportion of the total variations of y accounted for by the linear relationship fitted, often serves a useful purpose. The formula for working out R^2 is

$$R^2 = \frac{\hat{\beta} X'Y - \dfrac{(\Sigma Y)^2}{n}}{Y'Y - \dfrac{(\Sigma Y)^2}{n}}$$

where $\hat{\beta} X'Y - \frac{(\Sigma Y)^2}{n}$ = Explained sum of squares

and $Y'Y - \frac{(\Sigma Y)^2}{n}$ = Total sum of Squares

The null hypothesis that $\hat{\beta}_1 = \hat{\beta}_2 = \hat{\beta}_3 = ... \hat{\beta}_k = 0$ can also be tested by the F- ratio test given in the following form of the analysis of variance.

Analysis of Variance Table

Source of Variation	Sum of Squares	D.F.	Mean S.S.	F-ratio
Regression explained	$\hat{\beta} XY - \frac{(\Sigma Y)^2}{n} = A$	k–1	$\frac{A}{K-1} = P$	$F = P/Q$ $(K–1\ n–k)\ d.f.$
Residual	$Y'Y - \hat{\beta} X'Y = H$	n–k	$\frac{H}{n-k} = Q$	
Total	$Y'Y - \frac{(\Sigma Y)^2}{n}$	n–1		

This analysis of variance is equalent to the test of significance of R^2, as the F value given above can also be worked out as :

$$F = \frac{R^2/(k-1)}{(1-R^2)/(n-k)} \text{ for } (k-1, n-k)\ d.f.$$

Here if the value of F is insignificant, the explanatory power of the whole model is almost nil or in other words the population values of all the regression coefficients are zero i.e. $\hat{\beta}^1 = \hat{\beta}^2 = \hat{\beta}^3 = ... = \hat{\beta} = 0$. However, a significant value of F will suggest rejection of the above statement.

The values of R^2 in two problems of multiple regresions, having unequal numbers of observations and unequal numbers of variables cannot be compared because of the obvious reason. To make them comparable in such situations, the R^2 is adjusted for degrees of freedom and is denoted by $\bar{R}^2$ as given below :

$$\bar{R}^2 = 1 - \frac{n-1}{n-k}(1-R^2)$$

It is important to note that in the above formula, if k increases $(1–R^2)$ decreases, as R will increase with k. At the same time an incraese in k causes a decrease in $(n–1/n–k)$. Thus on R^2, the increase in the value of k has an inverse effect because of $(n–1/n–k)$ and has positive effect because of $(1–R^2)$. If the positive effect of an additional variable is more than its negative effect, the value of

$\bar{R}^2$ will increase. The value of $\bar{R}^2$, however, will decrease in the reverse case.

A full mathematically derivation of the concepts given above is given by Johnston (1960), Rao and Miller (1972) and Koutsoyiannis (1973).

Example

The concept of *F*-test, R^2 and $\bar{R}^2$ are further explained below, using the data in the last example.

Total Sum of Squares $= Y'Y - \frac{(\Sigma Y)^2}{n} = 120 - \frac{20 \times 20}{5} = 40$

Explained Sum of Squares $= \hat{\beta}' X'Y - \frac{(\Sigma Y)^2}{n} = 119.1885 - \frac{20 \times 20}{5}$

$= 119.1885 - 80.00 = 39.1885$

$$R^2 = \frac{39.1885}{40} = 0.9797$$

Thus a very large proportion of variations in *Y i.e.* 97.27% is being explained by these two variables only.

Analysis of Variance

Source	Sum of Squares	D.F.	Mean S.S.	F
Regression (Explained)	39.1885	3–1=2	19.5942	$F = \frac{19.5942}{0.4054}$ $= 48.3$
Residual	0.8115	5–3=2	0.4047	(2, 2) *d.f.*
Total	40.000	5–1 = 4		

$$\text{Also } F = \frac{R^2 / K-1}{\left(1-R^{2/n-k}\right)} = \frac{.9797/3-1}{(1.9797)/5-3} = \frac{.9797/2}{.0203} = 48.3$$

Note that both the values of *F* are same. As this value of *F* is significant at 1% level of significance all the population regression coefficients are not zero (*i.e.* the null hypothesis that $\beta_1 = \beta_1 = \beta = ...\beta_k = 0$ is rejected).

$$\text{Also } \bar{R}^2 = 1 - \frac{n-1}{n-k}\left(1-R^2\right) = 1 - \frac{5-1}{5-3}(1-.9797)$$

$$= 1 - \frac{4}{2} \times 0.0203 = 1 - .0406 = 0.9494$$

Problem of Multicollinearity

The assumption 4 of general linear model given above says that all the explanatory variables should be independent of each other. The reason for this assumption is that if some or all the independent variables are perfectly correlated the matrix $X'X$ cannot be inverted as in such case determinant of $X'X = 0$. A less extreme, but still very serious case arises when some or all of the explanatory variables are highly but not perfectly correlated.

In such cases the standard error of one of the two highly correlated variables will be over estimated and the standard error of the other variable will be under estimated. Hence the test of significance of their regression coefficient becomes unreliable and the analysis collapses.

This problem of inter-correlations among a set of independent variables is known as multicollinearity and is very frequently found in social variables. Thus in any problem of multiple regression analysis the researcher should be very careful about the presence of multicollinearity in the data and its consequences. In case the two or more variables are intercorrelated the safest solution is to replace one or few of them by some other variables which are independent. The regression analysis of a problem with multicollinearity is not however so simple. Here we have simply warned about the problem, as a detailed discussion on it is beyond the scope of this book.[1] Stepwise regression analysis as discussed below may sometimes help in handling it.

Stepwise Regression Analysis :

Whenever a multiple regression analysis is attempted, it is useful to know as to how the parameters get changed when new variables are added or substracted, one by one in the model. This procedure helps us in many ways.

Firstly, it tells us the contribution of an added or deleted variable in explaining the dependent variable (by seeing the changes in the value of R^2). Secondly, it helps to see whether the variable is worth including in the model or not (by seeing the changes in the value of $\bar{R}^2$). It also helps us in keeping a watch over the changes in the values of the regression coefficient and their standard errors. Such a useful procedure is known as stepwise regression analysis and is becoming increasingly popular among the social scientists. It may be forward or backward.

To explain as to how all these concepts of regression analysis (including the stepwise method) may be used in a real problem, a few results borrowed from Subbiah's[2] work are given below.

While explaining the agricultural productivity (in Rs. per hectare) of the districts of Tamil Nadu, the variables chosen by him in the forward approach are :

1. Value of agricultural produce in Rs. per hectare (Y)
2. Annual average rainfall in cms. (X_1)
3. Percentage of gross irrigated area to total geographical area (X_2)
4. Consumption of fertilizers per 100 hectare (X_3)

---

1. For a good discussion on multicollinearity, please refer to J. Johnston, Op. cit. pp. 159-168 and A Koutsoyiannis, A. Theory of Econometrices, Macmillan, 1973, pp. 225-249.
2. S. Subbiah : Environmental Technological and Institutional Determinants of Agricultural Productivity in Tamil Nadu Unpublished M. Phil dissertation, 1975. Centre for the Study of Regional Development, Jawaharlal Nehru University, New Delhi.

5. Number of Tractors per hectare of cropped area (X_4)
6. Percentage of agricultural workers (X_5)
7. Percentage of rural S.C. & S.T. population to total rural population (X_6)

The regression of Y on X is given in the first step for the independent variable that gives the maximum R^2. In the second step the variable which gives next highest value of R^2 is added into the previous regression equation. Any variable having high correlation with the previous variable (s) will aslo give a high value of R^2 but will not be included in the next step due to the fact that its part of explanation has already been explained by similar variable (s). Likewise the variables are added one by one and the entire analysis is carried out for each step. These results are given below :

Correlation Matrix

Y	X_1	X_2	X_3	X_4	X_0	X_6
1	18048	.44021	.37104	.1481	.72488	03006
	1	.82633	.19334	-.03104	.43557	31805
		1	.28924	-.04711	.73348	.49649
			1	.69438	.07365	.52376
				1	.3696	.54976
					1	.04393
						1

Results of Stepwise Regression Analysis

Variables	Regression Coefficient	S.E.	t	R^2	Increase in R^2	$\bar{R}^2$	F
Step 1							
x_5	7.363	2.122	3.328*	0.525		0.525	11.072*
Step 2							
x_5	6.689	1.475	4.535*				
x_3	36.306	10.559	.3438*	0.794	0.269	0.773	17.438*
Step 3							
x_5	9.570	1.723	5.554*				
x_3	43.484	9.159	4.747*	0.878	0.084	0.850	19.229
x_2	-2.480	1.060	-2.340**				
Step 4							
x_5	8.511	1.980	4.299*				
x_3	54.479	13.789	3.951*	0.895	0.017	0.855	14.927*
x_2	-2.363	1.058	-2.234**				
x_4	-9.780	9.223	-1.050				
Step 5							
x_5	7.804	2.387	3.269**				
x_3	55.201	14.514	3.803**				
x_2	-1.684	1.583	-1.064	0.901	0.006	0.843	10.925**
x_4	-7.744	10.250	-.756				

x_6	-1.913	3.181	-.601				
Step 6							
x_5	6.339	3.176	1.996				
x_3	55.355	15.096	3.667**				
x_2	0.404	3.268	0.124	0.910	0.009	0.835	8.508**
x_4	-6.822	-10.733	0.636				
x_6	-3.658	-4.063	0.900				
x_1	-0.906	-1.225	0.740				

* Significant at 1% level of significance (P<.01)
** Significant at 5% level of significance (P<.05)

The above results show that labour force (X_9) explains the maximum proportion of variations in agricultural productivity followed by fertilizer (X_3), irrigation (X_2), mechanisation (X_4) proportion of Scheduled Castes and Tribes (X_6) and the rainfall (X_1). The contribution of mechanisation, Scheduled Caste and Tribes and rainfall is however very low in increasing the value of R^2, as is clear from the column showing the difference in R^2, caused by each of them. A study of $\bar{R}^2$, however, shows that though the contribution of mechanisation is very poor in R^2 but it can be retained in the analysis as it has contributed a marginal increase in $\bar{R}^2$. The value of $\bar{R}^2$ decreases as S.C. and S.T. (X_6) and rainfall (X_1) are added into the model. This shows that their contribution in increasing the value of R^2 is not strong enough to counterbalance the reverse effect on the explanatory power of the model due to increase in the degrees of freedom (*n-k*). Hence, it is better not to carry out the analysis beyond the 4th step. In most of the computer packages, the option is given to include a variable only when its contribution to R^2 is by more than a specified value say 5 per cent (0.05).

The regression coefficients from step 1 to step 4 show a consistently significant values for labour force, and consumption of fertilizers at 1% level of significance. The regression coefficient of irrigation is, however, significant only at 5% level of significance as found in step 3 and 4. After step 4, the significance of regression coefficients do not remain consistent.

The value of *F*-ratio also becomes less significant after step 4. Thus the relationship as given in step 4 may be identified as an optimal fit. The results given in this step show that agricultural labour and consumption of fertilizers are the significant variables. The average change in agricultural production per hectare (*Y*) caused by a unit change in percentage of agricultural workers and in consumption of fertilizers per 100 acres is Rs. 8.511 and Rs. 54.479 respectively. Another significant regression coefficient (at 5% level) is that of irrigation which is consistently negative in 3rd and 4th steps. Further explanations have to be found for this, because usually irrigation is expected to have a positive effect on agricultural production. The last variable given in the 4th step is number of tractors per hectare of cropped area which is insignificant, and remains so in all the subsequent steps.

An important point at this stage is to note that as the analysis moves from step 4 to step 6, a sudden fall in the significant regression coefficient is observed. The probable reason of this could be a high correlation (.82633) between irrigation (X_2) and rainfall (X_1). This multicollinearity has disturbed the standard errors to a greater extent. As a consequence, the regression coefficient have become insignificant in step 6, though these regression coefficient are not different from those given in step 4.

Principal Component Analysis

Geographers are becoming increasingly interested in describing a complex spatial structure of a large number of socio-economic and other variables through some smaller number of underlying dimensions. In several studies, for example, the differentials in larger number of variables are described in terms of some directly unobservable dimensions like urbanization, industrialization and agricultural developments, etc. These underlying dimensions are extracted from the given set of structural variables on the basis of inter - correlations among them. The work of Mooser and Scott (1961), Soja (1968), and Berry (1970) etc. may be referred to in this connection.

The principal component analysis — a branch of factor analysis — is a technique designed primarily to synthesize a large number of variables into a smaller number of general components, which retain the maximum amount of descriptive ability. It permits a more economical description of the given set of structural variables and suggest some underlying dimensions (components), accounting for the statistical relationship among them. Morrison (1967) has described it as a method to discover those hidden factors which might have generated the dependence or covariance among the variables.

Principal component analysis essentially requires an orthogonal transformation of a set of inter-related structral variables into a new set of independent variables.

The mathematical formulation of the principal component analysis as developed by Hotelling (1933) is given below in a summary form.

Let $X = (X_1X_2.......X_p)$ be a set of p - vectors of standardized random variables having a good intercorrelations among them. The principal components of these p variables are such linear combinations of them which gives the maximum variance.

Thus, if this required linear function is

$$Y = a_1X_1 + a_2X_2 + ...+ a_pX_p,$$

the coefficient vector $a' = (a_1\ a_2..........a_p)$ must be such that :

(i) $S^2y = a'\,Sa$, (*i.e.* the variance of y) is maximum for all values of a and

(ii) $a'a = 1$ (a normalisation condition, only for the sake of mathematical convenience)

Where S is the variance - covariance matrix[1] of X and S^2y is the variance of Y.

---

1. A variance-covariance matrix, of the variables $x_1, x_2......x_N$ is a matrix whose diagonal elements show their variance and the off diagonal term Sij show the covariance between the variables xi and xj. These covariances are given by :

$$Sij = \frac{\Sigma(xi - \overline{xi})(xj - \overline{xj})}{n}$$

The objective of a principal Component analysis is to find out the values of the coefficient vector a' = (a_1, a_2.............a_p) which satisfies both the conditions given above.

The mathematical solution of this problem shows that '*a*' is one of the *p*-eigen vectors (normalised to unity) of the matrix of inter-correlations, *R*, among the original variables (X_1X_2.......X_p). It is important to note that as there are *p*-eigen vectors, the number of components derived in this way are exactly equal to the number of original variables *p*, and the original total variance[1] *p*, associated with (X_1X_2.....X_p) is preserved exactly in the total variance of the components (Y_1Y_2.........Y_p). The solution however, suggest that the variance of a component is equal to the eigen value (λ_i) of the eigen vector used for it. The descriptive power of each component is expressed as the ratio $\frac{\lambda_i}{p}$. The component which corresponds to the highest eigen value is known as the first principal component. The principal components which correspond to 2nd highest, 3rd highest, 4th highest........ and to the last eigen values are known as second, third, fourth and the *p*th principal components.[2] These principal components are statistically independent of each other.

It is generally found that only a few principal components having higher variances explain major portion of the total variance *p*. The rest of the principal components do not explain much of the total variations, because of their smaller variances. If we retain *r* such principal components corresponding to first *r* eigen values $\lambda_1\lambda_2$......λ_r (r<p) their descriptive ability is measured by the proportion :

$$\frac{\lambda_1 + \lambda_2 + \dots\dots\dots + \lambda_r}{p}$$

and is known as cumulative proportion of variations reflected by r principal components.

Factor Loadings

If the *p* elements of an eigen vector, corresponding to the eigen value λ_i and normalised to unity, are multiplied by $\sqrt{\lambda_i}$, they become the coefficients of correlation of the *i*th principal component with each of the *p* variables. These coefficients of correlation are also known as factor loadings. By inspecting the factor loadings of any principal component one can find out the variables having high correlations with that component. These correlations are used in interpreting a particular principal component and in giving any suitable name to it as an underlying dimension.

Thus, the steps required in any principal component analysis are :

1. Prepare an inter-correlation matrix *R* from the *p* variables given in the data matrix.
2. Work out the eigen values of *R*, normalised to unity and arrange them in descending order. Let these values be $\lambda_1 > \lambda_2 > \lambda_3 \dots\dots\dots > \lambda_p$.

---

1. Because x_1x_2...........x_N are *p* standardized variables each having zero mean and unit variance the sum of their variances is 1+1+............+1 (*p*-times) = *p*.
2. Note that the sum of their variance is $\lambda 1 + \lambda 2$...............λN = p, as we know that the sum of the eigen values of a matrix is equal to the trace of the matrix and the trace of a correlation matrix is p.

3. Take first few values of λ3 (say r values), find out the proportion

$$\frac{\lambda_1+\lambda_2+......+\lambda_r}{P}$$

If this value is satisfactory, say more than 70 per cent[1]. (it may vary from problem to problem) find out the eigen vectors corresponding to these eigen values.

4. Convert the original variables into standard scores and using the elements given in first eigen vector as weights, get the weighted sum of the standardized scores for each observation. The values so obtained are the scores of the first principal component. Similarly using the other eigen vectors the scores of 2nd, 3rd...and rth principal components can be worked out.

5. Multiply each eigen vector, used above, by the square root of their corresponding eigen values and give them as factor loadings.

To explain the whole procedure as given above, an exercise of a principal component analysis is given below with internediate results.

Example

In order to identify the dimensions along which the spatial variations in the economy of Rajasthan in 1970-71, can be studied, the varibales chosen are :

1. Net cropped area per agricultural workers (x_1).
2. Percentage of irrigated area to net cropped area (x_2).
3. Percentage of net cropped area to total geographical area (x_3).
4. Percentage of area under commercial crops to net cropped area (x_4).
5. Number of workers in registered factories per 10000 workers (x_5).
6. Number of workers in manufacturing (other than the registered factories) per 10000 workers (x_6).
7. Urban population per 10000 population (x_7).
8. Number of workers in trade and commerce per 10000 workers (x_8).
9. Number of registered vehicles per 1000000 population (x_9).
10. Length of railways per 10000 square Km. (x_{10}).
11. Length of roads per 10000 sq. Km. (x_{11}).
12. Number of beds in the hospitals per 1000000 persons (x_{12}).
13. Per capita consumption of electricity (x_{13}).
14. Percentage of literate to total population (x_{14}).

The data of these variables is given in Table 12.1.

1. Another simpler criterion as suggested by Kaiser is to retian all those eigen vectors whose eigen values are more than unity, see M.F. Kaiser, : "The Application of Electronic Computers for Factor Analysis", Educational Psychological Measurement, 1960, pp. 141-151.

The matrix of inter correlations, R, among them is worked out through the computer and is given below in Table 12.2.

The eigen values of the matrix R, have been worked out, in the second step. These 14 eigen values given in descending order are 5.6135, 3.1503, 1.7392, 1.0153, 0.6056, 0.4429, .4097, .3004, .2336, .2074, .0872, .0796, .0691 and .0454. Considering the 4th eigen value 1.0153 as almost unity, there are only three eigen values clearly greater than unity as 5.6135, 3.1503 and 1.7392. These eigen values account for $\frac{5.6135+3.1503+1.7392}{14}$ x100=75.01 per cent of the total variations in the data matrix.

The eigen vectors corresponding to the three eigen values given above, normalised to unify are given in Table 12.3. For working out the scores of first, second and third principal components, the 14 elements of each of the three eigen vectors are used as weights of the standardised values of the given 14 variables in the data matrix.

Multiplying each element of these eigen vectors by the square root of their eigen values, we get the factor loadings. These factor loading are also given in Table 12.3.

Table 12.3

Variables	Eigen vector normalised to unity			Factor Loadinds		
	I	II	III	I	II	III
1. x_1	0.9947	-.49757	.04521	.23567	-.88315*	.05962
2. x_2	.4910	.44687	-.08449	.11632	.79315*	-.11142
3. x_3	.05970	-.12301	-.63678	.14415	-.21834	-.83978*
4. x_4	-.11198	.45733	.05669	-.26532	.81172*	.07476
5. x_5	.35123	.17203	.11740	.83217*	.30534	.15482
6. x_6	.33373	.09302	-.24001	.79070*	.16510	-.31652
7. x_7	.37776	-.14189	.15714	.89501*	.25184	.20724
8. x_8	.38511	-.00828	.02318	91244*	-.01470	.03057
9. x_9	.30283	-.04183	-.01241	71749*	-.07425	-.01637
10. x_{10}	-18496	-.00961	-.60935	.43822	-.01706	-.80360*
11. x_{11}	.00606	.45164	-.03779	.01435	.80162*	-.04983
12. x_{12}	.31579	.08513	-.32590	74820*	-.15110	-.42979
13. x_{13}	.27345	.22710	.07787	.64788*	.40308	.10269
14. x_{14}	.38129	.07325	.01856	.90338*	.13002	.02447
Eigen Values	5.6135	3.1503	1.7392	5.6135	3.1503	1.7392
%Variance	40.09	22.50	12.42	40.09	22.50	12.42

*Significant at 1% level of significance.

Table 12.1
Data Matrix

District	x_1	x_2	x_3	x_4	x_5	x_6	x_7	x_8	x_9	x_{10}	x_{11}	x_{12}	x_{13}	x_{14}
Ajmer	1.7	2.03	48.7	13.6	383	212	656	3765	4701	201	1914	1791	74	30.3
Alwar	1.7	18.4	64.8	18.4	17	167	912	384	2480	156	1623	455	11	19.2
Banswara	1.2	5.6	39.8	25.2	7	87	507	242	851	0	1449	509	7	12.4
Barmer	5.4	0.8	44.9	1.1	23	89	726	279	1160	180	473	170	3	10.6
Bharatpur	1.5	25.1	65.7	20.8	67	161	1376	349	2823	309	1830	501	13	19.0
Bhilwara	0.9	40.9	31.2	26.8	99	159	1103	309	1389	85	1089	261	47	15.1
Bikaner	6.2	0.2	23.5	0.7	169	216	4138	675	5231	75	409	2214	59	25.8
Bundi	2.1	41.4	39.7	11.8	125	208	1461	315	1499	108	1416	350	78	16.0
Chittorgarh	1.2	26.9	33.3	29.5	37	158	1036	303	858	117	948	254	31	17.5
Churu	5.8	0.2	73.1	0.2	11	199	2959	444	1157	229	521	520	7	19.0
Dungarpur	0.9	10.2	32.3	5.5	10	107	589	270	773	122	1875	366	3	14.3
Ganganagar	4.3	40.5	64.8	10.1	130	245	1648	538	7559	260	708	303	25	20.2
Jaipur	1.8	25.0	59.3	8.0	204	345	3005	607	10316	318	1009	948	50	23.7
Jaisalmer	4.1	2.2	3.9	0.1	8	115	1450	267	3370	32	257	312	6	13.4
Jalore	4.1	5.0	66.8	6.3	9	127	443	384	750	119	721	231	3	10.1
Jhalawar	1.8	11.5	47.7	21.8	58	189	945	342	1087	52	1522	473	3	17.6
Jhunjhunu	2.7	2.9	76.6	0.9	35	183	1744	374	797	183	904	884	30	23.3
Jodhpur	4.8	2.2	52.1	3.9	175	232	3195	513	11167	156	857	1312	45	21.4
Kota	2.6	23.0	46.7	11.1	294	357	2405	593	7424	203	1386	547	147	25.3
Nagaur	3.4	1.6	69.9	6.2	74	146	1222	273	787	223	979	293	28	15.1
Pali	2.6	18.1	47.3	19.1	151	284	1118	483	1860	241	1338	525	7	17.2
Sawai Madhopur	1.6	18.5	47.6	14.5	57	166	1190	383	835	193	881	242	22	16.3
Sikar	2.7	6.4	71.4	1.4	4	271	1703	473	1673	326	1011	659	29	19.6
Sirobhi	2.0	24.8	31.2	13.2	16	234	1787	556	2074	125	1426	639	6	16.8
Tonk	2.8	15.3	63.4	8.1	14	242	1745	353	8708	124	900	379	5	15.4
Udaipur	0.8	33.6	20.8	16.1	77	182	1230	448	2777	148	1902	787	50	17.4

Table 12.1
Data Matrix

x_1	x_2	x_3	x_4	x_5	x_6	x_7	x_8	x_9	x_{10}	x_{11}	x_{12}	x_{13}	x_{14}
1	–.5778	.1558	–7200	–.0056	.0288	.4196	.2510	.2341	.600	–.7800	.2510	–.1371	.0383
	1	–.1741	.5839	.2863	.3002	–.1105	.1243	.1254	.1267	.4324	–.2015	.3906	.1146
		1	–.1969	–.0495	.2365	.0376	.0724	.0755	.6347	–.0405	–.1107	–.0911	.1643
			1	.0459	–.0967	–.3927	–.2188	–.2294	–.2206	.5485	–.2504	–.0461	–.1043
				1	.5804	.6635	.7023	.5429	.2559	.2320	.5945	.7630	.7624
					1	.5605	.7550	.6393	.5265	.4537	.3200	.5598	.6135
						1	.8043	.6162	.2463	–.1259	.8374	.4441	.8222
							1	.5954	.3853	.0264	.7356	.4596	.7990
								1	.2445	–.1349	–.4174	.3804	.5018
									1	.0558	.0268	.1575	.3820
										1	.4519	.2132	.1778
											1	.3014	.7638
												1	.5941
													1

Before working out the scores of the above three principal components, it is necessary to see that whether they can be interpreted as a meaningful dimension or not ? This interpretation part of the analysis is done through the factor loadings, which are the coefficients of correlation of a component with each of the given variables.

First Principal Component

The factor loadings of first principal component show that it has a significant positive correlation with workers in registered factories (X_5), workers in manufacturing (other than registered) (X_6), urban proportion (X_7), persons in trade and commerce (X_8), number of vehicles (X_9), number of beds in the hospital (X_{12}), consumption of electricity per capita (X_{13}), and the literacy (X_{14}). As these variables can be considered as the consequences of the industrialization and so this factor may be called as "Index of Industrial Development".

RAJASTHAN
SCORES OF FIRST PRINCIPAL COMPONENT - 1971
(Index of Industrial Development)

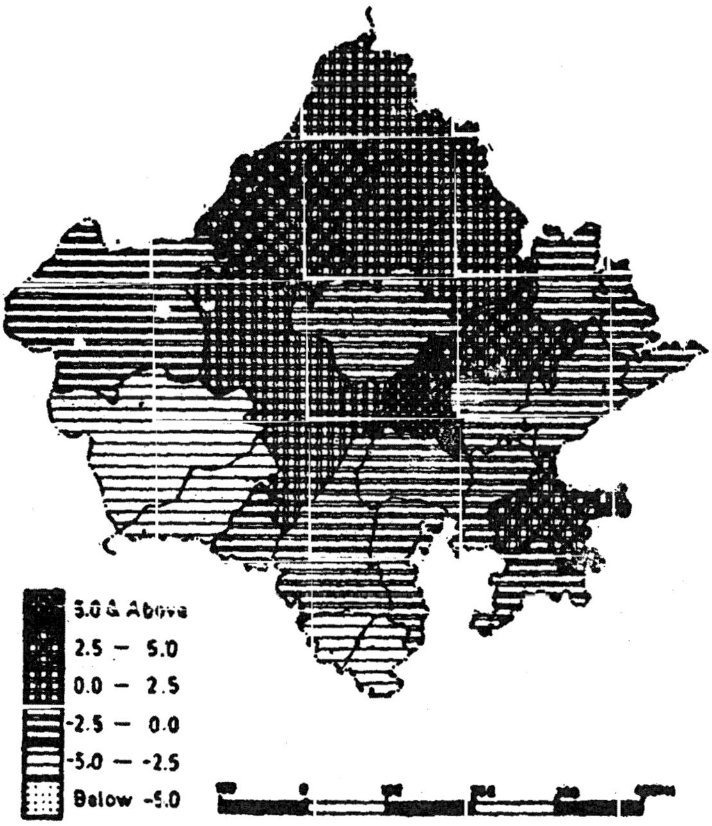

Fig. 12.1

RAJASTHAN
SCORES OF SECOND PRINCIPAL COMPONENT - 1971
(Index of Agricultural Development)

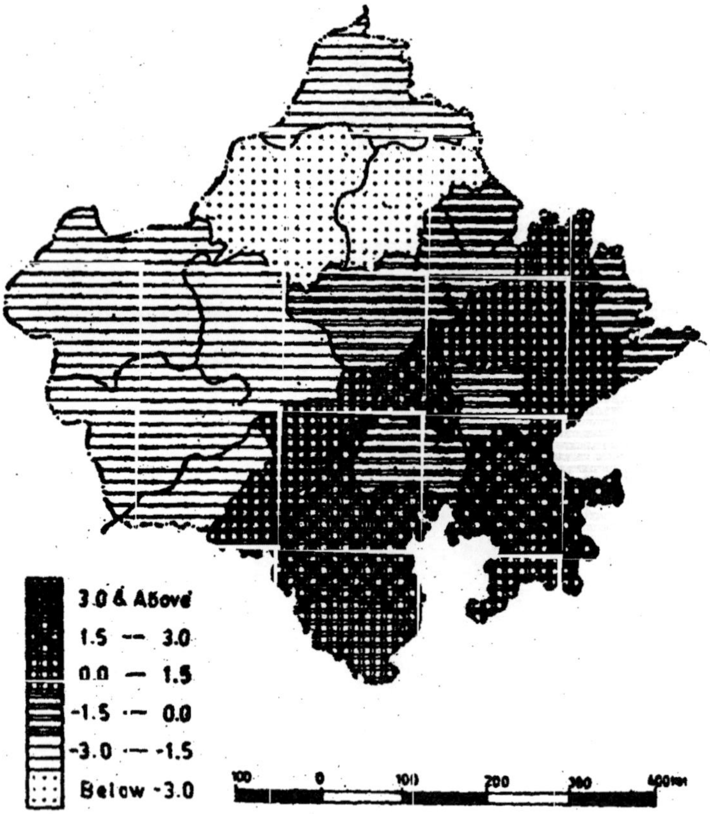

Fig. 12.2

Second Principal Component

The second principal component has positive significant correlation with irrigation (x_2), commercial cropping (x_4) and length of roads (x_{11}). It also has the negative significant correlation with per worker net cropped area (x_1). All these correlation indicates towards intensive cropping with good marketing facilities, suggesting a name for it as "Index of Agriculture Development".

Third Principal Component

The third principal component has only two significant negative correlations, with percentage of net cropped area to total geographical area (x_3) and length of railway per 10,000 sq. km. (x_{10}). Any factor based on its correlation with onnly a few variables, like here, can not be named precisely. However in the context of Rajasthan where topography is a major spatial variate, this factor may be

RAJASTHAN

SCORES OF THIRD PRINCIPAL COMPONENT - 1971

(Index of Physiographic Efficiency)

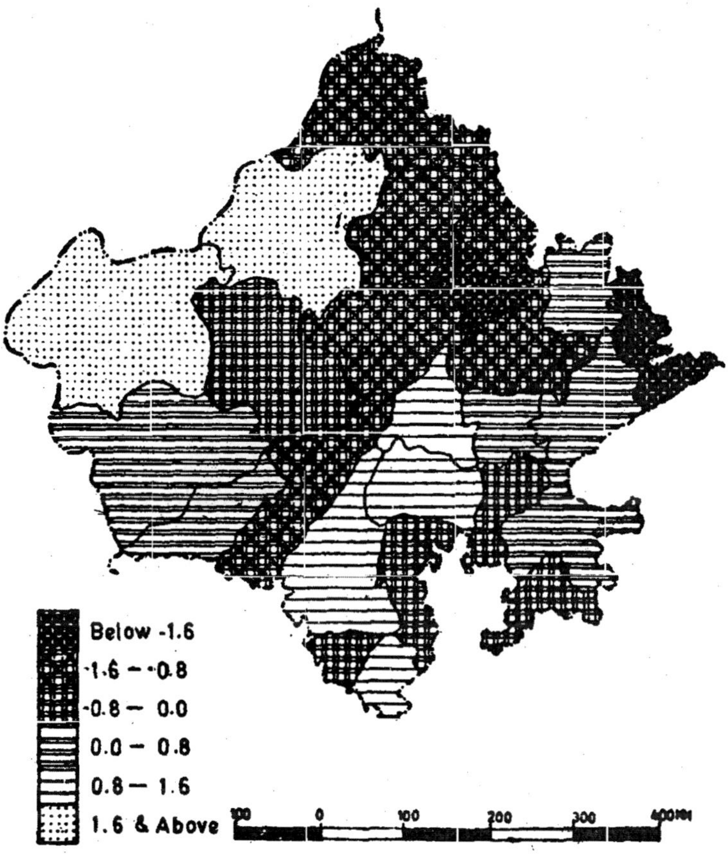

Fig. 12.3

named as "Index of Physiographic Inefficiency". In order to maintain the parity with the first two components we can call it as "Index of Physiographic Efficiency" also. But in this case, a higher value of the index will mean the lower efficiency and a lower value will show the higher physiographic efficiency. Thus the third principal component should be interpreted with extra care. If further precision in it is required, some new varibales should be added and the whole exercise should be repeated.

Once the number of principal component are chosen and their interpretation is also found theoretically consistent, the scores are worked out to see the position of each observation along these dimension (principal component). These scores are the weighted sum of the standarized scores of the given variables using the eigen value as weights.

The scores of the first three principal components in the present exercise have been worked out for all the districts and are given in Table 12.4.

The spatial variations in these three dimensions can also be shown by plotting these scores on the map. Figure No. 12.1, 12.2 and 12.3 show the values given in Table 12.4 on the map also.

Table 12.4
Scores of Principal Components

District	First Principal Component	Second Principal Component	Third Principal Component
1. Ajmer	5.168445	1.838338	1.273987
2. Alwar	-1.09266	.998635	-.002422
3. Banswara	-3.474585	.929030	1.525282
4. Barmer	-.607269	-2.850679	-.085956
5. Bharatpur	-.460891	1.606624	-1.813107
6. Bhilwara	-1.624433	2.553503	.91887
7. Bikaner	4.269229	-3.075681	3.338504
8. Bundi	-.360067	1.926189	.418784
9. Chittorgarh	-1.912324	1.799746	.622205
10. Churu	.443491	-3.307797	-1.158197
11. Dungarpur	-2.72910	.633815	.551027
12. Ganganagar	1.801503	-.163888	-1.683200
13. Jaipur	3.510901	.598643	-1.413757
14. Jaisalmer	-2.186483	-2.445210	2.505001
15. Jalore	-2.51270	-1.870447	-.597900
16. Jhalawar	-1.625572	1.003625	.614426
17. Jhunjhunu	.219083	-1.455950	-.879860
18. Jodhpur	2.423124	-1.801172	.494612
19. Kota	4.672642	1.871937	-.189774
20. Nagaur	-1.352070	-1.268463	-1.240544
21. Pali	.302488	.878744	-.911293
22. Sawai Madhopur	-1.356166	.415890	-45092
23. Sikar	.792264	-1.167644	-2.278125
24. Sirohi	-.143730	.741659	.591355
25. Tonk	-.004478	-.906423	.731278
26. Udaipur	.160628	2.516977	1.039154

Discriminant Analysis :

Identification of the significant regional variations among different socio - economic, demographic and other variables has always been an important concern of the regional geographers. Thus, given a set of well defined regions (or group of observation) it is worthwhile to study the direction or dimension along which major regional (or group) differential occur.

Regional analysts have recently started using discriminant analysis for tackling such problems. It identifies the dimensions along which the variations of the variables between the groups (regions) are maximum compared to their variations within the groups (regions). It also gives the intensity with which each variable tend to differ between the groups.

Before going into mathematical formulation of discriminant analysis, it will be helpful if the concepts of matrices sum of square of variables, within the groups (W) and between the groups (B) are discussed first, as below.

Let X_{ki} be the vector (set of values) of ith observation in kth group, k=1,2,........g; m_k be the vector of means in kth group and m be the vector of grand means (means of each variable for all the group observations). The matrices W and B, defined above are given by[1] :

$$B=\sum N_k\left(m_k-m\right)\left(m_k-m\right)'$$

$$W=\sum_{K-1}^{g}\sum_{i=1}^{N_k}\left(X_{ki}-m_k\right)\left(X_{ki}-m_k\right)'$$

Where N_k is the number of observations in kth group.

Now, suppose that a set of p vectors of variables X_1X_2..........X_p is given for well defined k groups (may be regions) and kth group has N_k observations. The problem of discriminant analysis amounts to finding out the dimension along which there is maximum inter-group variability among these variables compared to their with in group variability.

Let us assume that this required dimension is of the following linear form.[2]

$$Y=V_1X_1+V_2X_2+............+V_pX_p$$

A vector of weights $V'=(v_1v_2........v_p)$ may be derived which maximizes the discriminant criterion R, given as :

$$R=\frac{\text{Between group variability in Y}}{\text{With in group variability in Y}}$$

Statistically it has been shown that maximizing R is equivalent to maximizing

---

1. For a detailed discussion please refer to : W.W. Cooley, and P.R. Lohnes : *Multivariate Data Analysis,* Willey & Sons, New York pp. 224-226; 1971.
2. As the geometric concept of dimension or direction is closely related to the algebric notion of linear combination, please refer to Maurice, M. Tatsuoka, *Multivariate Analysis,* Willey & Sons. New York p. 157, 1971.

$$\lambda = \frac{V'BV}{V'WV} \qquad \text{....(2)}$$

With respect to vector V. The solution of this maximization problem gives λ as the eigen value of the non - symmetric matrix $W^{-1}B$ and vector $V' = (V_1 V_2 .... V_p)$, as the eigen vector[1] corresponding to the eigen value of λ.

To test whether the overall between group variability in the given variables is significantly greater than the within group variability, the F. ratio as given below can be used.

$$F = \frac{V'BV/(K-1)}{V'WV/(N-1)} = \frac{\lambda(N-K)}{(K-1)}$$

For $(K-1, N-K)$ degrees of freedom

Where total number of observations,

$$N = N_1 + N_2 + ...N_k$$

If F-ratio is found significant, the higher between group variability in the variables is ensured.

The elements of vector $V' = (V_1 V_2 .... V_p)$ may also be taken to indicate the intensity with which the corresponding variables have group differentials.

To illustrate the use of discriminant analysis in geography, the intermediate results of Aslam's work are given below :[2]

While deriving the basic stimulants of migration among Indian cities he took its 18 socio-economic and demographic indicators. Applying principal component analysis he extracted six principal components explaining about 82 per cent of the total variations. The name given to these six principal components are :

1. Long distance industrial pull (X_1)
2. Youthfulness of migrants (X_2)
3. Rural push with weak industrial pull (X_3)
4. Short distance industrial pull (X_4)
5. Old age/Return migration (X_5)
6. Service Pull (X_6)

To test the hypothesis that the intensity of the overall operation of these six factors vary from the cities of one type of dominant economic functions to another, he used the scores of these six

1. For derivation please refer to M.M. Tatsouka, op. cit. pp. 157-161.
2. Aslam Mahmood. "Patterns of Migration into Indian Cities–A Multivariate Analysis", *The Manpower Journal,* Vol. XI, No. 2, July-Sept. 1975, Institute of Applied Manpower Research, New Delhi.

components as variables (p=6). He further divided the cities into four groups (K=4) of different functional types as :

1. Cities with dominant industrial functions and low service (17 cities = n_1).
2. Cities with dominant industrial functions and moderate service (23 cities = n_2).
3. Cities with dominant service functions and moderate industry (27 cities = n_3).
4. Cities with dominant service functions and low industry (20 cities = n_4).

He then applied the discriminant analysis in the fashion given above. The highest eigen value: λ and its corresponding eigen vector of the matrix $W^{-1} B$ as worked out by him are given as

$$\lambda = 0.4230$$

$$V' = [-0.3322 - 0.0998 - 0.1834 - 0.2086 - 0.0504 + 0.7636]$$

So the value of F-ratio is

$$F = 0.4230\frac{(87-4)}{(4-1)} = .4230 - \frac{83}{3} = 11.703$$

$$\text{d. f.} = (83, 3)$$

The F-ratio is significant at 1% level of significance *i.e.* the variations of the six factors (stimulants of migration) taken together between the cities of similar economic functions are significantly larger than their variation within the groups.

The weights (elements of vector V') of the discriminant function

$$Y = -.3322X_1 - .0998X_2 - .1834X_3 - .2086X_4 - 0504X_5 + 7636X_6$$

show that in terms of group differentials, service pull is most important followed by the long distance industrial pull and the short distance industrial pull in the given order. As the weights of other factors are not relatively higher, they may be considered as less important in showing thc group differentials.

Discriminant analysis in India context has also been used by Ahmad (1965) and Biplab (1971). The work of Casetti (1964) and King (1961) may also be reffered to as the examples of application of discriminant analysis in geography. Anderson (1958), Cooley and Lohnes (1962), Kendell (1957) and Rao (1952) (1965) also provide excellent discussion on the analysis from different points of view.

In this age of Personal Computers (PCs) use of techniques of multivariate analysis has become very popular. Use of Computer Software Packages such as SPSS, SAS and STATA etc. has simplified their application dramatically.

REFERENCES

1. Ahmad, Qazi : "Indian Cities : Characteristics and Correlates" *Research Paper No. 102*, Department of Geography, Chicago University, Illinoins (1965).

2. Anderson, T.W. : *Introduction to Multivariate Statistical Methods*, John Wiley & Sons, New York (1958).

3. Berry, B.L.J : An Inductive Approach to the Regionalization of Economic Development in Ginsburg, N. (ed.) Essays on Geography and Economic Development, Chicago University, (1970), pp. 78-100.

4. Biplab Dasgupta : "Socio - Economic Classification of Indian Districts - A Statistical Approach", *Economic and Political Weekly*, 14th August (1971).

5. Casetti, E. : Classificatory and Regional Analysis by Discriminent Iterations, technical Report No. 12, Computer Application Earth Sciences Project, Deptt. of Geography, North-Western University.

6. Cooley, W.W. and Lohnes, P.R. : *Multivariate Data Analysis* John Wiley and Sons, New York (1971).

7. Hauser D.P., "Some Problems in the use of stepwise Regression Technique in Geographical Research" *The Canadian Geographer* Vol. XVIII, 1, 1974.

8. Hotteling, H. : Analysis of a Complex Statistical Variables into Principal Component, *Journal of Educational Psychology* (1933), Vol. 24, pp. 407-441.

9. Johnston, J. : *Econometric Methods*, McGraw - Hills, New York, 1960.

10. Kendall, M.G. : *A Course in Multivariate Analysis*, Charles Griffin, London (1957).

11. Koutsoyiannis, A. : *Theory of Economics*, Macmillan, 1973.

12. King, L.J. : "Discriminatory Analysis of Urban Growth Patterns in Ontario and Quebec, 1951-1961" Annals of Association of American Geographers (1967), Vol. 57, pp. 556-576.

13. Mooser, E.A. and Scott; W. British Towns : *A Statistical Study of their Social and Economic Differences*, Oliver and Boyd 1961.

14. Morrison, D.F. : *Multivariate Statistical Methods*, McGraw - Hills Inc. (1967), New York (1967), pp. 221-225.

15. Rao, C.R. : *Advanced Statistical Methods in Biometric Research*, John Wiley New York (1952).

16. Rao, C.R. : *Linear Statistical Inference and its Application*, John Wiley New York (1965).

17. Rao, P. and Miller R.L. : *Applied Econometrics*, Prentice Hall India, 1972.

18. Soja, E.W. : *Geography of Modernization in Kenya*, Syracuse University Press, 1968.

APPENDIX - I

Random Sampling Numbers

20 17	42 28	23 17	59 66	38 61	02 10	86 10	51 55	92 52
74 49	04 49	03 04	10 33	53 70	11 54	48 63	94 60	94 49
94 70	49 31	38 67	23 42	29 65	40 88	78 71	37 18	48 64
22 15	78 15	69 84	32 52	32 54	15 12	54 02	01 37	38 37
92 29	12 18	27 30	30 55	91 87	50 57	58 51	49 36	12 53
45 04	77 97	36 14	99 45	52 95	69 85	03 83	51 87	85 56
44 91	99 49	89 39	94 60	48 49	06 77	64 72	59 26	08 51
16 23	91 02	16 96	47 59	89 65	27 84	30 92	63 37	26 24
04 50	65 04	65 65	82 42	70 51	55 04	61 47	88 83	99 34
32 70	17 72	03 61	66 26	24 71	22 77	88 33	17 78	08 92
03 64	59 07	42 95	81 39	06 41	20 81	92 34	51 90	39 08
62 49	00 90	67 86	83 48	31 83	19 07	67 68	49 03	27 47
61 00	95 86	98 36	14 03	48 88	51 07	33 40	06 86	33 76
89 03	90 49	28 74	21 04	09 96	60 45	22 03	52 80	01 79
01 72	33 85	52 40	60 07	06 71	89 27	14 29	55 24	85 79
27 56	49 79	34 34	32 32	60 53	91 17	33 26	44 70	92 14
49 05	74 48	10 55	35 25	24 28	20 22	35 66	66 34	26 35
49 74	37 25	97 26	33 94	42 23	01 28	59 58	92 69	03 66
20 26	22 43	88 08	19 85	08 12	47 65	65 63	56 07	95 85
48 87	77 96	43 39	76 93	08 79	22 18	54 55	93 75	97 26
08 72	87 46	75 73	00 11	27 07	05 20	30 85	22 21	04 67
95 97	98 62	17 27	31 42	64 71	46 22	32 75	19 32	20 99
37 99	57 31	70 40	46 55	46 12	24 32	36 74	69 20	72 10
05 79	58 37	85 33	75 18	88 71	23 44	54 28	00 48	96 23
55 85	63 42	00 79	91 22	29 01	41 39	51 50	36 65	26 11
67 28	96 25	68 36	24 72	03 85	49 24	05 69	64 86	08 19
85 86	94 78	32 59	51 82	86 43	73 84	45 60	89 57	06 87
40 10	60 09	05 88	78 44	63 13	58 25	37 11	18 47	75 62
94 55	89 48	90 80	77 80	26 89	87 44	23 74	66 20	20 19
11 63	77 77	23 20	33 62	62 19	29 03	94 15	56 37	14 09
64 00	26 04	54 55	38 57	94 62	68 40	26 04	24 25	03 61
50 94	13 23	78 41	60 58	10 60	88 46	30 21	45 98	70 96
66 98	37 96	44 13	45 05	34 59	75 85	48 97	27 19	17 85
66 91	42 83	60 77	90 91	60 90	79 62	57 66	72 28	08 70
33 58	12 18	02 07	19 40	21 29	39 45	90 42	58 84	85 43
52 49	70 16	72 40	73 05	50 90	02 04	98 24	05 30	27 25
74 98	93 99	78 30	79 47	96 62	45 58	40 37	80 76	84 41
50 26	54 30	01 88	69 57	54 45	69 88	23 21	05 69	93 44
49 46	61 89	33 79	96 84	28 34	19 35	28 73	39 59	56 34
19 64	13 44	78 39	33 88	62 03	36 00	25 96	86 76	67 90
64 17	47 67	87 59	81 40	72 61	14 00	28 28	55 86	23 38
18 43	97 37	68 97	56 56	57 95	01 88	11 89	48 07	42 07
65 58	60 87	51 09	96 61	15 53	66 81	66 88	44 75	37 01
79 90	31 00	91 14	85 65	31 75	43 15	45 93	64 78	34 53
07 23	00 15	59 05	16 09	94 42	20 40	63 76	65 76	34 11
90 98	14 24	01 51	95 46	30 32	33 19	00 14	19 28	40 51
53 82	62 02	21 82	34 13	41 03	12 85	65 30	00 97	56 30
98 17	26 15	04 50	76 25	20 33	54 84	39 31	23 33	59 64
08 91	12 44	82 40	30 62	45 50	64 54	65 17	89 25	59 44
37 21	46 77	84 87	67 39	85 54	97 37	33 41	11 74	90 50

APPENDIX - II

Values of mod. t with a probability of being exceeded in random sampling
v=number of degrees of freedom

			Level of Significance		
i.f.	0.50	0.10	0.05	0.02	0.01
1.	1.000	6.31	12.71	31.82	63.66
2.	0.816	2.92	4.30	6.97	9.92
3.	0.765	2.35	3.18	4.54	5.34
4.	0.741	2.13	2.78	3.75	4.60
5.	0.727	2.02	2.57	3.37	4.03
6.	0.718	1.94	2.45	3.14	3.71
7.	0.711	1.90	2.36	3.00	3.50
8.	0.706	1.86	2.31	2.90	3.36
9.	0.703	1.83	2.26	2.82	3.25
10.	0.700	1.81	2.23	2.76	3.17
11.	0.697	1.80	2.20	2.72	3.11
12.	0.695	1.78	2.18	2.68	3.06
13.	0.694	1.77	2.16	2.65	3.01
14.	0.692	1.76	2.14	2.62	2.98
15.	0.691	1.75	2.13	2.60	2.95
16.	0.690	1.75	2.12	2.58	2.92
17.	0.689	1.74	2.11	2.57	2.90
18.	0.688	1.73	2.10	2.58	2.88
19.	0.688	1.73	2.09	2.54	2.86
20.	0.687	1.73	2.09	2.53	2.85
21.	0.686	1.72	2.08	2.52	2.83
22.	0.686	1.72	2.07	2.51	2.82
23.	0.685	1.71	2.07	2.50	2.81
24.	0.685	1.71	2.06	2.49	2.80
25.	0.684	1.71	2.05	2.40	2.79
26.	0.784	1.71	2.06	2.48	2.78
27.	0.684	1.70	2.05	2.47	2.77
28.	0.683	1.70	2.05	2.47	2.76
29.	0.683	1.70	2.04	2.46	2.76
30.	0.683	1.70	2.04	2.45	2.75
35.	0.682	1.69	2.03	2.44	2.72
40.	0.681	1.68	2.02	2.42	2.71
45.	0.680	1.68	2.02	2.41	2.69
50.	0.679	1.68	2.01	2.40	2.68
60.	0.678	1.67	2.00	2.39	2.66
00.	0.674	1.64	1.96	2.33	2.58

APPENDIX - III

1% Points of F

v1 / v1	1	2	3	4	5	6	7	8	9	00
1	40.52	4999.5	5403	5625	5764	5859	5982	6106	6235	6366
2	98.50	99.00	99.17	99.25	99.30	99.33	99.37	99.42	99.46	99.50
3	34.12	30.82	29.46	28.71	28.24	27.91	27.49	27.05	26.60	26.13
4	21.20	18.00	16.69	15.98	15.52	15.21	14.80	14.37	13.93	13.45
5	16.86	13.27	12.06	11.39	10.97	10.67	10.29	9.89	9.47	9.02
6	13.75	10.92	9.76	9.15	8.75	8.47	8.10	7.72	7.31	6.88
7	12.25	9.55	8.48	7.85	7.45	7.19	6.84	6.47	6.07	5.65
8	11.26	8.65	7.59	7.01	6.66	6.37	6.03	5.67	5.28	4.86
9	10.56	8.02	6.99	6.42	6.04	5.80	5.47	5.11	4.73	4.31
10	10.04	7.56	6.55	5.99	5.66	5.39	5.06	4.71	4.33	3.91
11	9.65	7.21	6.22	5.87	5.32	5.07	4.74	4.40	4.02	3.60
12	9.33	6.93	5.95	5.41	5.06	4.82	4.50	4.16	3.78	3.36
13	9.07	6.70	5.74	5.21	4.86	4.62	4.30	3.96	3.59	3.17
14	8.86	6.51	5.56	5.04	4.69	4.46	4.14	3.80	3.43	3.00
15	8.68	6.36	5.42	4.89	4.56	4.32	4.00	3.67	3.29	2.87
16	8.53	6.23	5.29	4.77	4.44	4.20	3.89	3.55	3.18	2.75
17	8.40	6.11	5.18	4.67	4.34	4.10	3.79	3.46	3.08	2.65
18	8.29	6.01	5.09	4.58	4.25	4.01	3.71	3.37	3.00	2.59
19	8.18	5.93	5.01	4.50	4.17	3.94	3.63	3.30	3.92	2.49
20	8.10	5.85	4.94	4.43	4.10	3.87	3.56	3.23	2.86	2.42
21	8.02	5.78	4.87	4.37	4.04	3.81	3.51	3.17	2.80	2.36
22	7.95	5.72	4.82	4.31	3.99	3.76	3.45	3.12	2.75	2.31
23	7.88	5.66	4.76	4.26	3.94	3.71	3.41	3.07	2.70	2.26
24	7.82	5.61	4.72	4.22	3.90	3.67	3.36	3.03	2.66	2.21
25	7.77	5.57	4.68	4.18	3.85	3.63	3.32	2.99	2.62	2.17
26	7.72	5.53	4.64	4.14	3.82	3.59	3.29	2.96	2.58	2.10
27	7.68	5.49	4.60	4.11	3.78	3.56	3.26	2.93	2.45	2.13
28	7.64	5.45	4.57	4.07	3.75	3.53	3.23	2.90	2.52	2.06
29	7.60	5.42	4.54	4.04	3.73	3.50	3.20	2.87	2.49	2.03
30	7.56	5.39	4.51	4.02	3.70	3.47	3.17	2.84	2.47	2.01
40	7.31	5.18	4.31	3.83	3.51	3.29	2.99	2.66	2.29	1.80
60	7.08	4.98	4.13	3.65	3.34	3.12	2.82	2.50	2.12	1.60
120	6.85	4.79	3.95	3.48	3.17	2.96	2.66	2.34	1.95	1.38
00	6.64	4.60	3.78	3.32	3.02	2.89	2.51	2.18	1.97	1.00

APPENDIX - III

SIGNIFICANCE POINTS OF THE VARIANCE - RATIO F

5 per cent points

v1 / v2	1	2	3	4	5	6	8	12	24	00
1	161.40	199.5	215.7	224.6	230.2	234.0	238.9	243.9	249.0	254.3
2	18.51	19.00	19.16	19.25	19.30	19.33	19.37	19.41	19.45	19.50
3	10.13	9.55	9.28	9.12	9.01	8.94	8.84	8.74	8.64	8.53
4	7.70	6.94	6.59	6.39	6.26	6.16	6.04	5.91	5.77	5.63
5	6.61	5.79	5.41	5.19	5.05	4.95	4.82	4.68	4.53	4.36
6	5.99	5.14	4.76	4.53	4.39	4.28	4.15	4.00	3.84	3.67
7	5.59	4.74	4.35	4.12	3.97	3.87	3.73	3.57	3.41	3.23
8	5.32	4.46	4.07	3.84	3.69	3.58	3.44	3.28	3.12	2.93
9	5.12	4.26	3.86	3.63	3.48	3.37	3.23	3.07	2.90	2.71
10	4.96	4.10	3.71	3.48	3.33	3.22	3.07	2.91	2.74	2.54
11	4.84	3.98	3.59	3.36	3.20	3.09	2.95	2.79	2.61	2.40
12	4.75	3.88	3.49	3.26	3.11	3.00	2.85	2.69	2.50	2.30
13	4.67	3.80	3.41	3.18	3.02	2.92	2.77	2.60	2.42	2.21
14	4.60	3.74	3.34	3.11	2.96	2.85	2.70	2.53	2.35	2.13
15	4.54	3.68	3.29	3.06	2.90	2.79	2.64	2.48	2.29	2.07
16	4.49	3.63	3.24	3.01	2.85	2.74	2.59	2.42	2.24	2.01
17	4.45	3.59	3.20	2.96	2.21	2.70	2.55	2.38	2.19	1.96
18	4.41	3.55	3.16	2.93	2.77	2.66	2.51	2.34	2.15	1.92
19	4.38	3.52	3.13	2.90	2.74	2.63	2.48	2.31	2.21	1.88
20	4.35	3.49	3.10	2.87	2.71	2.60	2.45	2.28	2.08	1.84
21	4.32	3.47	3.07	2.84	2.68	2.57	2.42	2.25	2.05	1.81
22	4.30	3.44	3.05	2.82	2.66	2.55	2.40	2.23	2.03	1.78
23	4.28	3.42	3.03	2.80	2.64	2.53	2.38	2.20	2.00	1.76
24	4.26	4.40	3.01	2.78	2.62	2.51	2.36	2.18	1.91	1.73
25	4.24	3.38	2.99	2.76	2.60	2.49	2.34	2.16	1.96	1.71
26	4.22	3.37	2.98	2.74	2.59	2.47	2.32	2.15	1.95	1.69
27	4.21	3.35	2.96	2.73	2.57	2.46	2.30	2.13	1.93	1.67
28	4.20	3.34	2.95	2.71	2.56	2.44	2.29	2.12	1.91	1.65
29	4.18	3.33	2.93	2.70	2.54	2.45	2.28	2.10	1.90	1.64
30	4.17	3.32	2.92	2.69	2.53	2.42	2.27	2.09	1.89	1.62
40	4.08	3.23	2.84	2.61	2.45	2.34	2.18	2.00	1.79	1.51
60	4.00	3.15	2.76	2.52	2.37	2.25	2.10	1.92	1.70	1.89
120	3.92	3.07	2.68	2.45	2.29	2.17	2.02	1.83	1.61	1.25
00	3.84	2.99	2.60	2.37	2.21	2.09	1.94	1.75	1.52	1.00

APPENDIX - IV

Values of x^2 with probability P of being exceed in random sampling
v=number of degrees of freedom

v \ P	0.20	0.10	0.05	.02	0.01
1	1.64	2.71	3.84	5.41	6.63
2	3.32	4.61	5.99	7.82	9.21
3	4.64	6.25	7.81	9.84	11.34
4	5.90	7.78	9.49	11.67	13.28
5	7.29	9.24	11.07	13.39	15.09
6	8.56	10.64	12.59	15.03	16.81
7	9.80	12.02	14.07	16.62	18.48
8	11.03	13.36	15.51	18.17	20.09
9	12.24	14.68	16.92	19.68	21.67
10	13.44	15.99	18.31	21.16	23.21
11	14.63	17.28	19.68	22.62	24.73
12	15.81	18.55	21.03	24.05	26.22
13	16.98	19.81	22.36	25.47	27.69
14	18.15	21.06	23.68	26.87	29.14
15	19.31	22.31	25.00	28.26	30.58
16	20.46	23.54	26.30	29.63	32.00
17	21.62	24.77	27.59	30.99	33.41
18	22.76	25.99	28.87	32.35	34.81
19	23.90	27.20	30.14	33.69	36.19
20	25.04	28.41	31.41	35.02	37.57
21	26.17	29.62	32.67	36.34	38.93
22	27.30	30.81	33.92	37.66	40.29
23	28.43	32.01	35.17	38.97	41.64
24	29.55	33.20	36.42	40.27	42.98
25	30.68	34.38	37.65	41.57	44.31
26	31.80	35.56	38.88	41.86	45.64
27	32.91	36.74	40.11	44.14	46.96
28	34.03	37.92	41.34	45.42	48.28
29	35.14	39.09	42.56	46.69	49.59
30	36.25	40.26	43.77	47.96	50.89